BEHAVIOR PROBLEMS IN PRESCHOOL CHILDREN

'Behavior Problems
in Preschool Children,

CLINICAL AND DEVELOPMENTAL ISSUES

Susan B. Campbell, PhD
University of Pittsburgh

THE GUILFORD PRESS
New York   London

© 1990 The Guilford Press
A Division of Guilford Publications, Inc.
72 Spring Street, New York, NY 10012

Printed in the United States of America

This book is printed on acid-free paper.

Last digit is print number: 9   8   7   6   5   4   3   2   1

Library of Congress Cataloging-in-Publication Data

Campbell, Susan B.
    Behavior problems in preschool children: clinical
and developmental issues / Susan B. Campbell.
      p.   cm.
    Bibliography: p.
    Includes index.
    ISBN 0-89862-395-2
    1. Behavior disorders in children. 2. Child development.
3. Preschool children—Mental health. I. Title.
    [DNLM: 1. Child Behavior Disorders. 2. Child Development.
3. Child Development Disorders. 4. Child, Preschool. WS 350.6
C191b]
RJ506.B44C36 1990
618.92'89—dc20
DNLM/DLC
for Library of Congress   89-16838
                                                  CIP

To Hallie, my constant companion, whose difficult behavior has helped me reach a new level of empathy for parents of hard-to-manage preschoolers.

Acknowledgments

A number of people have contributed to the work reported in this book, as well as to the preparation of the book itself. Special appreciation is expressed to Lin Ewing for her dedication to the study, her clinical sensitivity and concern, and her support and friendship over the past 10 years. Emily Szumowski's many contributions to the project are also gratefully acknowledged, as are her helpful editorial comments on drafts of early chapters. Other graduate students and research staff contributed to various phases of the research and critically reviewed specific chapters. In particular I wish to thank Clare Flanagan who reviewed the entire manuscript for clarity and helped assemble the references; Cindy March for feedback on selected chapters; and Anna Marie Breaux, Diane Gluck, and Patricia Huszar for their help on various phases of the research. Deborah Bremer and Donna Bickel helped conduct the 9-year follow-up assessments. The National Institute of Mental Health has provided funding for my research and I am grateful to various Institute staff and grant reviewers who, over the years, have recognized the importance of longitudinal research on difficult preschoolers and their families. This work has been supported by NIMH Grant Number 32735.

Special recognition goes to the many families who have participated in this work and have grappled with the challenges of raising difficult children. I hope that they have benefited from their association with the Project and that the insights that they have provided will ultimately benefit other children and families as well. The case studies described throughout this book are based on these families. However, family circumstances have been extensively disguised to protect their identities and fictional names have been used.

My colleague and friend Russell Barkley first suggested to Seymour

Weingarten of The Guilford Press that he contact me about a book on preschoolers and I thank him for this. Seymour's patience and support have been especially important, as I juggled the many demands on my time and missed many deadlines. He has been consistently tactful, understanding, and humorous, despite his eagerness for me to finally finish!

Special thanks and gratitude go to John E. Bates and an anonymous reviewer for helpful comments on an earlier draft of this book. Both spent their Christmas vacations meticulously reading and critiquing both content and style and this book is much improved because of their input.

Finally, to my current graduate students who have often found me unavailable, preoccupied, and overwhelmed, I appreciate your tolerance and understanding. I hope that I will be just a bit more accessible in the coming months.

Susan B. Campbell
Pittsburgh, PA

Preface

Three-year-old Jamie L was expelled from preschool after frequent fights with other children. He seemed to have a "chip on his shoulder," and the "rough and tumble" play and toy struggles so common in preschool classrooms tended to escalate and become a serious fight whenever Jamie was involved. Jamie seemed to lose control with other children; he was able to share toys and play quietly for only a few minutes at a time. If Jamie and some other boys were playing with trucks, Jamie was always the one to start the crashes, which got increasingly wild. In the sandbox it was always Jamie who threw the sand in someone's face or grabbed the shovel from another child. Jamie got into fights almost daily, and at times he would get angry enough to bite, kick, and hit anyone who would not let him have his way. This also included the teacher. After a month in school, the teacher became worried that Jamie might seriously harm another child, and she asked Jamie's mother to keep him at home.

Jamie's mother was shocked and dismayed at this request. She knew that Jamie was a difficult child, hard to discipline, explosive, and prone to temper tantrums. He had been hard to handle since early infancy, but she really wanted to believe her pediatrician's reassurances that Jamie was just going through a difficult period of development and that she need not worry. Mrs. L and her husband agreed that Jamie was a handful, but they wavered between seeing his difficult behavior as "just a phase" and as a sign of more serious problems to come. There were many possible explanations for Jamie's unruly behavior in preschool. Maybe the preschool teacher simply didn't understand how to handle him. Maybe she was too strict. Maybe she didn't intervene soon enough when he was beginning to get wound up and overexcited. Maybe a school with more structure would be better for him. Or maybe at age 3, he just wasn't ready for a preschool program.

By contrast, 3-year-old Annie adapted well to preschool and loved it. Her teacher saw her as bright and sociable, although somewhat dependent and anxious. She followed the school routines well and got along fine with other children. Annie's mother, however, had a different opinion; she found Annie virtually impossible to manage and the daily temper tantrums and constant battles were getting her down. She had enrolled Annie in preschool to give herself a break and was surprised at the teacher's report of Annie's good adjustment. Annie seemed to store up all her anger and defiance for her mother. She seemed a different child with other adults and was "Daddy's girl," putting additional stress on an already fragile marriage.

⌐ These vignettes describe typical problems encountered in the preschool period and raise a number of questions that developmentalists and parents alike must confront. It is obvious why parents would be upset by behavior similar to this in their preschooler, but it is less clear whether they need to worry about its long-term implications. Is it important for the pediatrician, developmental specialist, or mental health professional to intervene with children similar to Jamie or Annie? Are they just going through a difficult period or does their angry and uncontrolled behavior presage later, more serious problems? Even if the current problems are outgrown, what about the toll such children can take on parental self-esteem and marital harmony? Or are the problems themselves reflections of marital dysfunction, family distress, or inappropriate approaches to child rearing? Are Jamie's problems more likely to persist than Annie's or vice versa? Or are they each likely to develop persistent problems, but of a different type? For example, will Jamie be likely to develop into an aggressive and/or hyperactive child? Will Annie develop problems with relationships or become a depressed or withdrawn adolescent? ⌙

In this book an attempt will be made to address these issues, drawing on theoretical viewpoints and evidence from the fields of child development, developmental psychopathology, and clinical child psychology. The focus will be on late toddlerhood and the preschool period, with a particular emphasis on distinguishing those problems of early childhood that may be typical and transient from those that may be signs of a more persistent disorder. I will explore problem behaviors in young children, such as Jamie and Annie (roughly ages 2½ to 5), who may be going through a difficult and explosive, albeit temporary, developmental transition, or who may be showing early signs of more serious psychopathology with the potential to impede developmental progress. These are the children who confront parents, preschool teachers, pediatricians, and mental health professionals with particularly complex diagnostic and treatment decisions. Prognostic predictions about such children are especially risky and based on limited empirical data. Nevertheless, surprisingly little attention has been paid in the childhood psychopathology literature to the problems of the hard-to-manage preschooler and his/her development over time.

The reasons for the neglect of this age group are complex. First, it is particulary difficult to distinguish between what is and what is not "normal" at this stage of development. Because it is widely accepted that the period between 2 and 5 years of age is one of extremely rapid developmental change and because there are wide individual differences in the rates at which such change occurs, it has been considered reasonable to assume that early problems will be outgrown. Thus, difficult toddlers are often seen as just going through the "terrible 2's" and aggressive 3-year-olds are viewed as just learning how to operate in the peer group. However, some recent work calls these conclusions into question (e.g., Campbell, Ewing, Breaux, & Szumowski, 1986; Kohn, 1977; Richman, Stevenson, & Graham, 1982; Sroufe, 1983). Some children with problems in the preschool period continue to have significant difficulties later on. These persistent problems may reflect child characteristics, family dysfunction, or a combination of child and family factors. Conversely, early problems that are transient may indicate merely a perturbation in development and/or the influence of developmentally appropriate and effective parenting. Therefore, it is important to determine which child characteristics in combination with which family factors are associated with the amelioration of early difficulties, and which appear to be associated with the development of more long-standing psychological disorders (Sroufe & Rutter, 1984; Thomas, Chess, & Birch, 1968).

Theoretical debates within developmental psychology have focused on issues of continuity and change over time. Some developmentalists believe that early development is crucial and that experiences in the first 3 years of life determine the course of social and cognitive development thereafter (e.g., Bowlby, 1969; White, 1985); others emphasize the plasticity of young children's behavior (e.g., Kagan, 1984; Kagan, Kearsley, & Zelazo, 1978); still others assume that both continuity and change occur, but certain key experiences can influence developmental outcome (e.g., Sameroff & Chandler, 1975; Sroufe, 1979). Within the child psychopathology field, the debate hinges on issues of risk and resilience. Which factors place children at risk for problems, and what determines whether children exposed to one or more risk factors will be resilient enough to overcome negative early experiences? These are extremely important questions for professionals concerned with the development of young children to consider because the answers will ultimately influence the nature of prevention programs and the types of advice it is reasonable to give to parents.

Some of these theoretical issues will be examined in Chapter One. One particular theoretical approach, the transactional view of development (Sameroff & Chandler, 1975), will be explored as it relates to problem behavior in young children. The transactional view will be supplemented by a discussion of the child's social context—family, peer group, and wider social network (Bronfenbrenner & Crouter, 1983; Parke & Slaby, 1983). Questions of continuity and change will also be considered because they are among the central issues that developmental psychopathologists must address (Sroufe & Rutter, 1984). In Chapter Two the development of toddlers and preschoolers will be discussed, with a focus on the major developmental tasks of this age period: exploration and environmental mastery; separation–individuation and the development of autonomy; the establishment of internalized standards of control; and advances in cognitive functioning, including language and memory. The establishment of autonomy, self-awareness, and self-regulation are viewed as normal, but critical, developmental transitions that children must negotiate. If they are dealt with successfully, the children are likely to develop into competent and psychologically healthy youngsters; difficulties coping with one or more of these tasks may set the stage for the onset of problems. Chapter Three will explore clinical issues relevant to an understanding of symptomatic behavior in young children, including the epidemiology of behavior disorders, factors influencing referral, and diagnostic issues. Several case histories will also be presented to illustrate the nature of behavior problems in early childhood. These cases are derived from a longitudinal study of hard-to-manage toddlers and preschoolers who have been followed to elementary school (Campbell, Breaux, Ewing, & Szumowski, 1984; Campbell & Cluss, 1982; Campbell, Ewing, et al., 1986; Campbell, Szumowski, Ewing, Gluck, & Breaux, 1982). The role of family factors, sibling relationships, and the establishment of relationships with peers will be addressed in Chapters Four, Five, and Six, including illustrations with case material. Treatment issues will be considered in Chapter Seven; course, outcome, and prognostic indicators will be discussed in Chapter Eight with case material used to highlight salient findings. Chapter Nine will summarize the major points and address social policy implications.

Contents

CHAPTER ONE

Theoretical Issues

Although several theorists have attempted to account for either cognitive development (e.g., Piaget) or psychosexual development (e.g., Freud) with comprehensive theories, large-scale theories have played a relatively small role recently in the field of child development (Miller, 1983). This is particularly true in the area of social development, the topic emphasized in this book. Rather, small-scale models describing particular developmental processes within individuals (e.g., memory, friendship) or more inclusive models integrating behavior and social influences across different domains and levels of analysis (e.g., ecological models and transactional models) have dominated the field. This shift in emphasis from grand theories to models, which are more closely tied to empirical findings (Miller, 1983), appears to reflect the complexity of multiply determined developmental processes and the failure of any extant theory to account adequately for the variety of factors that interact to determine the direction of development in an individual. Because this book is concerned primarily with the wide range of social factors that influence the development of young children, the focus will be on the more inclusive transactional and ecological views of development that currently predominate in the field (Bronfenbrenner & Crouter, 1983; Parke & Slaby, 1983; Sameroff & Chandler, 1975).

In addition to a consideration of models of development, certain key theoretical issues must be addressed because they have profound implications for the conceptualization of developmental change in both "normal" and disturbed populations, as well as for etiological formulations of childhood problems. One major debate within development psychology and child psychopathology revolves around issues of continuity and change. How well does earlier behavior predict later behavior? What changes as development proceeds and what remains stable?

It is now well established that developmental stability reflects more than a link between a particular behavior that is evident in early infancy and that same behavior later on. Rather, the focus has shifted to more general questions, such as whether earlier behavior predicts later behavior at all and whether qualitative or stylistic aspects of an individual's behavior show evidence of stability. Some theorists argue that one can predict at least certain aspects of a child's development from knowledge of earlier behavior and social influences. Other theorists disagree and assert that developmental change is both so irregular and so profound that developmental course is not predictable. The question of predictability is a central one for developmental psychopathology because the early identification of children with problems and the delineation of prognostic factors rest upon the assumption that development is at least partially predictable from knowledge of earlier behavior and the caretaking environment.

Before proceeding with this discussion, several terms must be defined. *Continuity* will be used to refer to general similarities in behavior or personality over time, whereas *discontinuity* refers to a lack of demonstrated stability in behavior or personality characteristics. *Predictability* will be used to indicate a theoretically meaningful relationship between earlier and later behavior, whether or not the behaviors themselves are similar. Knowledge of earlier behavior may allow prediction of later behavior, despite developmental changes in the manifestations of the behavior itself, or earlier behavior may lead, in predictable ways, to the appearance of a different behavior. Finally, the terms *qualitative* and *quantitative* will be used to characterize the nature of developmental change. Quantitative change indicates an increase in capacity with development, although the behavior remains the same in terms of underlying processes and overt manifestations. Qualitative change refers to the reorganization and modification of behavior with development, leading to profound alterations in underlying processes. It is hoped that the meaning of these terms will become clearer during the ensuing discussion of these theoretical issues.

In addition to debate about whether or not developmental course can be predicted, there is a related debate on the nature of developmental change. What changes with development? Some would argue that developmental change reflects a quantitative increase in certain skills or processes, such as memory capacity or sociability, that is, the capacity to remember facts or events increases such that older children remember more of them. Others would argue that developmental change is qualitative. Children may remember more with development, but their increased capacity reflects a reorganization of memory processes and a change in the nature of memory strategies rather than an increase in the number of stimuli that can be remembered. Similarly, in the area of social development, children's increased capacity to play cooperatively with peers may be conceptualized as a quantitative increase in the acquisition of social skills, such as a larger repertoire of social approach behaviors, or, alternatively, as a reorganization of the cognitive structures that are thought to underlie the ability to cooperate with others, such as perspective taking and means–end thinking. At a logical level, continuity positions might be seen as allied with notions of quantitative change, whereas a discontinuity view would appear to fit with the idea that change reflects complex reorganizations. This is more or less the case, although the debates around these two related issues have become both heated and complex (e.g., Brim & Kagan, 1980; Kagan, 1984; Overton & Reese, 1981; Sroufe, 1979).

A third theoretical issue revolves around the nature–nurture question. Although either/or formulations of this issue are no longer widely accepted, the question of how biological and environmental factors interact to produce either normal or pathological development remains important. In most theoretical models of abnormal development, some attempt is made to address this issue. In particular, diathesis–stress models of adult psychopathology implicate both biological vulnerabilities and psychosocial stressors as central to the development of both schizophrenia and depression (e.g., Zubin & Spring, 1977). Similarly, transactional models of development focus on the interaction among biological and environmental determinants, while allowing for qualitative changes in behavioral and social factors as a function of development. These changes in turn may alter the nature of the organism–environment interaction.

In this chapter, these theoretical issues will be discussed and the implications of one or another position for the development of behavior disorders in young children will be addressed. This will be followed by a discussion of transactional and ecological models as they apply to developmental psychopathology. In the context of illustrating the implications of these various issues and models, the role of infant temperament and mother–infant attachment will be examined as well because both are seen as possible early precursors of childhood problems according to some theoretical models of abnormal development.

Continuity–Discontinuity and the Nature of Developmental Change

Decades of research in child development have been devoted to investigating continuity in behavior over time. For example, much early research attempted to predict later IQ from measures of infant functioning or to find personality traits, such as dominance or shyness, which were stable over time (e.g., Bayley & Schaefer, 1964; Kagan & Moss, 1962). It was assumed that simple knowledge of early behaviors would allow one to predict later functioning. As stage theories of development emphasizing qualitative change and reorganization (such as the work of Piaget) came to dominate the field, the notion that one could find continuities in development became suspect (e.g., Overton & Reese, 1981; Sameroff & Chandler, 1975). Thus, Overton and Reese have argued that the profound transformations in cognitive structures and in behavior that characterize development make it unrealistic to expect to find consistencies over time, a view that has been echoed by Kagan and his colleagues (Kagan et al., 1978). Some developmental theorists see qualitative change as synonymous with development and argue that the role of the developmentalist is to describe and attempt to explain the nature of developmental transitions rather than to search for elusive developmental continuities. Indeed, it is nearly impossible to discuss developmental continuity or discontinuity without also addressing the question of quantitative or qualitative change.

The discontinuity view arose partly as a reaction to the optimism of the early 1960s, when it was assumed that early experience determined later development (e.g., Hunt, 1961) and that the provision of appropriate cognitive stimulation in early childhood, especially to less "advantaged" children, would predictably lead to concomitant improvements in intellectual functioning. This view spawned intervention and enrichment programs, such as Head Start, which were expected to have more widespread and long-lasting positive effects than have been demonstrated. Yet, some studies have found that children considered to be at risk for delayed development function adequately even in the absence of intervention (e.g., Kagan & Klein, 1973). Similarly, a number of studies have failed to find the predicted link between pregnancy and/or delivery complications (reproductive risk) and deviant development (see Sameroff & Chandler, 1975, for a review). These findings have led some theorists to question whether the importance accorded to early experience has been exaggerated and to argue that developmental course is both less continuous and less predictable than was once supposed (e.g., Kagan, 1984; Sameroff, 1975).

Other researchers and theorists assume that development does show predictability, not in terms of the continuity of specific behaviors (see Kagan, 1971), but more generally in terms of certain attributes that cut across the domains of both cognitive and social functioning (e.g., Plomin, 1982; Sroufe, 1979; Thomas, Chess, & Korn, 1982) or reflect similar underlying cognitive processes (Bornstein & Sigman, 1986). These authors argue that within some general and broad parameters, knowledge of early behavior and the caretaking environment allows one to predict certain outcomes. Sroufe (1979) terms this the "coherence" of development. Thus, the issue becomes one of predictability rather than behavioral continuity. Furthermore, predictability can be demonstrated despite developmental transformations that reflect the qualitative reorganization of developmental processes. For example, a secure infant–mother attachment in infancy predicts competence in problem solving in toddlerhood and in the peer group in preschool (Sroufe, 1983). Sroufe suggests that the organization of behavior changes to meet developmental challenges, but the general approach to new developmental tasks remains consistent or coherent across development. From this perspective, specific behaviors would not logically be expected to show consistency. Temperament researchers likewise hypothesize that certain enduring personality characteristics can be identified in early infancy and that they shape, to some extent, the course of later development (e.g., Plomin, 1982; Thomas et al., 1968, 1982).

One complication in the study of change and continuity revolves around how one defines consistency in behavior and what denotes transformation and reorganization (Lewis & Starr, 1979). If one behavior is a necessary precursor of a later behavior, does that imply continuity, even if the later behavior differs considerably from the earlier one as, for example, in the shift from babbling to language? This is a particularly difficult problem when one attempts to relate infant behavior to later functioning because qualitative aspects of many behaviors do show dramatic change. How does one define behavior at vastly different developmental levels to investigate continuity? For example, how would one look for continuity in a disposition similar to sociability over time? Which behaviors would define it at 3 months? 3 years? Which behaviors in infancy might logically be considered early precursors of social engagement at school entry? Lewis and Starr (1979) argue that an understanding of continuity or discontinuity depends upon interpretation and level of analysis. Conclusions will vary according to which constructs are selected for study, how they are defined in terms of specific behaviors at different ages, how the chosen behaviors are measured, the time intervals between measurements, and how the data are interpreted.

Others agree that the interpretation of the data will reflect a preexisting stance or world view (e.g., Kagan, 1984; Overton & Reese, 1981). Kagan suggests that a continuity perspective is one that we ourselves bring to the data to provide some order and meaning to experience. The babbling to language example illustrates this issue well. If it were demonstrated that frequency of babbling in infancy was correlated moderately, but significantly, with some measure of language development obtained at the age of 3 years, would that be interpreted as evidence for continuity or for change? The continuity theorist would argue that it showed consistency in the use of vocalization as a means of communication and that the early babbling laid the groundwork for later verbal development. However, the discontinuity theorist would argue that the vocalizations and babbling of infancy had been so transformed and reorganized over the course of the ensuing months that it would be meaningless to talk of continuity between the babbling of an infant and the communicative and syntactically correct speech of a preschooler. From this perspective, the apparent continuity (i.e., as reflected in a measure of statistical association) would not lie in the child's behavior, but would probably best be explained as an example of environmental continuity. An evaluation of the caretaking environment over time would probably reveal consistencies related to the encouragement of differing types of age-appropriate vocal communication. Continuity might be found in the fact that maternal behavior encouraged vocalization, but the specifics of maternal behavior would change with the child's development, for example, from contingent responses to babbling and cooing in infancy, to facilitating labeling in toddlerhood, to reframing sentences and asking questions during the preschool period.

The continuity–discontinuity debate is further complicated by the fact that examples of continuity, transformation, and coherence abound in development. No one would expect continuity in certain behaviors, for example, smiling or crying, because it is obvious that they change their meaning with development and other behaviors (e.g., separation distress at maternal departure) drop out of the typical repertoire completely. For instance, smiling or crying in a 3-month-old is interpreted differently from smiling or crying in a toddler, despite the consistency in the topography of the behavior. One would not necessarily expect frequency of smiling at 3 months to predict frequency of smiling or even more general sociability at 2 years. Similarly, one would not expect the intensity of separation protest at 8 months to predict shyness at preschool age. These are examples of social behaviors that are highly age-determined where transformation and reorganization are the rule.

Although transformation and reorganization characterize some aspects of social and cognitive development, there is some evidence for stability in certain behavioral dispositions. For example, there is evidence that activity level in early infancy predicts activity level in the preschool period (Korner et al., 1985) and that activity level in preschoolers predicts activity level at school entry (Buss, Block, & Block, 1980; Campbell, Breaux, Ewing, & Szumowski, 1986; Halverson & Waldrop, 1976). Even for this apparently circumscribed aspect of behavior, the focus is not on continuity in specific behaviors because activity is measured differently in infants and preschoolers. Rather, the continuity lies in the finding that children who are in the higher ranges on some measures of infant activity are somewhat more likely than less active infants to score at higher levels on measures of activity obtained in preschool as well.

Three issues are embedded in this statement. First, these studies show only moderate stability in individual differences (McCall, 1977). Children maintain some similarity in rank order over time, but the behavior itself may or may not be stable. Developmental changes mean that behaviors are manifest differently (e.g., from the restlessness of an infant to the running and jumping of a preschooler) and are therefore measured differently. Thus, whatever continuity is implied is really consistency in behavioral style or intensity of response. Second, because at best studies find only moderate correlations (around .30 to .40) between earlier and later behaviors, interpretations depend upon the theoretical predispositions of the beholder. These correlations may be interpreted as demonstrating continuity because there is some relationship between activity in infancy and activity later, or they may be interpreted to reflect discontinuity because the relationship is only moderate. Third, as McCall argues, even when we can demonstrate stability of individual differences, we are not shedding light on the process of development. Studies that examine the stability of individual differences do not clarify how a child develops from a squirmy infant to an active and energetic preschooler.

Studies also suggest coherence in other general aspects of personality and social relations. This coherence probably reflects a combination of consistency in certain behavioral dispositions within children and certain stable characteristics of the caretaking environment. For example, studies suggest that fussy and difficult behavior in infancy may translate into defiance and confrontation in toddlerhood, particularly when mothers use relatively intrusive and angry methods of discipline (Lee & Bates, 1985). Other studies indicate that hard-to-manage preschoolers are more likely than more subdued and tractable preschoolers to continue to have difficulties in elementary school, especially when the quality of the mother–child relationship is negative and conflicted (Campbell, Breaux, Ewing, & Szumowski, 1986; Richman et al., 1982; Thomas et al., 1968). Work by Sroufe and his colleagues suggests that when mothers are responsive to their infants' communications and facilitate exploration of the environment, their infants are more independent and invested in problem solving in toddlerhood, suggesting coherence at the positive end of the spectrum as well (Matas, Arend, & Sroufe, 1978).

Taken together, these recent studies and theoretical perspectives suggest that the issue is not one of behavioral continuity per se, but consistency along some general dimensions of social and cognitive functioning. Stated differently, these studies document some coherence within the flux of development (Thomas et al., 1982), mediated in part by certain stable aspects of the environment. Furthermore, studies of problem children suggest that predictability may be better at behavioral extremes than with behaviors in the moderate range (Campbell, Ewing, et al., 1986; Richman et al, 1982). Children who are extremely active or irritable or noncompliant may be more likely to continue to respond maladaptively than children who are only average or slightly above in their activity level or noncompliance. Children at the extremes of irritability or noncompliance may also be more sensitive to stable but negative environmental influences or more disorganized by environmental instability (e.g., Crockenberg, 1981; Egeland & Farber, 1984; Lewis, Feiring, McGuffog, & Jaskir, 1984; Richman et al., 1982).

Similarly, at the positive end of the distribution, children who are more easy-going and compliant are more likely to show consistency on these dimensions of behavior, particularly in the context of supportive parenting (Lee & Bates, 1985; Matas et al., 1978), and they may be less disorganized by environmental instability (Thomas et al., 1968).

These issues have obvious implications for the study of psychological disorder in young children and for approaches to intervention. Early identification of children at risk for disorder is predicated on the idea that behavior is predictable. Preventive and therapeutic interventions are based on the assumption that problems may persist in the absence of treatment (i.e., that maladaptive behavior is often stable, but in the face of appropriate environmental interventions, change and transformation are possible). An extreme continuity view might lead to the conclusion that early behavior was unchanging and that interventions were fruitless. At the other extreme, a strongly held discontinuity view would appear compatible with the notion that problems are likely to be outgrown in the absence of treatment, as part of a normal developmental transition. Although some behaviors, such as aggression, appear to be relatively resistant to treatment, providing support for a continuity position (Loeber, 1982), some children at high risk for psychopathology appear to develop normally (Garmezy, 1987), providing support for the competing discontinuity view. Extreme adherence to either position, however, is probably an oversimplification: it seems clear that a more complex view, which highlights the interaction among child characteristics and environmental factors, will be necessary to identify children at risk and to pinpoint directions for intervention.

The Transactional Model of Development

Most current etiological models of adult psychopathology are considered "interactionist" because they incorporate both genetic–biological and environmental factors (e.g., Zubin & Spring, 1977). According to this view, both a biological diathesis or vulnerability and environmental stress are necessary to precipitate the onset of disorder. Thus, a genetically vulnerable individual might not break down if the environment were generally supportive and free from strain; similarly, even in the face of severe stress, some individuals continue to function well, presumably because they are biologically "resilient." The combined effects of faulty genetics and a poor environment are seen as necessary to produce the disturbed behavior. While this model has much appeal and successfully accounts for much of the data on schizophrenia and manic depressive illness, it is basically static and fails to allow for developmental change.

The transactional view, as outlined by Sameroff (1975), incorporates both organismic and environmental determinants in continual and mutually interactive flux over time. There are several basic premises that underlie this view. First, development is assumed to be discontinuous and characterized by qualitative change and reorganization. Second, consistent with current notions of child development (e.g., Kagan et al., 1978; Lerner, 1982; Scarr & McCartney, 1983), the young child is seen as an active organizer of experience, participating in his/her own development. Third, interactions between young children and caretakers are viewed as bidirectional (Bell, 1968); that is, children's responses to stimulation from adults, as well as their influences on the behavior of adults are important. Fourth, neither child characteristics nor the environment are considered static. Both are changing over time in a mutually regulated and reciprocal fashion. Fifth, strong, biologically based self-righting tendencies are assumed to be present in all but the most severely damaged infants; that is, movement is inherently toward normal development.

Taken together, then, the process of development is seen as an active and dynamic one in which the infant moves toward more complex functioning as cognitive and social processes reorganize with each new phase of development. Whereas maturation plays a central role in this process, especially early on (McCall, 1981), the role of the environment is likewise central and it takes on added importance with development (Sameroff, 1975). In particular, the importance of a responsive and appropriate caretaking environment, which changes over time to meet the infant's developmental needs, cannot be overemphasized. For example, responsive caretaking in the early weeks would involve accurately reading the infant's cues regarding hunger, fatigue, and the need for cuddling. By 8 months, the infant's needs expand dramatically to include a variety of requirements for social and cognitive stimulation and the availability of a safe environment that facilitates the exploration of objects. From a transactional view, the infant's requirements and the response of the caregiver change over time in a mutually regulated and reciprocal fashion. Stress and strain at one point in development may give way to more adaptive functioning as the infant overcomes a difficult developmental hurdle (e.g., weaning) or the mother learns to anticipate the infant's needs more accurately (e.g., by not letting him/her become overtired or overly hungry). Thus, changes in either member of the dyad will feed back to influence the relationship in a dynamic and adaptively regulated system.

Therefore, given a reasonably responsive and adequate caretaking environment in which mutual adaptations can occur, the odds favor good outcomes. Thus, an infant who is only moderately developmentally delayed is likely to overcome early deficits if the caretaking environment is generally appropriate and stimulating, thereby facilitating development. However, a moderately delayed infant born into an unresponsive or neglectful environment would be less likely to overcome early initial problems. In the absence of environmental supports for development, one might predict continuing decline in cognitive functioning as well as the onset of signs of emotional distress. Similarly, an irritable and unconsolable infant need not develop into a behavior problem toddler unless the caretaking environment is unable to accommodate to his/her needs. Exceptional outcomes are due only rarely to deficits solely in the infant but usually derive from "some continuous malfunction in the organism–environment transaction across time which prevents the child from organizing his world adaptively" (Sameroff, 1975, p. 282). One potentially traumatic experience, such as anoxia at birth or the death of a parent, would not be expected to lead inexorably to poor outcome. Rather, chronic negative or inappropriate parenting, particularly of a vulnerable infant, would be expected to predict continuing problems. Knowledge of infant characteristics alone or of the caretaking environment alone would not be sufficient to predict outcome except in the most extreme cases; furthermore, a longer term view would be needed because only more chronic maladaptation would be associated with long-term negative consequences. According to this view, the focus is on multiple determinants of development and complexity of their interactions over time. Both child characteristics and factors in the caretaking environment, what Sameroff and Chandler (1975) have termed the "continuum of caretaking casualty," need to be entered into the equation predicting outcome.

The transactional model presents a reasonably optimistic view because it suggests that most children will be able to overcome early problems and that interventions focusing on the child, the primary caretaker, or better still, their interaction over time would be sufficient to reverse a trend toward deviant development. It also suggests that it is possible to identify those infants or young children most at risk for disorder. Finally, this model makes it clear that the caretaking environment should be the major focus of preventive and therapeutic efforts.

Ecological Models of Development

The focus of child development research has been primarily on the child and the primary caretakers, usually the parents. Recently, however, child development researchers have become concerned with the child in a broader social context, that is, as a member of a family, peer group, wider social network, community, and culture. Thus, the focus has been broadened to consider a range of direct and indirect influences on the developing child and on the family in which he/she lives (Belsky, 1981, 1984; Bronfenbrenner & Crouter, 1983; Cochran & Brassard, 1979; Parke & Slaby, 1983). As with the transactional model, the metaphor is that of mutually regulated and interacting systems, but at varying contextual levels (e.g., those that directly impinge on the individual, such as the family and peer group, and those that indirectly influence behavior, such as prevailing cultural beliefs about child rearing).

An ecological perspective is based on the assumption that multiple factors have a direct impact on the child, and these and other factors also influence the quality of caregiving the child receives from parents. For instance, within the family it is necessary to consider the quality of both father–child and mother–child relationships. In addition, the quality of the marital relationship is likely to influence the child (Belsky, 1981, 1984). Furthermore, these effects should be both direct and indirect. The overall climate of the home (e.g., whether it is generally warm and supportive or fraught with tension) would be expected to have a direct effect on the child's sense of security and comfort (Cummings, Zahn-Waxler, & Radke-Yarrow, 1984). In addition, marital stress is likely to impinge upon the child indirectly through its effects on parents who, because they are upset or preoccupied, may be less available to their children. The complexities of these interacting relationships become even more complicated when a second child is born. The availability of extended family or close friends, for example, would also be expected to have both direct and indirect effects on the child, by providing additional adult attention and stimulation to the child and by providing social support to parents.

Cochran and Brassard (1979) suggest that all people outside the household who engage in regular social exchange with family members have the potential to influence a child's development. Direct influences include the opportunity to interact with different individuals and thus learn about new roles, styles of interaction, or new activities. Children develop close relationships with network members, such as regular babysitters or close friends of the family. Network members also have an indirect impact through their relationship with parents. For example, they may provide them with emotional, material, or informational support, which has a positive effect on the family; they may also model more appropriate child-rearing behaviors. Members of the wider network might also have a negative impact on the children if, for example, they took parental attention away from them or served as negative role models.

Community and cultural influences are also seen as relevant (Bronfenbrenner & Crouter, 1983). For example, physical aspects of the community such as the availability of playgrounds and the safety of the neighborhood, community resources such as the availability and quality of preschool or day-care settings, the nature and availability of work for parents, and educational and medical institutions have all been hypothesized to influence the quality of the child's environment and hence development, as have the availability of less formal social structures such as clubs, parent groups, church groups, and so on. In other words, a range of factors are seen as influencing the quality of life, and these factors should converge to affect the child's development. Focus on these wider sociological concerns stems in part from the recognition by some developmentalists that much laboratory research and theory lacked "relevance," that is, an awareness of the myriad of factors that played a part in children's lives.

An ecological perspective is generally inherent in most clinical approaches. It would be rare for a clinician, regardless of theoretical orientation, not to obtain information on a child's family environment and the resources available in the family and wider community to support the child's growth and development. Differences arise in the use to which such information is put in clinical practice and in the focus of treatment. However, developmental psychologists are now trying to systematize and evaluate empirically issues that clinicians routinely attend to in assessing a child and family.

Insecure Attachment as a Possible Precursor
of Child Disorder

Much recent work on the early parent–infant relationship has been
conceptualized within the framework of attachment theory (Bowlby,
1969; Ainsworth, 1969), an integration of psychoanalytic, cognitive,
systems, and ethological views on the nature of the child's affective bond
with its parents. Briefly, attachment theorists argue that infants have a
biologically based propensity to become attached to one or two primary
caretakers and that adults, likewise, have a biologically based tendency
to care for and nurture helpless and dependent members of the species.
Within this framework, inborn infant behaviors such as crying and
clinging are assumed to promote and maintain proximity to caretakers,
thereby protecting the infant from exposure or harm and also ensuring
sustenance. Attachment develops over the course of the first year,
progressing from indiscriminant responsiveness to any adult to a highly
specific and goal-directed emotional bond with the primary caregivers,
usually the parents. (Despite a growing interest in the role of fathers,
most research on attachment to date has emphasized the infant's
emotional bond with his/her mother.) Once a focused attachment to the
mother develops, the infant's behavior becomes organized around the
goal of maintaining proximity to her when in unfamiliar surroundings
or when tired or upset. She thus serves as the major source of comfort,
protection, and support in times of stress. The attachment figure also
serves as a secure base for exploration of the environment, facilitating
the infant's mastery of the physical and social world.

   According to this view, the attachment figure plays a central role in
the infant's cognitive and social development as well as the development
of a sense of self. It is argued that when the attachment figure is available
and responsive, the infant will be more likely to develop a sense of
security and trust. Because the world appears predictable, the infant
learns that he/she will be protected and cared for. Expectancies about
self-efficacy and worthiness as well as the availability of others are
thought to derive from early experiences with responsive attachment
figures (see Bretherton, 1985). However, unavailability and/or un-
responsiveness on the part of attachment figures are seen as resulting in
heightened anxiety as the infant learns that the world is unpredictable,
threatening, or rejecting and that basic needs for nurturance and
emotional support will not be met consistently. Within this framework,
then, unresponsive, rejecting, or capricious caretaking may lead to

insecurity and lack of basic trust; the infant, preoccupied with maintaining proximity to a caregiver who is not available or is only inconsistently so, may develop into an anxious, clingy infant who is easily distressed, and difficult to calm; infants whose mothers are rejecting may learn to avoid emotional and physical contact and become sober and withdrawn or angry and explosive (Ainsworth, Blehar, Waters, & Wall, 1978; Bowlby, 1969, 1973; Bretherton, 1985).

As noted earlier, attachment theorists take relatively strong positions on the continuity issue. Sroufe, in particular, has argued that the attachment relationship lays the groundwork for much subsequent development and that coherence stems from the way an infant's behavior is organized vis-a-vis the attachment figure. Individual differences in attachment derive from maternal behavior, primarily her responsiveness to infant cues and communications and her availability as a source of comfort during the first year of life. Individual differences in infant characteristics, for example, in irritability or consolability play a role in some formulations of attachment (e.g., Campos, Barrett, Lamb, Goldsmith, & Stenberg, 1983) but not others (Sroufe, 1985).

Some research studies demonstrate that individual differences in maternal behavior in early infancy predict the quality of the infant–mother attachment relationship that develops during the first year (e.g., Ainsworth et al., 1978; Belsky, Rovine, & Taylor, 1984; Crockenberg, 1981; but see Goldsmith & Alansky, 1987, for a more conservative interpretation of these findings). In addition, knowledge of whether the infant is securely or insecurely attached may have implications for social and cognitive development across contexts and over the life span, although this issue is also the subject of some debate (e.g., Lamb, 1987, vs. Sroufe & Fleeson, 1986). In particular, when assessed in toddlerhood and at preschool age, infants who were insecurely attached at 1 year have been found to be less competent in problem solving, less compliant with maternal requests, less sociable in the peer group, and more disorganized and deviant in their play with peers. Thus, according to this view, the quality of the early caretaking environment has profound and long-term influences on the child's development. Attachment theorists also argue that attachment in infancy has important implications beyond early childhood. Bowlby, for example, has suggested that the attachment relationship is the prototype for later intimate relationships; Ricks (1985) and others (Sroufe & Fleeson, 1986) have suggested that parents who have themselves been rejected as infants will in turn be unresponsive to their infants, establishing an intergenerational pattern of insecure attachment in some dysfunctional families. The relationship between insecure attachment in infancy and toddlerhood and later behavior problems has also been the subject of recent research and debate. Some studies suggest a link, with resistant and avoidant infants showing patterns of anger, aggression, and noncompliance, or social withdrawal and depression, in the preschool and early elementary school years (Lewis et al., 1984; Sroufe, 1983). In other studies, no relationship between insecure attachment and later behavior problems has been found (see Bates & Bayles, 1988, for a review, but see Greenberg & Speltz, 1988, for a somewhat different perspective).

The determinism inherent in attachment theory has been challenged, along with the argument that any observed coherence in development from infancy through preschool derives almost totally from early maternal behavior. Clearly, this aspect of attachment theory seems at odds with the position put forth by some (e.g., Kagan, 1984) that developmental psychologists have put too much emphasis on continuity and on the overriding importance of early experience. Thus, Kagan and others have countered that the coherence that has been demonstrated reflects not the irreversible impact of early experience, but endogenous infant characteristics and relatively stable aspects of the environment. The debates on these issues are beyond the scope of this book. The interested reader is referred to Bates (1987), Campos et al. (1983), Goldsmith and Alansky (1987), Kagan (1984), Lamb (1987), and Sroufe (1985). However, it appears that infant behavior as well as other factors contribute both to the quality of the attachment relationship observed at 12 months and to its stability over time.

Several studies have suggested that the links between early attachment and later behavior are mediated in part by characteristics of the infant and aspects of the mother's social network and her life circumstances. For example, in one study, the combination of infant irritability and low social support was associated with the development of an insecure attachment, presumably because mothers under stress had fewer resources to allow them to cope responsively with a difficult infant (Crockenberg, 1981). However, infant irritability in the context of adequate support was not associated with insecure attachment (see also Bates, Maslin, & Frankel, 1985). Other studies have suggested that environmental disruption is associated with changes in the quality of the attachment relationship (Vaughn, Egeland, Sroufe, & Waters, 1979). Securely attached infants became insecure as their environments became less stable and their mothers less available to meet their needs.

Finally, Lewis et al. (1984) have found that environmental stress interacts with early mother–infant attachment to predict good versus poor outcome at the age of 6 years. Although insecure attachment was associated with higher ratings of symptomatology, this held true only for insecure children living in stressful life circumstances.

Thus, the relationship between early attachment and later functioning appears to be transactional. As an infant's needs change, the nature of maternal responsiveness and of the attachment relationship may change in predictable ways; furthermore, ecological variables, such as the availability of support for the mother, appear to have an impact on child outcome, presumably indirectly through their impact on the mother and her ability to respond appropriately to meet her child's needs for support and nurturance. Furthermore, on the basis of available evidence, it appears that a poor mother–infant relationship is reflected in early insecure attachment, and this may well be a risk factor for a range of later problems in socioemotional development, especially in the absence of alternative attachment figures or in the context of chronic family instability or disruption. However, contrary to the deterministic arguments of traditional attachment theorists, insecure attachment in infancy need not lead inevitably to difficulties in later adjustment. In addition, some theorists (e.g., Campos et al., 1983; Kagan, 1984) argue that individual differences in infant characteristics will not only have an impact on the developing mother–infant relationship but also influence the direction of the young child's personality development more generally.

Temperament

- The concept of infant temperament has attracted much interest, as well as some recent controversy (e.g., Bates, 1980, 1987; Goldsmith & Campos, 1982; Plomin, 1982; Sroufe, 1985; Thomas et al., 1982). The issue of temperament and the role of temperament in the development of behavioral disturbance was first addressed by Thomas and his associates (Thomas et al., 1968). These authors developed one of the first truly interactive models of development in which they stressed the combined contributions of individual differences in infant behavior and the caretaking environment in determining social development. This work represented an early reaction to the environmentalism and the unidirectional view inherent in psychoanalytic formulations of childhood problems, and it has stimulated much recent research and theory within a transactional developmental model. Thomas et al. (1968) conducted an early descriptive, longitudinal study within this framework. They concluded that individual differences in infant characteristics interacted with child-rearing style to determine outcome. In particular, they stressed the importance of the "goodness-of-fit" between infant and caretakers as well as the active role the infant played in eliciting caretaking behavior from adults (see also Bell, 1968; Korner, 1971). Thomas et al. (1982) proposed that particular individual difference dimensions of infant behavior were, at least in part, constitutionally based and reflected stylistic aspects of infant behavior that were central to an understanding of early social development. These dimensions included regularity in biological functioning, threshold of response, intensity of reaction, quality of mood, adaptability, and activity level. Based on their typical patterns of behavior, some infants could be characterized as "difficult," that is, intense, negative, irregular, and slow to adapt to change. The combination of a difficult infant and an insensitive parent was seen as a risk factor for later deviant development, although Thomas et al. (1982) also noted that these interaction patterns were not fixed and that infant behavioral style could change as a function of environmental input. Thus, this theory directly raised issues of nature–nurture and continuity–discontinuity.

More recent debates have focused on the definition of temperament, its stability over time, the relative importance of constitutional and environmental influences on the expression of temperament, and whether infant difficultness is a risk factor for or precursor of later behavior problems. Thomas et al. (1968) defined temperament in terms of the "how of behavior" or stylistic aspects of social and cognitive functioning but did not take a position on its determinants except to assume that both genetic and environmental factors interacted to produce a child's characteristic response style. Thus, they argued that temperamental style was not necessarily immutable and unchanging because environmental events and parental caretaking styles would be expected to modify a child's inborn tendencies to behave in one way or another. Others have suggested, however, that the construct of temperament implies both constitutional–genetic determinants and stability over time (e.g., Bates, 1980, 1987; Buss & Plomin, 1975; Sroufe, 1985).

Goldsmith and Campos (1982) have recently synthesized a number of views of infant temperament. They define temperament as an individual differences construct that refers to stable personality dispositions, although the degree and nature of the stability may vary both across individuals and over time. In contrast to Thomas, who emphasizes the stylistic aspects of temperament, Goldsmith and Campos stress the affective and motivational aspects. Thus, according to this view, individual differences in intensity or threshold of affect expression may be reactive or may serve to initiate behavior. For example, infants differ in the speed and intensity of their response to annoying or aversive stimuli; some infants react slowly or fuss quietly, whereas others are quick to protest and may do so with great intensity. Infants also initiate social encounters that will vary as a function of the nature, intensity, and timing of their expressions of affect, be they positive, playful, and exuberant, or negative and demanding. Thus, Goldsmith and Campos consider temperament to reflect individual differences in the intensity and timing of emotional expression. As such, temperamental characteristics are not different from personality dispositions, a point also made recently by Plomin (1982) and Maccoby, Snow, and Jacklin (1984).

There is a general consensus that it is meaningful to talk about endogenous individual differences in infant behavior that are evident early (i.e., before differences in caretaking styles would be expected to have a profound effect) and influence the nature of parent–infant interaction in a bidirectional fashion. For example, Bates (1987) suggests that infant temperament is a useful construct because it highlights the role that infant characteristics play in socialization. Focusing attention on individual differences in infants helps to elucidate the processes by which different infants elicit different responses from primary figures in their social environment. Bates (1987) emphasizes fussiness, irritability, and negative mood in his conceptualization of the difficult infant, aspects of behavior that are more easily operationalized in observational studies of infant behavior and maternal caretaking (e.g., Crockenberg, 1981). Thus, infants who are fussy, demanding, and difficult to console may elicit anxiety, feelings of incompetence, and/or anger in their mothers, especially if their mothers are themselves preoccupied with other problems or are impatient or depressed. This initial clash of needs and feelings may abate as early feeding difficulties, such as colic, are overcome or as infants develop ways of soothing themselves; furthermore, initially stressed and anxious mothers may relax as they adapt to their infants' characteristics, gain confidence, or make better use of alternative caregivers to help them weather a difficult early developmental phase.

Yet, early mother–infant conflict may set the stage for more persistent problems in the relationship. For example, some mothers with irritable and demanding babies may become less responsive over time. Crockenberg (1981) suggests that this is the case when fussy infants are born to stressed and overwhelmed mothers with low social support. Lack of maternal responsiveness may lead, in turn, to increased demandingness on the part of an infant whose needs for social stimulation are not being met (Bates, 1987). Data from the longitudinal study by Bates (Bates, 1987; Bates & Bayles, 1988) suggest that difficult temperament, paired with a lack of affectionate and playful interaction with mothers in infancy, may fuel a cycle of demanding and coercive interaction. This pattern of interaction may become particularly problematic in toddlerhood, as young children's strivings for autonomy conflict with parental expectations for compliance, as well as with their own ambivalence and need for structure and security.

Whereas there is wide agreement that it is meaningful to think about individual characteristics of infants, the stability versus modifiability of these individual difference parameters has been the subject of some debate. Within the context of developmental psychopathology, the question focuses primarily on whether infants who show difficult behavior over time can be identified and whether they are at increased risk to develop behavior problems. Findings from several longitudinal studies suggest that such children may indeed be at greater risk to develop problems. For example, Bates and his colleagues (Bates et al., 1985; Bates & Bayles, 1988) found that infant difficultness was predictive of behavior problems at the ages of 3 and 5 years in the context of low levels of maternal positive and playful interaction. However, as would be expected from a transactional model, not all difficult infants continued to have problems. These findings are consistent with those of Thomas et al. (1968) because they implicate both child behavior and the quality of the mother–child relationship in the persistence of problems.

The issue of infant temperament has somewhat different implications, depending upon whether one subscribes to a continuity or discontinuity view of development. From the continuity perspective, it would be concluded that difficult infants are more likely to continue to have problems in adaptation, especially in the context of an unsupportive environment. From a discontinuity stance, early infant difficultness would be viewed as a developmental phase with few necessary implications for later maladaptive behavior. However, advocates of both positions would probably agree that an extremely difficult infant living in a chaotic and rejecting family would be at high risk for behavior problems. Interpretations would differ in terms of the relative emphasis placed on child characteristics and family background factors in contributing to the persistence of difficulties.

A Final Common Pathway Model of Interacting Factors

The theoretical issues discussed in this chapter highlight questions about the determinants of problem behaviors in young children, the predictability of good versus poor outcome, the nature of developmental change, and the relative contributions of biological and environmental factors to the onset of deviant behavior as well as to changes in behavior with development. Although none of these theoretical debates can yet be resolved unequivocally, either because they are basically philosophical questions without definite answers or because the empirical data do not provide overwhelming support for one view over another, it is possible to draw together a working model of interactive factors. It is thus possible to synthesize a large body of empirical data and theoretical ideas that implicate a range of child, parent, family, and social context effects in the development and/or maintenance of behavior problems. Furthermore, empirical studies suggest that some factors are more important than others. However, it does not appear logical to suppose that the same factors are operative for all children. Rather, there are probably multiple pathways to the development of disordered behavior in young children. Thus, although within-child factors (such as biological vulnerability and difficult temperament) and parenting factors (such as child-rearing practices) are both implicated, different combinations of factors probably converge to produce disorder in each individual case and to determine whether or not a problem persists. This is especially likely with young children, who have a relatively limited repertoire of behaviors. Thus, temper tantrums, defiance, separation distress, or sleep disturbances may result from a variety of environmental stressors or developmental challenges both in biologically vulnerable children and in those without specific biological risk factors for psychopathology. The intensity of the disturbance and its ultimate outcome also will vary as a function of multiple factors in the child and the family environment.

Table 1.1 lists a number of factors that have been associated with the onset and/or persistence of problem behaviors in young children. This list is far from exhaustive. Furthermore, it is not clear in some instances

TABLE 1.1. Some Factors Associated with the Development of Behavior Problems in Preschool-Age Children

Child Characteristics	Parenting Skills
Biological risk/vulnerability	Insensitivity/unresponsiveness
Age	Unavailability
Gender	Limited or negative affective involvement
Irritability/difficultness	Inappropriate developmental
Uneven or delayed cognitive	expectations
development	Overly harsh or lax control strategies
Deficits in social cognition and/or social	
skills	Family Environment/Social Context
	Low educational level of parents
Family Composition and Interaction	Unemployment or underemployment
One- versus two-parent family	Limited financial/material resources
Marital distress	Low social support
Parental personality problems	Inadequate institutional support
Physical and psychological	Inadequate child care facilities
well-being/disorder	Family stresses outside the nuclear family
Interparental disagreement over	
child rearing	
Number of children	

whether the factor in question is a cause, a correlate, or a reaction to a problem. For example, problems may stem from early irritability and unconsolability (difficult temperament), the difficult temperament may be an early indicator of a problem, or the behaviors labeled difficult temperament may be a response to inept and insensitive caregiving. Similarly, harsh disciplinary practices may be of etiological significance, a symptom of a disturbed parent–child relationship that developed initially for other reasons, or a parental reaction to a child's lack of response to more low-key attempts at behavioral control. Although it is not possible to delineate specific factors that cause disorder and to differentiate them from concomitants of behavior problems in young children, a sufficiently large and robust data base exists to allow us to speculate on factors that are likely to be significant in some cases, but not all.

Table 1.1 highlights biological vulnerabilities that may underlie children's problems, as well as personality or temperamental factors, and developmental and behavioral competencies that may be associated with deviant development. These interact with child-rearing practices, the affective quality of parental behavior, and parental attitudes and

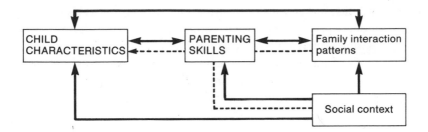

FIGURE 1.1. Model of interactive factors in the development of childhood problems. ――― Direct effects; ― ― ― indirect effects mediated by their impact on child rearing.

expectations to produce an ongoing parent–child relationship, which may or may not facilitate the child's optimal development. Other factors in the family environment are also seen as significant, including family structure (e.g., single- vs. two-parent; family size), the quality of the marital relationship in a two-parent family, the postdivorce arrangements and the role of the father in single-parent families, as well as parents' general personality characteristics and overall psychological adjustment. Finally, as noted earlier, social context effects also have an impact on the child.

Figure 1.1 illustrates the nature of the relationships among child characteristics, parental child-rearing strategies and behaviors, family interaction patterns, and social context effects. First, child characteristics and child-rearing behaviors influence each other as reflected in the bidirectional arrows. Similarly, patterns of interaction in the family will influence and be influenced by parenting behaviors and child characteristics. For example, marital distress, as reflected in frequent arguments, may be caused, in part, by disagreements over child rearing, which are fueled by a child's temper tantrums and disobedience. Family interaction patterns may also have indirect effects on the child, mediated by their impact on the parents and their child-rearing strategies. These indirect effects are depicted by the dashed lines. For example, marital discord may create tension in parents that spills over into harsh or inconsistent discipline. Finally, limited resources will likewise have both direct and indirect effects on children, by constraining their options and experiences and by influencing parental behavior. Models such as these are presented in more specific detail in several recent publications on parent–child relations and child development (Belsky, 1984; Parke &

Slaby, 1983; Schneider-Rosen, Braunwald, Carlson, & Cicchetti, 1985).
In the model proposed here, some combination of child characteristics
and parenting behavior are seen as the primary determinants of
problems, with family and social context effects exacerbating and/or
maintaining them. Family factors and social context effects may also lead
to the onset of transient disturbances, as exemplified by children's
reactions to divorce (e.g., Hetherington, Cox, & Cox, 1978; Wallerstein
& Kelly, 1980), but they are not likely to cause serious and long-term
difficulties in the absence of vulnerabilities in the child and/or problems
(ongoing or newly created) in the parent–child relationship. These
issues will be addressed in future chapters.

Summary

In summary, I have outlined several theoretical issues that appear
relevant to an understanding of the early development of young
children and to conceptualizations of problem behavior. General issues
that influence theoretical perspectives on development were addressed
first. Questions of interest included continuity in behavior over time and
the predictability of later behavior from knowledge of earlier behavior,
the nature of developmental change, and the combined contributions of
hereditary and environmental influences to developmental outcomes.
Although these complex theoretical issues cannot be unequivocally
resolved, the approach taken to them has a profound impact on one's
view of development. The adoption of a transactional perspective on
development implies the acceptance of both discontinuity and overall
developmental coherence or meaningful change, change that is primarily qualitative in nature, and is influenced by complex organism–
environment interactions, which themselves change over time in
reciprocal fashion. The addition of ecological variables to a transactional
model increases the complexities even further by including bidirectional
and indirect pathways of influence from sources beyond the nuclear
family and by considering factors other than those operating directly
within the parent–child relationship.

Such a theoretical perspective underlines the complexities inherent
in development and highlights the myriad influences that impinge upon
individual children. Predictions about which developmental pathways
particular children will follow and about probable outcomes at different
points in development are obviously difficult to make in the face of so

many interacting factors, most of which are changing over time. Although this dynamic perspective enhances our understanding of the general principles of developmental change, it makes clinical prediction more risky. Knowledge, even of a well-documented risk factor, may contribute little to prediction in the individual case. However, our increasing sophistication in conceptualizing the nature of development and in understanding the relative importance of various influences on development, both typical and atypical, suggests that examination of multiple risk factors may be a more fruitful approach. Furthermore, it is likely that children with similar histories will have different outcomes and children with similar outcomes may reach them by different developmental pathways, some more direct than others. An appreciation of this complexity is a necessary first step in describing and understanding the nature of development in young children with behavior problems, and ultimately, in devising effective treatments and predicting outcomes.

CHAPTER TWO

Developmental Issues

Wenar (1982) has suggested that problems in children can best be conceptualized as "normal development gone awry." Thus, it seems appropriate to examine the major developmental challenges of toddler-hood and the preschool years to suggest junctures at which development may proceed normally or may set the stage for the onset of problems. First, several aspects of infant development will be described briefly, followed by an overview of some of the main developmental achievements that occur from roughly 18 months to 5 years. This is meant to set the stage for the material that follows in ensuing chapters.

Among the major goals of early infancy are the development of state control and self-soothing ability, the establishment of routines, the modulation and coordination of motor activity, and the ability to focus attention on and to begin to derive meaning from environmental events (Kagan, 1984; Kopp, 1982; Sroufe, 1979). It is generally agreed that these early acquisitions are under strong biological–maturational control (Kagan, 1984; McCall, 1981; Olson & Sherman, 1983), although the role of the caretaking environment is also seen as central to the successful negotiation of these developmental challenges (Campos et al., 1983; Kopp, 1982; Sroufe, 1979). As noted in Chapter One, it is assumed that the sensitivity and responsiveness of caretakers will have a major impact on how well the infant is able to cope with environmental demands and the degree to which the infant will develop feelings of self-efficacy and competence. For example, the ability of infants to wait and soothe themselves when hungry is thought to derive, in part, from parental responsiveness because the baby's expectation that hunger and other needs will be met promptly will be determined by past experiences with predictable caregivers. Similarly, infants derive meaning from the repetition of environmental events and the predictability of outcomes, both of which are features of many adult–infant games. Kagan (1971, 1984) has written about the development of cognitive schemata for environmental events and the anxiety and distress attendant upon the violation of expectancies. Roughly between 6 and 8 months of age, infants develop a focused attachment to primary caregivers and begin to recognize that people and objects exist even when they are out of sight. At about this time they not only protest parental departures but may also show wariness or outright fear at the approach of strangers. These changes in behavior signal advances in cognitive and social development that set the stage for numerous other developmental attainments, as infants reach their first birthdays. A more detailed discussion of infant development is beyond the scope of this book. The interested reader is referred to Haith and Campos (1983), Osofsky (1987), and Stern (1985) for more theoretical and research-oriented discussions and to Stone and Church (1984) for a less technical description.

By the end of the first year or the beginning of the second, most children begin to walk and to use rudimentary language skills to communicate. These advances in motor coordination and symbolic processing usher in a period of rapid cognitive, affective, and social development. The hallmarks of this period include exploration and mastery of the environment and the development of autonomy and independence. By late toddlerhood and the early preschool period, the focus of parental expectations shifts to demands for greater self-control and the ability to play cooperatively with other children. The development of independence, self-control, and satisfactory peer relations occurs in tandem with marked advances in cognitive abilities. In particular, children begin to make sense out of their physical and social worlds and are able to convey their rudimentary understanding of the events in their environment in increasingly complex language. Brownell (1986, 1988) suggests that advances in self–other understanding and the ability to combine and sequence behavioral elements may underlie the profound cognitive and social changes that are evident during the second year. At this time children not only begin to sequence words into short sentences but also engage in smooth and reciprocal interactions with peers that involve complementary roles, to evidence role taking in early pretend play, and to modify their behavior in accord with the behavior of their partner.

Throughout the preschool period, children continue to demonstrate advances in cognitive and social development that are reflected in more complex reasoning and language skills, an emerging self-awareness and understanding of the feelings and thoughts of others, improved ability to balance one's own needs with the needs of partners during social interaction, and increased knowledge of the physical world. Overall, children's development across domains moves from concern with the concrete and physicalistic to an appreciation of more abstract and symbolic representations of experience. At the same time, as children become increasingly aware of the self as an autonomous agent, behavior becomes more organized and under the control of internal rather than external processes. In this chapter, we will discuss briefly some of the major developmental transitions that occur in social and cognitive development during the period from roughly 18 months to 5 years, with a focus on environmental mastery, pretend play, development of autonomy and self–other differentiation, self-regulation, language, and memory. The development of peer relationships, another major achievement of the preschool period, will be discussed in detail in Chapter Six.

All infants who experience normal, expectable caretaking, both physical and psychological, will show changes in behavior that signal the achievement of these development milestones, which appear to be invariant features of psychological growth. Thus, all normal and biologically intact toddlers explore the environment and begin to engage in pretend play; they develop some degree of autonomy and sense of self; they begin to use language to communicate and show gains in memory capacity; all normal preschoolers show major advances in cognitive and social-cognitive processing, self-control, and the ability to get along with other children. Individual differences in the ease or difficulty young children have coping with these milestones and transitions will be influenced by subtle aspects of parenting and the quality of the parent–child relationship. Individual differences also derive from variations in infant abilities and temperamental characteristics, for example, in such attributes as activity level, sociability, and mood. In keeping with a transactional model of development, it is assumed that reciprocal influences between child personality and caregiver responsiveness and sensitivity to developmental needs will contribute to the child's competence in each of these domains.

Cognitive and Social-Cognitive Development

First, some general issues in cognitive and social-cognitive development will be addressed. In keeping with current conventions, cognitive development will be used to refer primarily to reasoning about objects and abstract events that are not interpersonal, whereas the term social cognition will be used to refer to thoughts about social relationships and events (e.g., Shantz, 1983). Although a large body of research has traced the development of various cognitive skills in young children including their understanding of the physical properties of objects, number concepts, categorization abilities, and other aspects of abstract thinking and symbolic reasoning (see Gelman & Baillargeon, 1983, for a recent review), much of this work is beyond the scope of this discussion. However, in the context of understanding how young children reason about the world and about their relationships with others, it is worthwhile to touch briefly on a few issues. In particular, it seems important to discuss some general characteristics of thinking and reasoning in preschoolers. Then, preschoolers' ability to take another's point of view and their understanding of causality will be considered because they have a significant impact on children's social relations in the family and the peer group.

Much of our thinking about the cognitive development of children has been shaped by the theorizing of Jean Piaget (e.g., Piaget, 1926, 1928; an overview of Piagetian theory may be found in Flavell, 1963). Piaget proposed a stage theory of cognitive development in which children's logical reasoning progressed from the sensorimotor stage of infancy and toddlerhood (roughly to age 2), through the preoperational stage of the preschooler (roughly from ages 2 to 7), to the more advanced concrete operational stage of the school-age child. These stages are seen as universal in that all children go through them in the same sequence, although individual differences are apparent in the rate at which development proceeds. Furthermore, children's reasoning about a range of topics develops in parallel; consequently, children should be at roughly the same developmental point in, for example, their understanding of physical causality, conservation of quantity, categorization skills, and so on. Understanding of the physical world is thought to underlie young children's ability to correctly perceive the nature of social relations as well. Cognitive structures or schemata constrain the child's thinking at each level, and the coherence of functioning across domains is what defines a stage. With development and a shift to the next level of functioning, the child progresses through numerous qualitative changes in reasoning ability and understanding of the world.

According to Piagetian theory, preverbal infants and toddlers, who are functioning at a sensorimotor level, think mainly in terms of sensations and motor acts. Their thoughts are dominated by whatever is present in their immediate environment because they are only in the process of developing the cognitive schemata that permit them to represent events symbolically. Over the course of the first 2 years, infants move through various substages of the sensorimotor period during which they begin to recognize the familiar; they develop a rudimentary sense of cause–effect relations; they begin to behave purposefully; and they learn that objects have an independent existence, even when they are not in view (object permanence). These cognitive advances occur as a function of infants' intrinsic motivation to learn about the world, biological maturation, and infants' active engagement with the environment.

Piaget describes the preschooler as preoperational. Children at this stage of development are beginning to think symbolically as reflected in their rudimentary memory ability, their use of language, and their increased understanding of causality. However, Piaget emphasizes the constraints on children's thinking at this age. For example, preschoolers are described as egocentric or unable to distinguish between their own point of view and that of others; they tend to be easily distracted by the appearance of objects, even when these are obviously deceiving; also, they have difficulty coordinating information from several sources or attending to more than one dimension of a stimulus configuration at a time (Gelman & Baillargeon, 1983). These constraints lead to faulty logic and errors in understanding the world. Theorists working in the area of social development have adapted this framework to describe children's understanding of social phenomena, such as friendship relationships, family relationships, social perspective taking, and social conventions (e.g., Damon, 1977; Selman, 1981).

Although certain aspects of Piagetian thinking are still widely accepted, for example, notions of intrinsic motivation and cognitive structures that undergo qualitative change with development (Gelman & Baillargeon, 1983), other aspects of the theory have been called into question by new data. Thus, there is growing agreement that stage theories are not supported by the findings because children tend to advance in specific areas, especially those that are closely tied to their experience and knowledge base (e.g., Chi & Koeske, 1983); that is, advances are domain-specific, rather than general (Flavell, 1982); Gelman & Baillargeon, 1983; Turiel, 1978).

In addition, there is growing agreement that Piaget underestimated the abilities of preschoolers. Gelman and Baillargeon (1983) specifically asked whether it was appropriate to characterize preschool thought as preoperational. They concluded that "under certain conditions, even young preschoolers have a nonegocentric manner, ignore misleading perceptual cues, integrate information about states and transformations, and so on" (p. 172). Thus, when studies employ familiar situations and materials, those within the young child's frame of reference and experience, preschoolers evidence some degree of perspective-taking ability on some tasks assessing what another person is able to see, what another person feels, and what another person knows. In several studies even some 2-year-olds were able to perform correctly on visual perspective-taking tasks (see Gelman & Baillargeon, 1983, for a review of relevant studies).

Naturalistic observations of young children's problem solving, social interaction, and conversation are entirely consistent with this view. For example, Zahn-Waxler, Radke-Yarrow, and King (1979) observed that even toddlers and young preschoolers evidenced some degree of empathy and perspective-taking ability when witnessing the distress of others. Dunn and Kendrick (1982), in their study of siblings, also noted that toddlers and preschoolers were aware of the thoughts and feelings of siblings as reflected in both comforting and provocative behavior. As a final example, Shatz and Gelman (1973) reported that 4-year-olds modify their speech to use shorter sentences when talking to 2-year-olds. However, recognizing the state of another does not mean that young children will know what to do about it or will behave appropriately. Thus, in the Zahn-Waxler et al. study (1979) some children became agitated and upset by another's distress but were at a loss about what to do; others were solicitous, but their behavior still was egocentric in other ways. For example, giving a favorite teddy bear to an upset adult represents both perspective taking, as evidenced by the response to another's distress, and egocentrism, as reflected in giving a toy to an adult for comfort. Shantz (1983) notes that preschoolers have difficulty distinguishing between intentional and accidental events. Although they recognize or can sometimes infer the intentions of others, they have trouble understanding, for example, that someone might harm another person accidentally. Misconstruing another's intentions implies limited perspective taking, and it can lead to conflict.

Whereas naturalistic observations generally suggest that children are able to take the perspective of another very early, at least in some situations, interview studies of young children's awareness of relationships such as friendship are more consistent with a Piagetian view. Thus, when asked about their friends, preschoolers refer primarily to the fact that they play with them or they live nearby; they do not refer to enduring characteristics of others or of the relationship. This has been interpreted as evidence of the concreteness of the preschooler, as well as the egocentric nature of early relationships (e.g., Selman, 1981). However, observations of children's social interaction suggest a more differentiated view of relationships with peers (e.g., Corsaro, 1981; Gottman & Parkhurst, 1980). Children's choices of playmates are influenced by a range of factors, both cognitive and affective, and ties between peers can be intense, even if children cannot articulate the reasons for their choices or why they like some children and dislike others. Discrepancies between these different sources of data probably reflect constraints imposed by the linguistic development of preschoolers, their understanding of the questions asked in interview and laboratory studies, and the fact that what guides early behavior, including relationships, may be implicit rather than explicit (Gelman & Baillargeon, 1983). Children's friendships will be addressed in more detail in Chapter Six, which deals with peer relationships.

Piaget also suggested that preoperational children's notions of causality were extremely primitive. Although they might be able to recognize a short causal sequence that was explicit and immediate, with one visible event causing another (e.g., a ball knocking over a toy), preschoolers would not be expected to understand that causal mechanisms might exist even if they were not seen. In a series of experiments, Gelman and her students (see Gelman & Baillargeon, 1983) have demonstrated that 4- and 5-year-olds are able to use their knowledge of the world to make logical inferences about physical causality in specific laboratory situations, even when they do not observe the causal event directly (various events causing a jack-in-the-box to pop up). Moreover, preschoolers in these studies appeared to understand the sequence of events: causes must precede events. In the highly structured and relatively concrete situations devised by Gelman and her coworkers, these young children were able to identify a causal mechanism. Although this indicates causal reasoning at a more advanced level than is predicted by Piagetian theory, it still does not mean that preschoolers are generally able to infer cause–effect relationships in the more abstract situations assessed by Piaget. As noted above, preschoolers also are able, under some conditions, to infer the intentions of another's behavior, also an example of causal reasoning, albeit in the social domain. However, it is unclear how well children at this age infer idiosyncratic intentions, as opposed to those that are common, familiar, and, therefore, reflect more general social knowledge rather than an ability to anticipate the causes of another person's behavior in a highly specific situation (Shantz, 1983).

In general, then, preschoolers appear to be much more advanced in their reasoning and representational skills than is suggested by Piagetian theory. Furthermore, appropriately designed laboratory studies as well as observations of young children's real-world behavior confirm that they are more sophisticated, at least within their own realm of experience and knowledge, than earlier work suggested. However, it is also clear that preschoolers remain more concrete than older children and their knowledge in one area may not generalize to other related areas. As preschoolers reach school-age, they become more abstract in their thinking and better able to make inferences about the world and other people. Increases in conceptual skills are partly a reflection of increased knowledge of the world, a wider range of experiences, and strides in communicative competence. Much of this early knowledge is gained through exploration of the environment, a major developmental task of infancy and toddlerhood.

Environmental Mastery

As infants' motor skills improve to permit visually directed reaching and the purposeful grasping of objects, interest in the physical world becomes a central focus of their waking hours. Infants reach for, examine, mouth, drop, and bang objects—all part of the early repertoire of exploratory behavior. With somewhat more advanced motor and cognitive abilities, two objects are banged together, objects are placed one inside the other, and containers are filled and emptied as infants practice emerging skills; they experiment with gravity and also explore the size, shape, texture, and taste of various inanimate objects. The increasing complexity of early play and its importance for early cognitive development has been described in detail by Piaget and others (see Rubin, Fein, & Vandenberg, 1983). In this context, infants learn about cause–effect relations and their ability to control some aspects of their environment.

As infants become mobile, they are in a position to explore ever-widening areas and to exert more control over what things capture their interest. At this point in development, some parents begin to have difficulties balancing their own needs for order and control, as well as their concerns for their infant's safety, with the infant's need to explore. Parents sometimes find that their cuddly infant is now hell bent on opening every cupboard and drawer and that they are unable to keep up with the flurry of activity. Whereas some parents appropriately view this as an important developmental phase, others may begin to engage in battles with their child, and it is at this point that some parents, rightly or wrongly, become concerned about overactivity. At the other extreme are withdrawn, passive, or timid babies who rarely venture out to explore. These infants may have more limited experiences as a result of their lack of interest in mastery, and this may influence their later cognitive and social development.

It is generally accepted among developmental theorists that young children have an intrinsic motivation to explore and master the environment (Hunt, 1961; White, 1959), that curiosity about the world is a normal and healthy facet of children's behavior. Mastery is most clearly illustrated by the tendency of infants and toddlers to repeat and practice newly acquired skills, such as climbing stairs or stacking objects. At the same time, interest has focused on individual differences in engagement with the environment, or mastery motivation, which encompasses both persistence in exploration and competence (Yarrow, McQuiston, MacTurk, McCarthy, Klein, & Vietze, 1983). Early caretaking experiences are thought to be one determinant of variations in mastery motivation. For example, attachment theorists consider maternal responsiveness to have a major impact on infants' exploratory competence. Infants and toddlers who feel secure and nurtured will have more energy available to invest in exploration and more curiosity about the world. Sure of their mothers' availability, they will use her as a secure base for exploration, returning from time to time to check in with her, but showing interest in independent play (Ainsworth et al., 1978).

Other aspects of maternal behavior also appear to be related to mastery motivation and exploratory competence. For example, mothers who provide the infant or toddler with opportunities to explore, who support autonomy by permitting independent play and rewarding success experiences, and who encourage exploration without being intrusive or controlling appear to raise toddlers who are more invested in environmental mastery and more adept at negotiating the environment (Cassidy, 1986; Frodi, Bridges, & Grolnick, 1985). Yet, parents who are unable to tolerate their young child's tendency to explore or who are overly directive and controlling, thereby thwarting the child's independent attempts to learn about the world, may be setting the stage for a variety of subtle problems, both social and cognitive. It appears that toddlers' ability to master the physical environment has implications for their more general feelings of self-worth and autonomy, another major developmental issue of toddlerhood. In addition, with development, exploration gives way to pretend play, which is also seen as central to both cognitive and social development.

Pretend Play

The development of pretend play is intertwined with the development of language and representational abilities, and observations of the play of toddlers and preschoolers provide a window into their spontaneous language, thought, and role taking. Numerous theorists underline the importance of play in young children's development (see Rubin et al., 1983, for a review). In particular, Erikson (1963) considers play as one means by which the young child begins to master the environment, whereas Piaget considers pretend play as enhancing cognitive and social development by allowing the child to experiment with deferred imitation, role taking, and other more advanced cognitive skills and, thereby, consolidating newly assimilated cognitive schemata. Others have emphasized pretend play as a social activity, as facilitating symbolic development, and as contributing to the development of the self-concept. Pretend play is also used as a therapeutic tool to understand the concerns and conflicts of young children. Furthermore, more advanced and elaborated pretend play is associated with greater competence in other areas, including language, creativity, and social skills.

Pretend play first emerges, in rudimentary form, at about 13 months of age when children can be observed to make believe they are engaged in a familiar activity, such as eating, drinking, or sleeping. Such acts are usually short-lived and they rely on concrete props, for example, a cup or a toy cup, if the act is drinking. By 18 months, the child is able to act upon another object in pretend play. Instead of feeding herself, she will feed her doll. Rubin et al. refer to this as the shift from self-referenced to other-referenced play. At the next level, that of active other, the child pretends that the doll is the active agent; that is, the doll is feeding itself. Studies reviewed by Rubin et al. indicate that children's play follows this developmental sequence from 12 to 30 months of age. Furthermore, as a more advanced play form emerges in the child's repertoire, earlier forms disappear. In addition, early symbolic play consists of single events, but as play becomes more complex in terms of who is the active agent, it also incorporates more complex sequences of actions and activities. The doll is not only fed but also burped, bathed, and put to bed. Thus, the child is also practicing familiar sequences of events or scripts that figure prominently in his/her understanding of the world (Rubin et al., 1983). Children are also better able to use substitute objects as props in play, an advance that illustrates another facet of representational ability. A block can stand for a cup and the child can make believe that the doll is drinking from a cup. Most 24-month-olds are able to incorporate both sequential actions and substitutions in their play.

After the third birthday, pretend play takes up an ever-increasing portion of children's spontaneous play time. According to Rubin et al. (1983) in group situations, such as preschools, children rarely engage in solitary pretend play, but cooperative dramatic play sequences are common. Furthermore, children who are familiar with one another are more likely to engage in pretend play than newly acquainted pre- schoolers (Gottman & Parkhurst, 1980), presumably because a certain level of comfort is necessary before children are willing to move beyond their own identity and let their imagination take over. Garvey (1977) observed pairs of acquainted 3- to 5-year-olds in a laboratory playroom well equipped with toys likely to elicit pretend play. She reported that fairly complex dramatic sequences were evident even in the 3-year-olds, but that older children participated in longer and more elaborate pretend interactions. Most of the imaginary play of preschoolers revolves around a relatively limited number of common themes that are well known to children, reflecting their social milieu and shared social knowledge. According to Garvey (1977), children tended to take on particular types of roles: relational or family roles predominated (mommy, daddy, baby), followed by functional roles, that is, those defined by an activity or occupation, such as teacher, bus driver, or doctor. Children across the 3- to 5-year age range took on these roles. 4- and 5-year-olds were also more likely to play imaginary characters, such as a dragon or Batman. All of these forms of dramatic play require a transformation of identity. Garvey also observed play sequences in which the child played himself but incorporated absent characters; for example, she describes a delightful sequence in which a 4$\frac{1}{2}$-year-old engages in a long telephone conversation with an imaginary friend about a sick teddy bear. In this instance, the props (toy phone) appeared necessary to scaffold the pretend sequence in the absence of role adoption and a willing play partner.

Pretend play usually involves the assignment of complementary roles, a plan of action, and the use of props (Garvey, 1977). The adoption of complementary roles implies perspective-taking ability, as does the give and take necessary for a truly interactive sociodramatic interaction. Furthermore, children often switch back and forth between the pretend character and their real self, with the real self narrating or directing the play (e.g., "Now the mommy is going shopping" or "You say, 'Don't do that!,' okay?"). These shifts are usually indicated by voice changes (the child's real voice for the directions and a high pitched baby voice or a grown up voice for the role, depending upon whether the character is a baby or a mommy). In addition, dramatic play sequences not only involve complex sets of role appropriate interactions but also exaggerated affect expression, such as mock anger or concern, and other modifications in speech. For example, a child playing mommy will often talk in shorter sentences to the "baby," consistent with the way adults talk to infants. These shifts also indicate that the play is pretend, older preschoolers may also make this explicit by specifically asking a peer to pretend something. Here, too, there is evidence not only of perspective taking but also of a clear distinction between fantasy and reality, although it has been erroneously assumed that preschoolers have difficulty distinguishing between the real and the make-believe. Although this may be the case when they are observing the fantasy of others, for example, on TV or in a movie, they certainly are aware of the differences when they themselves are engaged in the pretend activities.

The pretend play described by Garvey (1977) and others (see Rubin et al., 1983) reflects a large store of knowledge about people, relationships, and activities, as well as an ability to step outside the self and practice various roles. When younger children engage in these forms of sociodramatic play, they are likely to follow social conventions literally, and any variation from traditional expectations is likely to provoke a discussion about what is appropriate ("Daddies don't cook!"; "My daddy does!"; preschoolers seem to be surprisingly sexist), or to result in a switch in roles or a change in the activity. Older preschoolers are better able to adapt to a wider range of variations in a particular role.

Moreover, role enactments in older children are more reciprocal; younger children may act out their roles, but they tend to do so with less attention to the other's behavior and verbalizations (see Rubin et al., 1983). Finally, older preschoolers are more likely to negotiate role assignments and reassure each other that it is "just pretend," something that 2-year-olds and young 3-year-olds do not appear to do.

These advances appear to be important hallmarks of normal cognitive and social development. Children integrate experiences, express feelings, practice roles, and differentiate between reality and fantasy in the context of sociodramatic play. In clinical practice, play therapy is based on the premise that the themes expressed in children's play mirror their feelings, conflicts, preoccupations, and interpretations of reality, much of which they are not capable of expressing directly (e.g., Axline, 1969). Despite the emphasis on play therapy and the reliance on fantasy play in both the assessment and treatment of psychological distress in preschoolers, surprisingly little systematic research has been conducted on the fantasy play of clinically identified preschool children (Rubin et al., 1983). Thus, it is unclear whether some disturbed preschoolers show delays in the development of pretend play, are reluctant to engage in fantasy, or use fantasy as a way of escaping from an unsupportive or threatening environment. Despite the reliance on fantasy in clinical practice, it is not known, except at an anecdotal level, whether some children really do express their concerns through play or what the implications of individual differences in this are for under-standing and treating problems. However, because the development of pretend play is associated with major advances in language abilities and other symbolic processes, as well as with other changes in the quality of peer interactions, it seems logical to hypothesize that extremely bizarre fantasy play or the inability to engage in pretend play might be a signal of "development gone awry." For example, preschoolers who engage in extremely aggressive or disorganized fantasy play may be indicating that they are having difficulties coping with new expectations, environ-mental changes, or other stresses or developmental transitions. At the other extreme, children who are unable to engage in pretend play may lack certain symbolic or language abilities, raising concerns about cognitive-developmental delays, or they may be showing signs of social withdrawal and emotional constriction.

In summary, the appearance of pretend play marks another major advance in cognitive development. By early in the second year, children are beginning to use their representational and emerging language abilities in their play. By the age of 2 years, they are engaging in more complex representational and sequential activities. By late in the third year, role playing allows children to engage in a variety of sociodramatic play sequences that are thought to enhance social cognitive abilities, such as role taking and perspective taking as well as awareness of self–other differentiation and feelings of self-esteem. The failure of children to engage in pretend play by the age of 4 years or their tendency to engage in highly aggressive or bizarre fantasy play may be an indicator of problems in development or adaptation.

Separation–Individuation and the Development of a Sense of Self

At the same time that toddlers are engaged in intense exploration, they are grappling with another major developmental hurdle, the establishment of a separate identity. It is the combination of this need to explore and the need to test the limits of one's independence that is often termed the "terrible 2's." Just as exploratory competence and mastery of the environment have roots in early infancy and are mediated by the quality of the early mother–infant relationship, theorists interested in the development of self-awareness emphasize the role of the early care-taking environment in facilitating the emergence of a sense of self and in determining the nature of individual differences. Although a thorough discussion of the major theories is beyond the scope of this chapter, interested readers are referred to Lewis and Brooks-Gunn (1979) and Harter (1983a). It is worth noting, however, that theorists since the turn of the century have emphasized the role of social interaction in the development of self-identity and self-esteem (see Harter, 1983a).

More contemporary theorists, whether they espouse a cognitive-developmental perspective (Lewis & Brooks-Gunn, 1979), favor attachment theory (Bowlby, 1969), or work from more psychodynamic orientations (Erikson, 1963; Mahler, 1968), also emphasize the importance of the caregiving environment and the role that responsive caregivers play in the child's development of self-esteem, an independent identity, and an awareness of the self as an active agent who can have an impact on the environment, both physical and social. Erikson (1963) proposes that basic trust derives from responsive early care, which in turn permits secure toddlers to assert their independence without fear of rejection and to feel competent about their ability to exert some control over their environment. From the perspective of cognitive-developmental (Lewis & Brooks-Gunn, 1979) and attachment theories (see Bretherton, 1985, 1987), infants' experiences with consistent, responsive, and contingent care set the stage for the development of expectancies about the predictability of others and their availability, which in turn influence feelings of self-efficacy. The infant whose signals are responded to promptly and consistently learns that he/she has control over the social environment. However, infants whose signals are often ignored or who are responded to inconsistently learn that their needs and behaviors do not have an impact on the behavior of others and they do not develop expectancies that their needs will be met. Their "internal working models" (Bretherton, 1987) or schemata of the self and relationships, which are based on their past experiences with unresponsive or rejecting care, lead them to perceive themselves as incompetent and unworthy and to view others as untrustworthy, leaving them with few resources and limited motivation to assert their in-dependence. In Erikson's terminology, a lack of basic trust in early caregivers is translated into fearfulness, incompetence, and feelings of limited control in toddlerhood. Instead of feeling autonomous and able to cope with a range of new challenges, such toddlers would be expected to doubt their abilities and to feel shame both as a result of their own perceived ineptness and the anticipated rejection by significant others who have failed to support their developmental needs.

Before toddlers can assert their independence and autonomy, they must develop a sense of self that is independent from primary caregivers. Both cognitive-developmental (Lewis & Brooks-Gunn, 1979) and psychodynamic theorists (Mahler, 1968) propose that infant self-awareness develops in a sequence of stages. In early infancy, infant and environment are merged and the infant is unable to distinguish between the "me" and the "not me." With advances in motor, cognitive, affective, and social development, the infant gradually begins to differentiate between the self and others until, somewhere between 18 and 24 months, the toddler recognizes that he/she is distinct from primary caregivers. Harter (1983a), based on the work of Lewis and Brooks-Gunn (1979), distinguishes between the self as an active, independent, causal agent and the self as an object of self-knowledge. This parallels other aspects of social and cognitive development in which active, overt, or concrete advances precede more symbolic and internal representational ones. According to the framework outlined by Harter

(1983a), infants initially have no awareness of themselves as distinct from others, but by about 9 months, they are beginning to recognize that their behavior has independent effects on other people and objects. This awareness emerges at the same time that infants begin to engage in more complex reciprocal play and turn taking with adults, to act on objects by throwing, banging, and mouthing, to show clear awareness of the permanence of objects and people who are not in their immediate view, and to show a rudimentary appreciation of physical causality. Thus, the feedback inherent in turn taking and object play, as well as the representational skills implied by object permanence and the reasoning ability inherent in causality underline the complex advances in cognitive and social development at this age. By about 12 months, infants begin to recognize that they can have effects on the environment that are different from the effects that others can have, an awareness that is probably fueled by their increased mobility and their beginning ability to communicate their wants with rudimentary language.

As representational skills become more sophisticated, during the first half of the second year, toddlers begin to have some awareness of specific features of the self. For example, toddlers can recognize themselves in mirrors or in pictures and begin to identify body parts on the self and others. By the latter half of the second year, toddlers can also appreciate unique features of the self and can label pictures of the self by name, gender, and other simple attributes. This also implies an ability to conceptualize "me" from "not me" and, therefore, to recognize that others possess attributes that are different from one's own. However, at this stage, toddlers would be likely to have only a relatively rudimentary appreciation of this concept and to recognize only concrete and obvious attributes, such as gender, size, and age (baby, child, adult). This is the stage that Mahler describes as the rapprochement phase of separation–individuation in which the toddler's growing awareness of separateness from mother is associated with increased separation distress, anger, frustration, and noncompliance, which may reflect ambivalence over independence versus dependence.

In a longitudinal study of development in toddlers over the second year, Kagan (1981) defined several converging signs of growing self-awareness, as well as awareness of others as distinct individuals. He emphasized increases in "mastery smiles" indicating satisfaction with one's own accomplishments, as well as distress at the inability to carry out an adult's request, thereby eliciting feelings of incompetence. By the latter half of the second year, Kagan also noted an increase in children's interest in directing adult activity in game-like interactions, another indication of toddlers' growing sense of autonomy and self-efficacy. Finally, Kagan documents the increased use of self-descriptive speech from 22 to 27 months, including descriptions of ongoing activities, statements specifically referring to the self using "I," "me," and "mine," and references to internal states (e.g., "want," "hurt," "like").

By the beginning of the third year, Mahler's resolution phase, the toddler has adapted to this separateness and is better able to tolerate his/her independence because cognitive-developmental advances in language development, symbolic representation, and reasoning make it easier to bridge periods of maternal absence and because the child is increasingly involved in independent play activities, often in the company of age-mates.

Parents are often uncertain about how to cope with this developmental transition point because once cooperative and positive youngsters may go through a period of irritability and anger reflected in frequent tantrums, crying spells, and oppositional behavior. At this point, children may be oppositional just for the sake of saying "no!," and parents may waffle between flexibility and rigid limit setting. It seems important for parents to recognize that this is a normal developmental phenomenon and that their children are experimenting with limits, their own and others, as well as asserting their independence, sometimes by failing even to go along with things they want to do. Parents need to feel comfortable setting limits because testing often indicates a young child's need for some guidelines about acceptable behavior from significant others, but limits that are flexible and not confrontative. Too often parents let their toddlers gain control, either by engaging in a battle of wills, by failing to set clear and consistent limits, or by not setting any limits at all. Other parents overreact to defiance from their toddler. Unable to tolerate any challenges to their authority, they set limits that are too harsh, leading to escalating confrontations that may have a negative impact on the quality and tone of the parent–child relationship. The difficulties of this developmental period are often exacerbated by the birth of a sibling, which may further fuel a toddler's tendencies to be noncompliant, negative, and attention seeking. The way that parents handle this difficult period of development may be critical because the child may become increasingly demanding in the face of either inadequate or strict limits, and this may set the stage for ongoing parent–child conflict.

As children mature, however, this phase of negativism and noncompliance is usually replaced by a more reasonable period of increased interest in the world and in peer relationships. The phase of separation–individuation has been successfully negotiated and the child's self-awareness continues to become both more complex and more differentiated as social comparisons are made and children become increasingly aware of the thoughts and feelings of others. The development of peer relationships and social-cognitive awareness become primary.

Self-Regulation

Related to self-awareness and the development of autonomy and independence is the development of self-regulatory ability. Indeed, self-control and self-regulation obviously depend upon self-awareness and one's sense of self because self-awareness and self-reflection would appear to be necessary for the internal regulation of behavior. Self-regulation, like self-awareness, is seen as developing through qualitatively distinct phases, with children moving from concrete and externally mediated control attempts to more internally mediated self-regulation (Kopp, 1982). There is general agreement that self-regulation, whether it is defined in terms of compliance, modulation of behavior, inhibition of situationally inappropriate behavior, or the ability to wait for desired events, depends upon the awareness of what constitutes acceptable behavior and derives from socialization experiences (Kopp, 1982).

It is important to point out that most conceptualizations of behavior problems in childhood focus on deficits in self-control. For example, Achenbach and Edelbrock (1978), in their description of childhood disorders, discuss patterns of overcontrol (e.g., social withdrawal) and undercontrol (e.g., overactivity, aggression, noncompliance). It is well known that in early childhood the bulk of problems about which adults complain are characterized by undercontrol (Achenbach & Edelbrock, 1978; Campbell, 1989), and they can be construed as failures to develop internalized standards of socially appropriate behavior and/or to use these standards to guide behavior. The Blocks' (Block & Block, 1980) theory of personality development likewise focuses on ego control as one major bipolar dimension of personality functioning. Overcontrolled individuals are tight and lack spontaneity, whereas undercontrolled individuals tend to be explosive, active, and aggressive. Both individual child characteristics and patterns of child rearing are implicated in the development of ego control (Harter, 1983a).

Despite the importance accorded to self-control by personality theorists and clinical psychologists (see Harter, 1983a, for a review), there has been relatively little attention paid to its early development. The work of Kopp (1982) is the one notable exception to this neglect. She has outlined a theoretical model of the cognitive and social antecedents of self-control in infancy as well as its emergence during toddlerhood and the preschool period. Consistent with a transactional model of development, Kopp (1982) suggests that early modulation of behavior as well as later self-regulatory abilities derive both from individual differences in infant characteristics that have biological–constitutional roots and from the quality of caretaking. With development, as self-regulation becomes more internalized, socialization processes within the family and cognitive processes within the child become especially salient determinants of individual differences in self-control.

Kopp proposes that modulation of physiological arousal in the early months and infants' organized responses to environmental stimuli during the first year depend largely on constitutional factors and parents' abilities to provide predictable routines, to respond appropriately to infants' communications, and to prevent overwhelming frustration. Through most of the first year, infants are able to modulate their reactions when supported appropriately by parents, but their behavior does not have an intentional quality and it is dependent upon ongoing events. By the end of the first year, however, infants begin to comply with parental requests and can even anticipate the need to perform or inhibit particular motor acts, such as not touching something dangerous or fragile. Kopp argues that certain cognitive-developmental advances in object permanence and recognition memory must necessarily precede the emergence of this early form of control, which involves compliance with social demands and the expectations of caregivers, goal-directed behavior, intentionality, and rudimentary awareness of the self. It is assumed that this form of self-control occurs in only a limited number of situations that are predictable, and they are associated with relatively clear external controls. Furthermore, although children know that they should not do certain things, they are not likely to understand the reasons for the prohibitions. Anyone who has ever been around toddlers can think of examples of this form of control, for instance, the child who knows that the stove or a valuable china teapot is off limits. The self-initiated and coordinated behaviors that characterize certain games, particularly when turn taking and complementary roles are involved, also require control over one's behavior as well as some degree of self-awareness and anticipation of the reactions of the partner (Brownell, 1986; Kopp, 1982). Furthermore, there is accumulating evidence that the strategies parents use to gain compliance and direct behavior are important determinants of children's willingness to comply (Maccoby & Martin, 1983). Thus, firm, clear, consistent, and appropriate limits appear more effective than inconsistent, ambiguous, or harsh attempts at control.

By the end of the second year, Kopp (1982) notes that true self-control emerges as children are able to comply with expectations and can inhibit impulses in the absence of external constraints. This advance in behavioral control appears to depend upon more advanced representational thinking and more complex memory development, including evocative or recall memory. Both are seen as cognitive prerequisites if children are to begin to monitor their own behavior in accordance with social rules in the absence of constant adult reminders. Language development also plays a role. In the second year, children use language to describe their ongoing behavior and this may sometimes aid them in initiating or inhibiting a specific behavior (Kagan, 1981). Kopp (1982) distinguishes between the early, self-generated self-control of which toddlers are capable, which tends to be relatively inflexible and tied to specific situations, and the more advanced self-regulation of the preschooler. By about the age of 3 years, children are able to engage in more complex, adaptive, and long-term self-regulatory behaviors. Kopp suggests that this form of self-regulation may involve self-reflection and planning strategies. Language may also be used to verbalize plans or prohibitions; therefore, advances in language development may aid in self-regulation. Certainly, the complex routines that preschoolers follow and their ability to function cooperatively with peers and teachers in nursery school and day-care suggest fairly marked gains in socially appropriate regulation of self-help skills and social interaction. At this stage, too, children are able to apologize for transgressions and to recognize when others are behaving in unacceptable ways, suggesting both some degree of self-reflection and the internalization of standards of behavior. Throughout the preschool years, children acquire greater control over impulses and more awareness of the limits of socially acceptable behavior. Related to these advances are the development of conscience and morality, the idea that behavioral control and definitions of right and wrong often involve more than social convention; that is, they stem from higher precepts, such as not harming others or violating their trust.

Individual differences in child personality and child-rearing strategies appear to be associated with differences in self-regulation (Harter, 1983a; Maccoby & Martin, 1983). For example, children who are more irritable and easily aroused may have a more difficult time controlling impulses and tolerating frustration, and these difficulties may be exacerbated if their parents are themselves impatient and explosive. As already noted, children's problems in early childhood and beyond often reflect difficulties with internalized standards of behavior as indexed by noncompliance, overactivity, aggression toward peers, defiance of authority, and a limited ability to tolerate frustration or delayed gratification. Findings from longitudinal studies also suggest that early deficits in self-control may persist (e.g., Block & Block, 1980; Richman et al., 1982), although clinically significant difficulties tend to reflect a constellation of problems that may indicate a lack of internalized standards and concern for the rights and/or feelings of others. Although relatively little is understood about the processes influencing the development of self-regulatory abilities in clinical populations of young children, it does appear that parental approaches to discipline, their own strategies of conflict resolution and self-control abilities, and the quality of relationships within the family are all crucial backdrops against which to view children's problems in the early development of self-control.

Language Development

It has often been noted that the main characteristic that differentiates the human form other primates is the capacity to use spoken language to communicate. Over the course of the first 36 months of life, children move from being preverbal and unable to comprehend spoken language to being able to communicate using complex and syntactically correct sentences (Shatz, 1983; Stone & Church, 1984). The major transitions in cognitive functioning that occur over the first 3 years are dramatized by a consideration of the accomplishments made in language development. Language development is intricately tied to conceptual development and the more general capacity to represent reality with symbols (Clark, 1983; Kagan, 1981; McCall, 1979). The ability to make connections between objects without actually acting upon them develops at about 13 months, and the capacity to think about their relationship to one another, even when they are not present (i.e., by representing them mentally), appears to consolidate during the latter part of the second year (McCall, 1979). These two developmental transitions also herald the development of language, first the appearance of single words at about 12 months, followed by the ability to put two words together at about 24 months.

Although the relationships between cognitive and language development has been the subject of some debate, Clark (1983) argues that there are cognitive constraints on language development. She suggests that children learn words that map onto conceptual categories that they have already mastered at a representational level. Furthermore, the ability to think symbolically, that is, to recognize that something (such as a word) can stand for something else, would appear to be a cognitive prerequisite for language. Language develops in a highly predictable sequence that is invariant across children regardless of their linguistic and cultural background, suggesting that early language development is under strong maturational control and dependent upon the growth of brain structures (Clark, 1983). Furthermore, this sequence is clearly consistent with the view that cognitive developmental advances either precede or emerge simultaneously with early linguistic competence, rather than language preceding cognitive transitions. For example, the child's ability to link two objects in thought and to sequence two events in pretend play appear at about the same time that toddlers begin to put two words together, somewhere around 24 months (Brownell, 1988; Kagan, 1981; McCall, 1979).

Young infants vocalize to express distress and pleasure and they respond to the sound of the human voice, localizing sounds in the early weeks of life. In the early months infants play with sounds and are able to discriminate between differing consonant–vowel combinations. The cooing of the young infant gives way to babbling as infants practice making various sound combinations. By the latter half of the first year, infant babbling takes on the cadence of the child's own language and by about 8 to 10 months, children are able to understand some simple commands and names for familiar people and objects. By 12 months, most infants have a vocabulary of a few simple words, although they may only be recognizable to those familiar with their idiosyncratic use of a particular speech sound to designate a particular object, person, or category of objects or people (e.g., "Da" for Daddy or for all men). Infants' first words are almost universally object words that signify familiar people and things in their immediate environment (e.g., mama, ball, doggie, bottle), although some properties of objects are also learned early (e.g., hot). By 18 months, children tend to have words for people, common animals, vehicles, toys, food, body parts, and household objects. In addition to nouns, children also begin to acquire vocabulary to describe situations and states (Clark, 1983). For example, they begin to use verbs such as go, eat, and sleep, as well as words that describe other aspects of situations or states, such as broken, up, and little. These words all describe ongoing experiences, as well as familiar objects and events in concrete terms (Clark, 1983). At about 18 months, toddlers also use one-word utterances to imply an entire sentence. For example, "all-gone" may mean that the milk, ice cream, or whatever is all finished.

Once children begin to use words to communicate, they show a rapid increase in vocabulary, primarily an increase in the acquisition of object words. This language spurt at about 18 months has been called the naming explosion because children may triple their functional vocabulary in just a few weeks (Gopnik & Meltzoff, 1988). Children going through this stage of language acquisition may go around the house asking constantly "What's that?" in an active attempt at vocabulary building. Another feature of early language is the use of what has been termed overextensions (Clark, 1983); that is, a word may be used to refer to a range of objects that are perceptually similar or that belong to a larger class of things. The word is being used in a more overinclusive manner than it would be in adult speech, but the errors are usually logical. For example, a toddler may refer to dogs, horses, cows, and sheep as "doggie" until more differentiated terms are learned. Clark (1983) notes that overextensions may account for up to 30% of vocabulary usage during the period from 12 to 30 months but that overextensions systematically drop out of the vocabulary as word knowledge increases. She interprets these as approximations that young children use when they do not have adequate vocabulary but still wish to communicate. As they learn the appropriate word (e.g., "horsey"), they do not need to rely upon the inappropriate use of the word "doggie." Underextensions are also apparent, although less well documented. Thus, children may use a word such as "kitty" to refer to a specific cat, rather than to the class of animals that adults call cats.

Roughly at the time of their second birthday, toddlers begin to put words together into two-word sentences. This is a major transition in language development and ushers in a new period of language complexity. At this time children begin to create sentences on their own.

Shortly after the appearance of two-word sentences, sentence length increases. At this time, too, children increase their use of self-referent statements, including descriptions of their own internal states. These advances in language development underline the reciprocal relationships among self-awareness, self-regulation, and language competence (Kagan, 1981). By the third birthday, children are speaking in increasingly complex sentences that may include clauses and connectives, as well as statements of causality, descriptions of past events, and planning for the future. Thus, while early vocabulary is focused almost exclusively on concrete objects or ongoing events in the here and now, by 36 months, children are able to use language to convey information about internal states, relationships, and other abstractions.

It is generally agreed that, similar to the motivation to explore, the motivation to become verbal is intrinsic, a given of development. Furthermore, the capacity to develop language appears to be inherent in brain structure, although exposure to the language of the culture is an obvious prerequisite to its development (Clark, 1983). However, children are not taught language as such. Rather, the combination of physical maturation and environmental exposure combine to lead first to the recognition of speech sounds, then to comprehension, and finally to the production of language. Thus, children spontaneously learn the phonemics as well as the syntax and semantics of their native language without direct instruction. They also learn the cadence and can mimic the prosody of their native language before they can produce a comprehensible sentence. In addition, children learn the basic rules of grammar and apply them diligently. This is evident in the logical errors that young children make, for example, in forming plurals or past tenses (e.g., feets, mans, bringed, goed) (see Stone & Church, 1984). Finally, it is worth emphasizing the point that children construct new sentences all the time by putting together in logical and appropriate sequence series of words that they have heard in other contexts. It is this creative aspect of language that has fascinated students of child development.

Although early language appears to develop relatively predictably given a wide range of normal experiences with caretakers, the language environment also plays an important role and this probably becomes more important as young children use speech to communicate (Shatz, 1983). Early adult–infant interaction often involves reciprocal vocalization, and this appears to set the stage for later language. There is no doubt that children must hear language if they are to learn to speak appropriately and at the expected time. Observations of adult–infant interaction also indicate that adults automatically adapt their speech to that of their young child. Thus, Snow (1972) described "motherese" or the tendency of adults, but particularly mothers, to use simple, well-formed sentences, more exaggerated voice inflections, and repetition when speaking to toddlers. There is evidence that children as young as 4 years modify their speech when talking to younger children, producing shorter and less complex sentences than they do when talking to adults or peers (Shatz & Gelman, 1973). Mothers also correct young children's speech, for example, by supplying the correct word ("That's not a doggie, it's a horse") and elaborating on a child's utterance. They also keep conversations going by adding new information. There is overwhelming evidence that communicative competence is influenced by the amount of conversation in the household and that conversations, even with prelinguistic infants, are important. However, the specific relationships between parental language input and children's later language competence are far from clear.

There are several clinical implications of marked delays in language development in young children. Whereas language delays are most obviously associated with more general delays in cognitive development, they are also frequently associated with behavior problems in children with normal abilities. Children referred to speech clinics because of language delays are likely to experience a range of behavior problems as well (Cantwell, Baker, & Mattison, 1979) and, conversely, children referred to child psychiatry clinics often have unsuspected language immaturities or disorders that may be overshadowed by their behavior problems (Cohen, Davine, & Meloche-Kelly, 1989). Both of these studies reported an overlap between language delays and behavior problems of roughly 50%. Furthermore, Richman et al. (1982) found an association between delayed language development and behavior problems in their epidemiological study of London 3-year-olds, and language delays were associated with reading and learning problems at the age of 8 years.

At the level of process, a language delay may be a sign of difficulty in expressive language that can have an impact on social development by influencing peer relationships, parent–child relationships, or teacher–child interaction. For example, children may tease, reject, or isolate a child with less developed speech or speech that is hard to understand. Such youngsters may have difficulty participating in social games that involve dramatic roles and conversation. Parents may become impatient with children who misunderstand instructions or who do not easily communicate their wishes or thoughts. Parents and teachers may underestimate the abilities of children with language delays or in other ways communicate to them that they are not competent. Children's impaired language abilities may also be one manifestation of an unstimulating or otherwise unsupportive environment. The relationships among language development, general cognitive development, social development in the peer group, and parent–child relationships are undoubtedly complex. Research is only beginning to delineate associations among these different facets of cognitive and social development. These constitute a first step that will naturally lead to the more interesting questions about developmental process.

Memory Development

The ability to learn language and to profit from experience is much dependent upon memory. Memory development in young children shows both qualitative and quantitative change over the period from infancy through preschool. Changes in memory, as in other domains of functioning, reflect both brain maturation and major advances in language and conceptual development. Theorists propose that memory depends upon information processing at different levels of analysis and organization (Ornstein, 1978). Thus, it has been suggested that at least a three-step process ensues: (1) stimuli are first attended to and perceived, (2) then they are encoded in short-term working memory, and (3) then they are integrated into long-term memory. From a developmental perspective, it has been assumed by some that memory structures do not change much with development beyond infancy but that cognitive developmental change and an increased knowledge base allow for the more efficient organization of information and the development of memory strategies (Ornstein, 1978).

Over the first few months of life, infants begin to derive meaning from environmental stimuli, and by 3 months they begin to recognize the familiar. This is evident from studies that rely upon infants' innate preferences for novelty and use looking time as an index of interest in unfamiliar compared with familiar stimuli. Six-month-olds have been found to recognize visual stimuli after a 2-week delay, a finding that is not surprising because infants at this age can recognize familiar people or favorite toys that they do not see daily. Furthermore, recent work by Rovee-Collier and associates (reviewed in Dachler & Greco, 1985) suggests that even very young infants have some degree of long-term memory and that earlier research has tended to underestimate the memory abilities of 2- and 3-month-olds. For example, these investigators found that 2-month-olds could remember a motor act (i.e., a foot kick that activated a mobile) after a 2-week period, while 3-month-olds could activate the mobile after a month long delay provided they were exposed first to the mobile.

Olson and Sherman (1983), in an extensive review of infant memory development, note the rapid changes in infant memory capacity over the first year of life as infants become better able to organize information about the world. They are able to rely on a growing knowledge base to help them make sense of new experiences and this organizational capacity facilitates the retention of information about familiar objects, people, and events. Diary studies provide evidence for fairly complex memory ability, as evidenced by expectancies, surprise, and recognition in young infants. Thus, by 12 months, infants give clear evidence of remembering both routine events and past experiences, such as visits to the pediatrician. More controlled research also demonstrates that 1-year-olds can recognize pictures shown only briefly in a large array. Furthermore, object permanence clearly relies on memory both for the hidden object and for its location.

Memory in young children also tends to be very context-specific (Daehler & Greco, 1985). It has been suggested that the improvements noted in memory between the ages of 2 and 5 years can be accounted for by conceptual development and an increase in the knowledge base, rather than by a change in the strategies children use (Daehler & Greco, 1985; Myers & Perlmutter, 1978). Both recognition and recall are facilitated when the to-be-remembered stimuli consist of objects or properties of objects that are familiar to the child, when they fit into categories that are well known to the child, or when they relate to familiar events or experiences in the child's life.

As in other areas of cognitive development, the nature of the task appears to influence the picture one gets of young children's memory capacities. The meaningfulness and importance of the information appear crucial. Diary reports indicate that 1-year-olds remember routines and games; 2-year-olds can remember sequences of events over several months when they are salient, such as a birthday party or a trip to the zoo. However, young children often may not distinguish between what they expect to happen on a trip to the zoo and the specifics of a particular trip to the zoo, making it difficult to assess specific recall as opposed to script knowledge, that is, the awareness of the typical sequence of events in familiar situations (Daehler & Greco, 1985).

In one study, Wellman and Somerville (1980) found that salience had a considerable influence on the memory capacity of toddlers and preschoolers. Two-year-olds and 4-year-olds were told to remind their caregivers either to buy candy or to hang up the wash. As might be expected, the children had no difficulty remembering the candy, although only one in five remembered the wash. Furthermore, delay intervals ranging from a few minutes to overnight did not make a difference. Because children were motivated to remember the candy, they did so, even after a relatively long delay interval; no age differences were obtained in this study, probably because the situation was meaningful to children in this age range and fit in comfortably with their daily routine.

There is also interest in the strategies that children use to help them remember, as well as their awareness of memory strategies or metamemory (Brown, Bransford, Ferrara, & Campione, 1983). Whereas Myers and Perlmutter (1978) specifically noted the lack of strategic memory in the preschoolers they studied on more traditional memory tasks that required children to recall pairs or groups of objects, Brown et al. (1983) take issue with this conclusion. They argue that even very young children use simple and concrete memory aids to help them in familiar tasks with clear goals. For example, Wellman, Ritter, and Flavell (1975) observed 3- and 4-year-olds on a memory for location task, in which a toy dog was hidden under one of three containers. One half of the children were told to wait to find the toy, and the other half were told to remember where it was. Children given the remember instructions used a variety of strategies, such as pointing at, looking at, or touching the appropriate container. Children who utilized some form of strategy remembered better than those who did not. Similarly, DeLoache, Cassidy, and Brown (1985) observed 18- to 24-month-olds on a memory for location task in which a toy cat was hidden and reached a similar conclusion. Although the strategies used by this age group are clearly concrete and external, rather than internal ones that might be used by older children, these studies provide beginning evidence for the spontaneous use of memory aids in young children.

Taken together, it is generally agreed that memory improves with development, probably as a function of cognitive and language development and the use of strategies to facilitate the organization and recall of information. Furthermore, children have an easier time remembering things that fit into their knowledge base; that is, if they can incorporate new information into a context, it is more readily assimilated and integrated into useful long-term memory. Preschoolers are just beginning to utilize strategies to facilitate memory, but these tend to be concrete and tied to familiar situations. Although it is difficult to link memory development to specific clinical problems, it seems obvious that memory abilities are a necessary and fundamental component of all other aspects of cognitive and social development. Mastery of the environment, the development of a sense of self, language development, and self-regulation all depend to some extent on children's ability to learn from past experience. Similarly, peer relations and relationships within the family will be shaped to some extent by children's abilities to remember past events and to develop expectations about the behaviors and personality characteristics of others.

Summary

In this chapter some of the major advances in cognitive and social development that occur during toddlerhood and the preschool years have been described. It should be evident from this discussion that exploration and pretend play, self-regulation and self-awareness, and memory and language development are all intricately intertwined, with advances in one domain partly tied to advances in another. Thus, for example, the ability to engage in pretend play implies some degree of stable self-image that permits the child to switch roles; the ability to engage in a mutually regulated interaction with another also rests upon self-regulatory ability, memory, and language, as well as a common core of organized knowledge about the social world. Moreover, it appears that participation in pretend play sequences with other children also serves to enhance self-awareness, social knowledge, and self-control. It also seems clear that the preschooler, although limited to some degree by experience and cognitive structures, is much more sophisticated about the world than earlier theorists believed. In particular, observations of children's spontaneous behavior in a range of social and problem-solving situations indicate that preschoolers are much less egocentric than was suggested even a decade ago. Finally, individual differences in these various developmental achievements appear to depend, in part, on environmental factors, particularly parental tolerance, sensitivity, and the provision of appropriate stimulation and opportunities to learn about the world.

When children's development in one or more of these domains does not proceed smoothly, this may reflect a transient problem, a reaction to a difficult developmental hurdle. However, a potentially benign or transient problem may have wider ramifications on a child's functioning, especially if it is not handled appropriately by significant adults. For example, a child who is having difficulty grappling with issues of separation and autonomy may also develop problems in self-regulation and in the peer group, and this may be more likely if parents deal with early conflicts over separation in an angry and authoritarian manner. When parents are sensitive to developmental stresses, they can usually help young children overcome potential difficulties and move on to the next developmental task. Unfortunately, not all parents are equally skilled at anticipating their children's developmental needs or appropriately interpreting irritable, explosive, or withdrawn behavior. Although many children progress despite less than optimal support from parents, others have a difficult time coping with the frustrations of development in the absence of help and guidance from significant adults. In these children potential problems with autonomy, self-control, or mastery may be exacerbated by parental insensitivity, ignorance, or rejection, leading to increasingly more severe problems or problems that surface each time the child confronts a new developmental challenge. Other children may have difficulty at some developmental transition points even with adequate to excellent parenting. However, the way that families manage the developmental tasks of toddlerhood and the preschool years may have implications for their children's later development.

CHAPTER THREE

Clinical Issues

Annoying Behavior or a Problem?

Jenny is riding a tricycle around the preschool classroom when Jerry arrives. Jerry wants it! He watches Jenny for a few seconds as she rides around the room, then dashes over to her, and tries to push her off the bike. The teacher intervenes.

Alan's mother just had a new baby and he has been particularly moody and unpredictable. One minute he is clinging and tearful, the next he is wild and defiant, throwing toys and disobeying.

Sarah is a leader in the classroom and is always the one to be the "mother" in the play house at nursery school. When Sandra wants to take turns, Sarah protests and refuses to play with Sandra, roughly pushing her out of the way. Sandra goes off tearfully to tell the teacher.

Jeffrey has been in preschool for a week and has refused to talk to or play with the other children. The teacher has never heard him say a word to anyone but his mother. He has consistently ignored the overtures of other children and spends his time either hovering at the edge of a group of children, watching their play, or off by himself in a corner playing with trucks. When the teacher attempts to engage Jeffrey in group activities, he withdraws even more.

Jill and her mother are in the supermarket and Jill is reluctant to stay in the shopping cart. It's no fun going shopping if you can't run around and touch things! When her mother insists that she sit in the shopping cart, Jill begins to throw groceries from the basket all over the floor of the meat department while crying and screaming. Her mother is mortified as people walk by and stare disapprovingly.

These are all familiar scenes to anyone who has had contact with young children. Certainly no one would consider these toy struggles, temper tantrums, or signs of sibling jealousy to be anything but typical behaviors. Indeed, studies suggest that these and a range of other behaviors that are troubling or annoying to adults are common in the general population of preschoolers. But when do temper tantrums or fights between peers become problems worthy of concern? Is Jeffrey's social isolation just an indication of excessive shyness in a new and overwhelming situation, something he will soon overcome, if left to adapt slowly? Or, is it a sign of a potentially more serious difficulty relating to others? If Jill was having frequent tantrums and was finally referred to a psychologist, would the behavior then become a symptom of a psychological disturbance? When an annoying behavior becomes something a parent cannot handle, does that make it a symptom of a child's behavior disorder or of a parent's problems setting limits? How does one distinguish among an annoying behavior, an age-specific problem behavior, and a symptom of disorder? In an attempt to provide some conceptual clarity, the terms worrisome or annoying behavior will be used throughout this chapter to refer to typical and age-appropriate behavior that may concern some parents; age-specific problem or problem behavior will be used to indicate an exaggeration in the frequency and/or intensity of typical behavior to an upsetting degree, something that may or may not be a sign of a more serious difficulty to come; and symptom or symptomatic behavior will be utilized to designate a problem of probable clinical significance.

These degrees of troublesome behavior overlap considerably, and it is difficult, if not impossible, to clearly differentiate them. Furthermore, different observers may interpret a particular behavior differently, giving the same behavior a different meaning or developmental significance. For example, toy struggles in preschool are seen by some psychologists as an important developmental step in learning the rules of social exchange and sharing. Parents, however, may become upset by frequent squabbles over toys between peers or siblings and worry that their child is not learning to share. Toy struggles, in and of themselves, therefore, might be considered annoying but healthy behaviors or age-specific problems, depending on the point of view of the observer. However, when they occur in the context of frequent aggressive encounters with other children, disobedience, and temper tantrums, toy struggles might be seen as a symptom of a more serious problem warranting treatment. Similarly, tantrums may be the hallmark of a

2-year-old's struggle to assert herself and establish some degree of independence and autonomy. Or, in the context of a variety of other problem behaviors indicative of more widespread aggression, noncompliance, and anxiety, the tantrums may be seen as symptomatic behavior. As a first step in attempting to differentiate between age-related behaviors and behavior problems in young children, a number of studies have assessed the frequency of behaviors considered annoying or problematic by adults; some of these studies have also looked at age changes and sex differences in target behaviors in an effort to clarify systematic variations in irritating or upsetting behaviors.

How Common Are Problem Behaviors?

Epidemiological studies and large-scale surveys have been conducted to examine frequencies of occurrence of specific potentially problematic behaviors in representative samples of children. Thus, researchers have asked parents and preschool teachers to rate large numbers of annoying and/or worrisome behaviors typically shown by children. These studies have found that most of the behaviors of interest, that is, those that might be considered symptomatic of disorder in some contexts (e.g., doesn't listen, is overactive, fights with other children, worries, or is shy), are very common. Thus, many, if not most, children will exhibit these behaviors some of the time in specific situations or at a particular period of development, although only a few children will show these behaviors at high intensities and/or frequencies. Other symptomatic behaviors are rare, exhibited by few children, even at low frequencies (e.g., steals, bizarre mannerisms), and when they are observed, they are more obviously indicative of a problem.

Most studies of this type have been conducted on children of preschool age or older, although a few have included younger children. It is not surprising that the nature of parental concerns about young children parallels expected developmental changes. Thus, Jenkins, Bax, and Hart (1980) examined parental concerns in a representative sample of parents of children ranging in age from 6 weeks to 4½ years. In infancy, concerns were relatively rare, with worries about sleeping, feeding, and crying predominant. Between the ages of 1 and 2 years, the total number of parental concerns began to increase somewhat, with feeding and sleeping difficulties still the major focus. Difficulties with bowel and bladder control emerged as parental worries at age 2. The number and intensity of parental concerns peaked at age 3 when the major complaints revolved around difficulties with management and discipline.

Other studies have likewise found that parents of young children frequently report concerns about toileting, eating habits, and sleeping problems. Relatively high proportions of parents of 3-year-olds also complain of more general problems with noncompliance, limited 3— self-control, and poor relations with siblings and peers. (Earls, 1980; Richman et al., 1982). For example, in an epidemiological study of 705 3-year-old children in London, Richman and her colleagues reported that 12.9% were described by their mothers as overactive and restless, 10.7% were seen as difficult to control, and 9.2% were seen as attention seeking. In a large-scale screening study of day-care attenders in rural Vermont, Crowther, Bond, and Rolf (1981) reported even higher rates of overactivity, low frustration tolerance, frequent fights with peers, and inattention in 3-year-old boys. It seems unlikely that such a large proportion of young children is showing clinically significant symptoms. Rather, these studies suggest that many of the behaviors that may indicate problems are also extremely common in the general population.

Both cross-sectional and longitudinal studies also reveal that the nature of children's problem behaviors changes with age. Thus, as noted above, management difficulties appear to peak at age 3 and to become 3— less troublesome thereafter. According to both maternal and teacher reports, other specific behaviors, including fears and worries, tantrums, overactivity, attentional problems, and fighting with peers, seem to decrease in both frequency and severity over the preschool years in nonclinical samples (Coleman, Wolkind, & Ashley, 1977; Crowther et al., 1981; MacFarlane, Allen, & Honzik, 1954). These findings from large-scale studies that indicate that some problem behaviors show age-related decreases have been interpreted to suggest that most problems in preschoolers are likely to be outgrown. However, studies have not examined systematically whether some problem behaviors are more likely to persist when they are initially at the extremes in intensity or frequency or whether some behaviors are more likely to persist in a somewhat different form at different developmental periods.

✓   Sex differences in the frequency and intensity of problem behaviors have also been examined. In general, boys are more likely than girls to be described as aggressive, overactive, inattentive, and disobedient, although findings are inconsistent about the age at which sex differences first appear. Three studies of preschoolers found only trivial sex differences in parent reports of problem behaviors (Campbell & Breaux, 1983; Earls, 1980; Richman et al., 1982). Crowther et al. (1981), on the other hand, reported that sex differences were apparent by age 3 on a large number of potentially symptomatic behaviors. Teachers rated boys in day-care as showing more destructive behavior, disruptive behavior, noncompliance, and peer problems, and lower frustration tolerance than girls. Although sex differences in young children's behavior require further research, the findings of Crowther et al. are consistent with a large number of studies of school-aged children, which indicate higher rates of aggressive and overactive behaviors in boys (Achenbach & Edelbrock, 1978, 1981; Werry & Quay, 1971).

Taken together, these studies indicate that behaviors that are considered indicative of psychological disturbance in some contexts are common in the general population, that certain behaviors show age-related increases or decreases, and that sex differences are often found in the frequency and severity of annoying or worrisome behavior.

A Relative Definition of Problem Behavior

The studies just discussed do not allow us to define normality or abnormality objectively, but they do place problem behaviors in a wider context. Knowing that 3-year-old Jamie is aggressive in preschool and that aggression in preschool is common among 3-year-old boys may lead us to conclude that Jamie's behavior is merely typical and need not be a cause for parental concern, beyond attempts to handle it in the present situation. However, such an evaluation will depend upon factors in the child's peer group and family, his overall pattern of behavior and its intensity in a variety of situations, and changes in his behavior over time. Isolated behaviors are probably less cause for concern than those that occur together with other maladaptive behaviors or within a troubled family milieu. Similarly, if we know that separation distress is rare by age 4, its presence does not permit us to conclude that a serious problem exists with long-term consequences for the child's development until other associated factors have also been examined. The presence of a disorder or an incipient disorder cannot be determined on the basis of one or two annoying and/or potentially symptomatic behaviors. The emphasis must be on the pattern of behavioral disturbance rather than specific symptoms. The frequency, intensity, and constellation of symptomatic behavior is relevant to a determination of whether a clinically significant problem exists, as is its wider family and social context.

Assessment of problem behavior is further complicated by differences in perceptions and interpretations of children's behavior as well as the variability in the behaviors children display in different settings and with different people. Thus, a child's toy struggles with peers, temper tantrums, or separation distress may worry one parent and be dismissed as typical behavior by another. In many families, fathers and mothers appear to perceive their children's behavior differently as evidenced by the relatively low agreement between parents on rating scales describing children's behavior (e.g., Achenbach, McConaughy, & Howell, 1987; Hubert, Wachs, Peters-Martin, & Gandour, 1982). In addition, children behave differently with different adults and in various settings. For instance, one child may be cooperative with new people or in preschool but noncompliant at home, while another is sociable at home but shy and withdrawn in preschool. Thus, it is necessary to assess a child's behavior from multiple perspectives, that is, within a developmental framework and from the vantage point of several significant adults in the child's environment. A relatively comprehensive assessment is needed if an accurate picture of the child's functioning is to emerge.

As already noted, the developmental supports available to the child from within the family must also be considered in an evaluation of problem behavior. Are parental expectations unrealistic, thereby exacerbating conflict during a difficult developmental transition? For example, are parents too rigid and demanding in setting limits at a time when the toddler is attempting to establish independence and autonomy, thereby creating a "battle of wills" that leads to frequent temper tantrums and bouts of noncompliance? Conversely, are parents reluctant to set limits for fear of thwarting their child's sense of self at a time when firm, consistent, but flexible guidelines are more congruent with the child's developmental needs? Are parents who are overwhelmed with their own problems unable to provide a stable, nurturing, and structured environment that fosters exploration and the development of self-awareness and self-control? Or is the child's behavior being misinterpreted as a problem by parents who lack an understanding of normal development?

In summary, particular behaviors may be typical or may be indicators of a potential problem. Assessment must focus on the child in a developmental and family context. It ultimately involves a decision as to whether the behaviors in question are age-appropriate, typical, and likely to be outgrown or the sign of a clinically significant problem. If the clinician judges the problem to be clinically significant, does it correspond to the usual patterns of aggressive or withdrawn behavior observed in young children? What meaningful clinical decisions can be made about treatment? Before an assessment can be conducted, someone in the child's immediate environment, usually a parent or preschool teacher, must be sufficiently concerned about the behaviors in question to make a referral to a mental health professional.

Factors Influencing Referral

Many children with problems, especially young children who are not attending preschools, probably do not reach mental health practitioners. Conversely, any one who has worked with young children and their families has seen children with age-appropriate difficulties who were brought in for help because of parental concern. Factors influencing referral patterns are complex and have not been investigated extensively. Thus, what follows is a distillation of clinical experience and is not based on empirical findings. However, it seems obvious that some combination of family, child, social, and cultural factors must converge to lead to referral in some cases and to work against referral in others.

At the first level, child behavior is obviously relevant. Children whose behavior is annoying to others are more likely to be referred than children whose behavior, even though equally disturbed, is quieter and less overt. Thus, children who are aggressive, disobedient, and overactive are more likely to be seen as a problem by parents than are quiet, withdrawn, and fearful children. Furthermore, it is likely that parents will seek help more readily if their child's exasperating behavior is apparent outside the home as well. Thus, the child who throws temper tantrums at home but is an "angel" around other adults will be less likely to be referred. Once a parent's concern is corroborated by the preschool teacher or the pediatrician, that is, when the behavior is both sufficiently annoying to others and evident across situations (e.g., home and preschool), help seeking is more likely. Furthermore, when the behavior problems are accompanied by cognitive and/or language delays, parents may be more motivated to seek help to understand the severity of the cognitive problem and to obtain remedial intervention. Clinically, it appears that cognitive and learning problems may be less threatening than behavioral ones or may be viewed by parents as more likely to require treatment.

Parents' previous experience with children, their implicit theories about the nature of development, their levels of tolerance for children's behavior, their developmental expectations, and their own definitions of normality will also influence their assessment of the need to seek help. Thus, for example, the parent who believes that early signs of disturbance are possible indicators of more serious, long-term problems (a continuity view) may be more likely to seek help than a parent who sees problematic behavior in preschoolers as merely a difficult phase of development (a discontinuity view). Similarly, parents with more limited tolerance for rambunctious and exuberant behavior may be more likely to seek a referral than parents who are more child-centered and tolerant of high levels of noise and activity.

In my own work, I have been struck particularly with the wide variation in parents' knowledge of normal development and expectations for their children's behavior. Tolerance levels, developmental expectations, and experience with children appear to interact in complex ways. Parents with unrealistic expectations and low tolerance may make excessive maturity demands on their preschooler, which may tax their child's competence or self-control, and they may seek help to "make their child behave." For example, parents with limited exposure to young children may be more likely to interpret sibling or peer squabbles as "meanness" and may have unrealistic expectations for sharing and harmony between young children. I have found sibling and peer difficulties to be a major concern of parents of young children. Yet, parents who are both tolerant and aware of developmental issues around sibling or peer conflicts may be overly lax about setting limits and allow toy struggles or other typical child conflicts to escalate to more serious fights, thereby providing inadequate guidelines for more appropriate conflict resolution (Zahn-Waxler et al., 1979). Parents with limited knowledge of development also may become unduly upset by the finicky and faddy eating habits that often characterize preschoolers, or they may worry that problems around toilet training will develop into rebellion and other more serious problems. Forcing these issues in an insensitive and heavy-handed manner can turn eating or toileting into a battleground (see also Brazelton, 1974) and lead to serious parent–child conflict, which ultimately leads to help seeking. However, whereas a discontinuity view and moderate levels of tolerance are probably adaptive for most children and parents, extreme adherence to one or both of these viewpoints may allow a parent to overlook or rationalize away a potentially serious problem.

Parental perceptions of child behavior as typical or potentially problematic are likewise influenced by a range of other factors, including their own history of child rearing, their family history of psychopathology, their own experience with the mental health system, and their attitudes toward it. For example, families with a severely disturbed adult member, such as an aunt or grandparent, may be more likely to seek help early on, even for relatively minor problems, as a preventive effort. Other families with a history of hyperactivity or learning problems in a close relative may be more likely to dismiss the need for help with the comment that "Joey is just like Uncle George was." Because Uncle George is now a successful businessman, they assume that Joey too will outgrow his early childhood problems. However, if Uncle George's early problems developed into more serious academic and interpersonal ones in adolescence, they may want to prevent the occurrence of problems similar to those they observed in their own family of origin while growing up. Similarly, parents' willingness to seek help will be influenced by their own experiences with problems and the helpfulness or lack thereof of their mental health contacts.

Additional family factors that influence referral patterns include marital status and the quality of the marital relationship, educational and occupational status, and emotional and material resources. For example, it is not uncommon for parents to seek help with child-rearing concerns as a ticket into marital or family therapy, although neither partner is willing or able to acknowledge marital problems. Yet, some disturbed parents with disturbed children may postpone referral because they need to feel supported before they are able to confront and deal with their child's difficulties. Still other families may avoid seeking help because they are afraid that their child's difficulties will reveal their own or because there is marked disagreement between the parents on the need for help. Thus, a complex range of factors influences help seeking in parents of preschoolers. However, there is almost no empirical research on the variables that influence the referral of young children, although some studies suggest that maternal anxiety and depression play a major role in determining which parents seek help (e.g., Gath, 1968; Shepherd, Oppenheim, & Mitchell, 1971). Once a referral is made, it is the task of the mental health professional to determine the severity of the problem, whether it is indeed serious enough to warrant intervention or whether it reflects an age-appropriate struggle with a developmental transition, requiring primarily parental understanding and support. If treatment does appear indicated, it will be necessary to decide whether the parents, the child, or the family should be the focus of intervention and what type of intervention appears most relevant (e.g., parent education, family therapy). These issues will be addressed more fully in Chapter Seven.

Attempts to Define Clinically Significant Problems

Clinicians agree that a definition of disorder in young children must include a pattern of symptoms that has been troublesome for some time, is evident in more than one situation, is relatively severe, and is likely to impede the child's ability to negotiate the important developmental tasks necessary for adaptive functioning in the family and the peer group. Thus, it is not the presence of specific problem behaviors that differentiates "normal" from "abnormal" but their frequency, intensity, chronicity, constellation, and social context. Thus, in one of the examples discussed earlier, toy struggles would not be interpreted as problematic if they occurred once in a while, were of short duration, or were apparent in a preschool-age child with few other problems. However, toy struggles might be considered more worrisome if they occurred frequently, were intense, escalated into more serious fights, and were initiated by a child who was in other ways difficult to control and seemed to be showing a general pattern of externalizing symptomatology. Richman et al. (1982) used a combined statistical and clinical approach in an attempt to identify children with clinically significant problems. They noted that roughly 15% of their sample was assessed as showing mild problems and another 7% as showing moderate to severe problems. Children identified as evidencing moderate to severe problems were described as exhibiting a range of symptoms of relatively marked intensity, which appeared to be interfering with their developmental progress and were having an impact on family functioning.

Although there may be moderate to good agreement among clinicians (Richman et al., 1982) about the presence or absence of a recognizable disorder in young children, accurate prognostic predictions are difficult to make. The teacher, the parent, and the psychologist may all agree that Jamie's behavior is disrupting the family and impairing his ability to venture into the peer group. But does that mean that in 6 months or 1 year he will still be having problems? There are few guidelines to assist the professional in making such judgments and the data on this question are somewhat conflicting (Campbell, Ewing, et al., 1986; Fischer, Rolf, Hasazi, & Cummings, 1984; Richman et al., 1982). As noted earlier, studies that examine the persistence of troublesome or annoying behavior in nonclinical samples of young children suggest that they most often disappear with development. Yet, longitudinal studies of young children with identified problems have been relatively rare. The few extant studies suggest that some problems are more likely than others to persist. These studies will be discussed in more detail in Chapter Eight. In general, however, there is some evidence that externalizing problems are more likely than internalizing ones to persist, particularly in boys, and that family factors appear to mediate outcome.

Dimensions of Behavior Problems in Young Children

Because it is obvious that isolated behaviors do not reflect disturbance, researchers have looked for clusters of behaviors that may occur together and define a typology of disorder. Across the age span from preschool to adolescence, two major classes of problem behavior have been identified in children (Achenbach & Edelbrock, 1978, 1981). These include a range of behaviors characterized by undercontrol that typically are high in annoyance value and/or the potential to hurt others. These have been termed "externalizing" because they are expressed outward against others or have an impact on the child's environment. Examples include overactivity, tantrums, fighting, destructive behavior, and disobedience. Behaviors reflecting overcontrol also tend to cluster together. They have been termed "internalizing" because they have their major impact on the child himself and appear to be an expression of social withdrawal, fearfulness, unhappiness, and anxiety. Unfortunately, internalizing behaviors are often ignored or not recognized by adults in the child's environment because they are usually less dramatic and less irritating to others than externalizing symptoms.

Hundreds of studies have confirmed these general clusters of behavioral symptoms, although the specific behavioral manifestations may vary as a function of age and developmental level (Achenbach & Edelbrock, 1981; Campbell, 1989). It is not clear whether these rather global typologies of internalizing and externalizing symptomatology are sufficiently precise in their characterization of children's problems to facilitate decisions about treatment or predictions about prognosis, or whether specific subtypes of internalizing and externalizing disorders must be the focus of clinical decision making. Debate has been particularly intense on the question of whether the specific attentional problems, impulse control deficits, and high activity level that characterize "attention deficit disorder" define a specific disorder or are merely reflections of more general problems with aggression and discipline. Likewise, it is not clear whether anxiety problems and mood disorders are distinct in young children as they are in adolescents and adults. Several studies, however, suggest that hyperactive–distractible behavior and aggressive–noncompliant behavior represent relatively independent clusters of externalizing behavior in preschoolers (Achenbach & Edelbrock, 1981, 1983; Behar, 1977), although children rated as overactive also tend to be rated as aggressive (Campbell, Breaux, Ewing, & Szumowski, 1986). Internalizing problems appear to cluster into social withdrawal, anxiety, depression, and somatic complaints (Achenbach & Edelbrock, 1981, 1983), although it has not yet been demonstrated that such specificity characterizes the behavior of young children who show internalizing symptoms. It is likely that problems appear more global in early childhood and become more specific and focused with development.

The categorization of problems in young children is particularly problematic, however. Although behaviors rated on checklists may cluster in relatively similar ways across the age range, the usefulness of either dimensional or categorical approaches with preschool-age children has not been examined systematically, raising a number of questions about the classification of problem behavior. Is a dimensional approach appropriate for the description of behavior problems in young children? Is it reasonable to apply a more categorical diagnostic approach, such as the DSM-III or DSM-III-R (American Psychiatric Association, 1980, 1987), to the description of young children's behavior problems? If so, are the categories designed for use with adults and school-age children applicable to preschoolers? And finally, which approach to the description and classification of young children's problems is more clinically useful and less stigmatizing?

Diagnostic Issues

Because the mental health professions have adopted the DSM-III
diagnostic system and are required to utilize this system for reimburse-
ment by insurance companies, this approach to diagnosis will be
scrutinized with particular care in this section. Although its appropriateness and usefulness with children have been the subject of some
controversy (e.g., Rutter & Shaffer, 1980), it has not been evaluated
specifically in terms of its applicability to the behavior problems of
preschoolers. It will be argued here that this diagnostic system has
severe limitations when applied to preschoolers, except in extreme cases
of pervasive and profound developmental and emotional disorder.
Although the authors of DSM-III and its recent revision (DSM-III-R)
wisely specified that certain childhood disorders, such as conduct
disorder and identity disorder, could not apply meaningfully to very
young children, other disorders are described more ambiguously, and
indeed diagnoses are being given to young children seen in clinical
facilities. However, the use of diagnostic labels, which are based on
unvalidated inclusion and exclusion criteria, would appear to "over-
medicalize" and overpathologize less severe (i.e., nonpsychotic or
nonautistic) problem behavior in preschoolers. DSM-III and its succes-
sor, DSM-III-R, do not provide adequate guidelines for determining the
developmental and clinical significance of those symptomatic behaviors
that define disorders, making them of questionable appropriateness for
use with preschoolers. In the discussion to follow, attention will be paid
only to the DSM-III (and DSM-III-R) categories that may apply to
preschoolers.

DSM-III Externalizing Disorders

Only two externalizing disorders, called disruptive behavior disorders in
DSM-III-R, could conceivably be diagnosed in children of preschool
age: attention deficit disorder and oppositional disorder. DSM-III states
that attention deficit disorder typically is apparent by age 3 (changed to
age 4 in DSM-III-R), an observation that derives primarily from
retrospective parental reports of early onset (Campbell, 1976; Ross &
Ross, 1982). Although accumulating evidence supports this contention
(e.g., Campbell, 1985), it is also clear that most active, inattentive, and
impulsive preschoolers would not meet either set of criteria (i.e.,

DSM-III or DSM-III-R) for attention deficit disorder at school entry (Campbell, Ewing, et al., 1986; McGee, Williams, & Silva, 1984). However, the potential to overdiagnose this disorder in young children is a cause for concern because the criteria that would differentiate between age-appropriate levels of activity, shifts in attention, and impatience are nowhere defined. It is indeed difficult to make a clear diagnostic decision when confronted with a rambunctious, curious 3- or 4-year-old whose parents cannot cope with his/her behavior.

Preschoolers who are learning about the world and how to master its complexities are expected to exhibit boundless energy, to attend readily to the new and novel, and to exhibit unrestrained enthusiasm and exuberance. When, therefore, does a shift in activity and interest signify curiosity and exploration, and when does it reflect a too-rapid change in focus and an inadequate investment of attention? When does excitable and impatient behavior indicate an age-appropriate need for external support and limit setting, and when does it suggest a failure to internalize standards necessary for the development of self-control? When do frequent toy struggles reflect a child's age-appropriate need for experiences in the peer group that facilitate sharing and turn taking, and when do they indicate excessive impulsivity and an inability to wait? Although both DSM-III and DSM-III-R specify that "developmentally inappropriate" inattention, impulsivity, and overactivity are required for a diagnosis of attention deficit disorder, this is a difficult decision to make in the absence of normative data defining age-appropriate behavior. DSM-III also notes the erratic nature of symptomatic behavior: "It is the rare child who displays signs of the disorder in all settings or even in the same setting at all times" (p. 42). Thus, the child who is an absolute terror in the preschool may be more controlled when alone with his mother; another hyperactive child may function well in the peer group but run wild in the supermarket where the temptation to sample everything in sight overwhelms her limited capacity for self-control; still other hyperactive youngsters may be able to focus attention on activities that capture their interest but may become easily bored if they are not provided with enough to do; finally, some youngsters have "good" days and "bad" days, demonstrating behavior that is highly unpredictable from day to day.

This discussion is meant to demonstrate the potential hazards of assigning diagnostic labels, with their implication of permanence, to young children because the probability is relatively high that problem behaviors will reflect a transient developmental phase rather than early symptoms of disorder. Although the duration criterion of persistent problems for at least 6 months may help to distinguish between transient problems and a potentially more serious disorder, few data exist to indicate whether this is a sufficiently long period of time for children's behavior to become reorganized and stabilized. Thus, it appears prudent not to rely heavily on this diagnostic label until more is known about the early course of symptomatic behavior in young children and the correlates of good and poor outcome. Furthermore, because DSM-III and DSM-III-R suggest that attention deficit disorder is often likely to persist, it appears particularly important in the absence of more complete longitudinal data to utilize extreme caution when making statements about prognosis to parents.

Oppositional disorder is likewise difficult to assess in preschoolers. The framers of DSM-III, in an attempt to acknowledge the importance of developmental issues, and with a nod toward "the terrible 2's," noted that oppositional disorder had its onset after the third birthday: "Oppositional behavior in 18-to-36-month-old children is part of a normal developmental phase. The diagnosis of Oppositional Disorder should be considered only if severe oppositional behavior persists beyond this period" (p. 64). However, the diagnosis of a "psychiatric disorder" seems excessive when one is dealing with a stubborn, provocative, or defiant preschooler who may be struggling with a need to establish autonomy in the face of inflexible parental strictures or may be confused and frustrated by overly lax parental guidelines for acceptable behavior. Because only two symptoms indicative of "disobedient, negativistic, and provocative opposition to authority figures," for a duration of at least 6 months are necessary for such a diagnosis, many youngsters who face a particularly difficult developmental transition at age 3 could qualify. Furthermore, if one relies entirely on parental report, the child with particularly intolerant parents may easily appear to meet criteria. Indeed, it may be the rare preschooler who never meets DSM-III criteria for this problem, given the lack of clear guidelines defining "argumentativeness," "stubbornness," and "provocative behavior." Moreover, epidemiological studies suggest that management problems and defiant behavior often reach their peak at age 3 ("the trying 3's") (e.g., Crowther et al., 1981; Jenkins et al., 1980; Richman et al., 1982).

Although the temptation to overdiagnose oppositional disorder in young children may be difficult to resist using DSM-III criteria, DSM-III-R represents a significant improvement. Five (rather than two) of nine symptoms are required for a diagnosis of "oppositional defiant disorder," and some of the symptomatic behaviors appear to be less characteristic of the trying 3's than was the case with DSM-III. However, developmental issues are sidestepped almost completely with two exceptions; problems must be more severe than in children of similar mental age. There is also the implication that the disorder does not appear in full-blown form in preschoolers. The authors note that "precursors may occur in early childhood" and that the disorder "typically begins by eight years," suggesting an age of onset somewhere between 5 or 6 and 8 years. However, this assumption is not stated explicitly.

DSM-III Internalizing Disorders

Internalizing disorders, such as avoidant disorder and separation anxiety disorder, are also deemed appropriate diagnoses to confer on preschoolers according to the guidelines specified in DSM-III and DSM-III-R. However, the distinctions among typical reactions and actual "disorder" have not been adequately addressed. Separation anxiety disorder is described in terms of excessive anxiety concerning separation from the attachment figure for a duration of at least 2 weeks. Although age of onset "may be as early as preschool age," the clinician is also warned that "in early childhood some degree of separation anxiety is a normal phenomenon" and that clinical judgment must be used to distinguish between this and the more severe form that characterizes disorder. Few guidelines are given to help in this distinction. It is also suggested that separation anxiety is most likely to develop after some life stress, such as a loss, illness, or a move. In young children, then, without the cognitive capacities to understand sudden and/or dramatic life change, it is not clear when we can reasonably talk about a "disorder" as opposed to an appropriate reaction to a stressful, confusing, and/or frightening event. Because young children may not be expected to cope easily with certain kinds of stressful events or to readjust quickly to major life change but instead may need the close support of an attachment figure to help them make the necessary transitions, the expression of anxiety through nightmares, physical symptoms, or separation protest may be adaptive rather than pathological. Thus, a 3-year-old who shows a major reaction to a loss or other major life change or upsetting event expressed as clinging and other signs of separation distress may be behaving in predictable ways that clearly do not warrant a diagnosis of a psychiatric disorder. However, in the absence of any identifiable event in the life of a young child who becomes virtually panic-stricken at the prospect of separation, such a diagnosis may be warranted; at the least, this fearful and incapacitating behavior may be evidence that something serious is going on in the family.

The diagnostic category avoidant disorder likewise raises problems. It is defined as "persistent and excessive shrinking from contact with strangers" which "may develop as early as two and a half years, after stranger anxiety as a normal developmental phenomenon should have disappeared." Again, it is unclear where one draws the line between a shy or "slow to warm up" 3-year-old and one who is showing signs of a potentially serious problem in interpersonal relationships. It is hard to imagine many 3-year-olds whose avoidance of strangers interferes with normal peer relationships, unless they are also showing more severe psychopathology and/or serious developmental delay, which would warrant a diagnosis of a problem much more pervasive than avoidant disorder.

General Developmental Considerations in the Diagnosis of Young Children

Because both DSM-III and DSM-III-R lack a strong empirical basis, especially in regard to behavior disorders in very young children, it does not appear appropriate to utilize these diagnostic labels with children younger than 5 years except in very clear and unambiguous cases. By age 5, children are becoming substantially more independent and cognitively competent; they show relatively good self-control and understand the nature of rules and regulations; they are well beyond the period when separation protest is expected; and, by then, peer friendships have become a central focus of their lives. Thus, the criteria outlined in DSM-III and DSM-III-R begin to make some sense developmentally. However, for the 2-, 3-, or 4-year-old who may fit one or another of these categories, the dangers of diagnosis would appear to far outweigh their benefits. The use of labels may suggest to parents and teachers that we know more than we actually do about etiology, prognosis, and likely course; a diagnosis may stigmatize a child as suffering from an "illness" or a "disorder" when they are really exhibiting behaviors that reflect inappropriate parenting, a normal developmental transition, or an age-appropriate reaction to a loss or other upsetting event that they cannot comprehend; a diagnosis may imply something about prognosis or treatment that is relevant to the school-age child but may not be appropriate for the younger child. Thus, the use of V-codes or the less stigmatizing adjustment disorder category would appear to be more appropriate for preschoolers in most instances in which a diagnosis is required for insurance or other administrative purposes. These caveats do not apply to a more severe disturbance, such as pervasive developmental disorder.

The dimensional, descriptive approach of Achenbach and Edelbrock seems far more appropriate for use with young children because age-related guidelines are available in the form of age and sex norms for the severity and clinical significance of parent-reported behavior. Furthermore, the use of parent rating scales implies nothing more than a behavioral description of the child; it does not include the supposition that one is dealing with a "mental disorder." The use of a dimensional approach permits one to measure change in behavior over time, as a function of development, and in relation to change in the child's environmental and social context. We may describe Jamie as somewhat more aggressive or more difficult to handle than the average 3-year-old without implying that he is suffering from a disorder or a permanent condition.

It seems important to draw a sharp distinction between prudent clinical practice and research needs. Although clinically it seems wise to eschew diagnostic labels when dealing with less severe behavior problems in preschoolers in favor of more general behavioral descriptors, it seems crucial that research proceed to examine the appropriateness of these widely used diagnostic approaches for young children. Such research, particularly if it has a developmental and longitudinal focus, will help us to understand the course and outcome of common childhood problems as well as their correlates and the changes in the clinical picture that occur with development. Etiological formulations will require longitudinal studies that focus on populations at risk to develop a specific disorder; the development of prevention and treatment approaches likewise will depend upon the careful delineation of groups of children with particular problems who can be evaluated over time; similarly, epidemiological studies will need to examine not only the prevalence rates of specific symptoms in young children but also the prevalence and correlates of clusters of commonly occurring problem behaviors that may define a disorder.

Overview of a Longitudinal Study of Problem Preschoolers

As noted earlier, research on the pattern and severity, developmental course, and family correlates of problem behavior in young children is sorely needed. In the absence of empirical data, it is difficult to know how to explain children's problems to parents, when to characterize problems as potentially serious, or what advice to give. The focus and nature of the most appropriate treatment is likewise not always obvious. In an effort to identify early behavioral markers for attention deficit disorder and related externalizing behavior problems in young children and to understand more about the early developmental course of problem behavior, my students and I have been involved in an early identification and follow-up study of hard-to-manage preschoolers.

We were initially concerned about the ethical implications of this work because we worried about overpathologizing the difficult behavior of young children. For example, we were uncomfortable acknowledging that a particular child was a problem for fear of fueling a self-fulfilling cycle of negative parental perceptions, discipline problems, harsh child-rearing practices, and escalating conflict. However, after years of clinical work with school-aged children and their parents, we were convinced that early signs of problems could be identified and that parents could be given some support and guidance in dealing with hard-to-manage preschoolers who are capable of creating chaos in a family. We were also convinced that some hard-to-reach school-age youngsters developed problems as a result of insensitive and inappropriate child rearing, excessive stress in the family, and a generally unhealthy psychological environment that failed to support them through difficult periods of development. As we have come to know the families in our study, it seems clear that problems in children and families are complex and multiply determined and that initial problems, their developmental course, and their outcomes reflect complex transactions among a constellation of factors that are probably different for each child and family. Although we have collected a huge amount of empirical data on the children and families who have participated in our study, much of which has been reported in journal articles and book chapters (Campbell & Cluss, 1982; Campbell et al., 1982, 1984; Campbell, Breaux, Ewing, Szumowski, & Pierce, 1986; Campbell, Ewing, et al., 1986), we also have a wealth of clinical material that may be of use to clinicians. I will first describe the study and then present more detailed information about several children who participated.

They were chosen as typical examples of problems apparent in early childhood. They illustrate different patterns of childhood symptoms, styles of family functioning, and strategies of child rearing that presumably have an impact on the child's development as a preschooler and on academic and social competence at elementary school age. They also suggest different initial causal mechanisms and different maintaining factors. Although etiological formulations remain speculative, it is generally agreed that similar clinical pictures may develop from diverse causes (e.g., Ross & Ross, 1982).

The children in our study do not consist of a representative sample of preschoolers who are difficult to handle. Because we were concerned about the ethics of labeling young children, we initially decided to recruit children through pediatric offices and preschools but to insist that parents initiate contact with the project. Thus, our sample is comprised of a self-selected group of parents who were seeking help because of problems managing their toddler or young preschooler. Parents with concerns about their child's activity level, defiance, poor impulse control, and difficulty playing alone were invited to participate in a study of development; free parent training groups were offered as an incentive. Children with grossly delayed language development, psychotic-like symptoms, clear indications of brain damage, sensory impairments, or a Stanford–Binet IQ below 75, were excluded from the sample. Children between 25 and 47 months of age who were in good physical health made up the sample of 46 parent-referred problem youngsters and 22 controls. Details of sample recruitment may be found in Campbell et al. (1982).

Initial assessment data were collected during a home visit, two visits to our laboratory playroom, and in the child's preschool classroom. Assessments included a structured interview administered to the child's mother, a series of questionnaires describing child behavior completed by both parents and by preschool teachers, observations of the child in the laboratory during free play, structured tasks, and interactive play with mother, and a naturalistic observation of the child's interaction with peers and teachers in nursery school. In addition, intelligence was assessed by the Stanford–Binet, and a delay task was administered as one index of impulse control. Measures of activity level, attention, compliance, and aggression were derived from the observations and questionnaires. A developmental and family history was obtained from the structured interview. Children were assessed again at the ages of 4 and 6 years on parallel but age-appropriate measures. Finally, they were followed up again at the age of 9 years, with an emphasis on the children's behavior at home and school as assessed by a structured interview with their mothers and questionnaires completed by mothers and teachers.

Initial parent reports indicated group differences on rating scales assessing hyperactive–distractible behavior and aggressive–noncompliant behavior; groups did not differ on scales assessing anxiety. Independent laboratory observations revealed that the free play behavior of problem youngsters was less focused and directed to toys than the play of comparison children. The play of the problem children was also characterized by more shifts in activity from object to object and by more involvement with objects in the room other than toys. Parent-referred problem children also moved around more and were less attentive during structured tasks than comparison children. They were more impulsive on a laboratory task assessing delay capacity, in which they were required to wait for a signal before finding and eating a cookie hidden under one of three cups (Campbell et al., 1982).

Those parent-identified hard-to-manage children who attended preschool were rated by their teachers as more hyperactive and aggressive than comparison children, but consistent with parental reports, not as more anxious; observations in their preschool classrooms indicated that they were also more aggressive with peers; problem boys were less compliant with teacher requests than were other children in the sample. Problem and control groups did not differ in their tendency to approach peers or to play cooperatively (Campbell & Cluss, 1982). It should be noted that teachers were informed only that children were in a study of the development of preschoolers; no mention was made of problem behavior.

Although the families of the problem children were, on average, from a lower social class and experiencing higher levels of psychosocial stress, including parental illness, marital dysfunction or disruption, financial difficulties, or problems with extended family, there were wide individual differences on these background measures. Finally, on measures of mother–child interaction obtained during a relatively unstructured free play period, problem children showed only a nonsignificant tendency to be more noncompliant or aggressive in their play. Mothers of hard-to-manage children were more likely than mothers of controls to be negative and controlling during this play observation (Campbell, Breaux, Ewing, Szumowski, & Pierce, 1986).

Parent report and laboratory measures were repeated 1 year later when children were 4 years old. As is often the case in longitudinal studies, there was differential attrition. Families lost to follow-up were primarily from the problem group; even within this group, they tended to be the most distressed and dysfunctional families in the sample (Campbell et al., 1984; Campbell, Ewing, et al., 1986). This means that many of the more difficult children in the sample or those who would be expected, on theoretical and clinical grounds, to have the worst outcomes were among the children most likely to drop out of the study. Indeed, those families lost to follow-up differed significantly from those who remained in the study in both social class and level of psychosocial stress (Campbell, Ewing, et al., 1986). Despite this differential attrition of 21%, groups continued to differ at the age 4 follow-up assessment.

Children who were identified as problems at age 3 continued to be rated as significantly more hyperactive and aggressive at age 4 but not as more anxious. They also were less focused in their play and they moved around more during structured tasks. On a laboratory task requiring them to delay searching for a cookie hidden under one of three cups until they received a signal from the experimenter, problem youngsters were still more impulsive. It is also important to note that despite these continued group differences, most children improved relative to their own initial performance, as evidenced by parallel developmental progressions in the two groups. Thus, as a group, the problem children became somewhat less active and impulsive, relative to their performance 1 year earlier, on several laboratory measures. These data indicate that children identified as hard-to-manage at age 3 continued to have more difficulties than comparison children when followed up 1 year later; thus, problems in the group as a whole did not appear to reflect only age-related activity or a transient developmental phenomenon. Furthermore, within the problem group children tended to maintain their rank order, with more active and impulsive 3-year-olds remaining more active and impulsive than their peers at age 4. For example, within the problem group, maternal ratings of aggression–hostility at ages 3 and 4 were significantly correlated, as were ratings of activity level; activity shifts during free play observed at ages 3 and 4 were likewise related, as were impulsive responses on the cookie task.

Early predictors of maternal ratings of problem behavior at age 4 were also examined. Lower social class and more negative and controlling maternal behavior observed in the laboratory at age 3 predicted higher ratings of hyperactivity and aggression at age 4. In addition, boys who had been more noncompliant and aggressive during play with their mothers at age 3 and who had been rated by them as more symptomatic at initial assessment continued to be rated as more active at age 4; negative child behavior and early aggression ratings, but not gender, also were associated with aggression ratings at age 4. These findings underline the relatively high degree of continuity in problem behavior, particularly in the context of a conflicted and negative mother–child relationship (Campbell, Breaux, Ewing, & Szumowski, 1986).

In addition to the assessment of children's behavior across situations, parents were offered the opportunity to participate in parent training groups that provided information about normal development and/or taught parents behavior management approaches. The developmental portion stressed the developmental tasks of late toddlerhood and the early preschool period (establishing autonomy, developing self-control, exploring the world, and learning to function effectively in the peer group) (Sroufe, 1979). The behavior management portion of the groups focused on learning to observe child behavior, on the use of praise and time out, rather than criticism and physical punishment, and on the use of age-appropriate activities as incentives and reinforcers for good behavior. More information about these parent training groups will be provided in Chapter Seven, which deals with treatment. However, it is worth pointing out here that attendance at a parenting group was not associated with differential outcome at age 4 follow-up.

Case 1: Jamie L

Jamie was briefly introduced earlier. His mother called the project after seeing our descriptive poster in her pediatrician's office. Jamie was then 3½ years old. During the telephone screening, Mrs. L stated that she was calling the project because of Jamie's problems in nursery school, primarily aggression with peers and wild and uncontrollable behavior. His preschool teacher had recently asked her to consider removing him from school. She also complained of Jamie's temper tantrums and defiance ("he doesn't take 'no' for an answer"), his overactivity ("always on the go; constantly moving"), and his tendency to get overexcited and out of control, especially when around other children.

During the home visit, Mrs. L was interviewed about Jamie's early development and current behavior. He was born full-term, weighing over 7 pounds but with some mild delivery complications. There was some mild fetal distress and the delivery involved the use of forceps. Jamie was described as an active infant who cried a lot and was difficult to calm. He was irregular in his sleeping patterns and tended to require less sleep than his mother expected, taking short naps but not sleeping for long periods. Feeding was not, however, a problem. Jamie could be calmed somewhat in early infancy if he was held and walked, but by 6 months of age he resisted physical contact. His parents first became worried about a problem when he was just over 1 year old. Their concerns focused on his high activity level and his difficulty settling down. By age 3, their concerns also included his aggression with peers, short attention span, excitability, and discipline problems.

These middle-class, well-educated, professional parents were extremely patient with Jamie and set clear and relatively consistent limits. They avoided the use of physical punishment, which they saw as upsetting Jamie, and leading to even poorer control than a firm but calm approach. Thus, they gave him a clear warning before sending him to his room to calm down. They also used a good deal of verbal reasoning with explicit rules. Mrs. L noted that Jamie became easily upset by changes in routine and did best when he was well prepared ahead of time for something new.

Jamie and his 1-year-old brother lived with both parents in a quiet, residential neighborhood. Their mother had taken a break from her career to stay at home with her children. Her husband was likewise very involved with the family and spent evening and weekend time with the children; this also served to give Mrs. L some needed time away from them. The marriage seemed stable and the climate of the home was warm and relatively relaxed under the circumstances. Jamie was clearly the main source of stress in the family because he needed frequent supervision. Mr. and Mrs. L agreed that Jamie was difficult and they used similar methods of discipline with him. They both were feeling frustrated and defeated by the time they contacted the project. Both parents rated Jamie well above the mean on measures of hyperactivity–distractibility and aggression–hostility.

Jamie was an appealing youngster with his red hair and freckles. He greeted the home visitors enthusiastically and quickly struck up a conversation with the examiner. On the Stanford–Binet, he scored in the very superior range of intelligence and his good language and reasoning ability were especially noteworthy. Despite his cognitive strengths, the examiner noted his short attention span, fidgetiness, need for structure, and tendency to leave his seat frequently. These observations were consistent with his behavior during the laboratory assessment of free play during which he shifted activities frequently and spent much of his time engaged with objects other than toys, such as locked cabinets. He was also more impulsive than average on the cookie task. During unstructured play with his mother, Jamie was moderately noncompliant, but Mrs. L's calm, warm, positive but firm approach was very effective in keeping him involved in elaborate and creative fantasy play. She was especially skilled at redirecting him to a new activity or at elaborating upon his ongoing fantasy play as ways of keeping him focused. Despite Jamie's difficult behavior, Mrs. L did not become confrontative. Jamie was eventually enrolled in a more structured preschool program and his parents participated in our parent training groups.

When Jamie was followed up at age 4, he showed some improvement in his ability to focus attention and to control himself, although he was still difficult to discipline, restless, easily bored, and aggressive with peers. In the interim the family had moved to a new house, but otherwise the family situation was unchanged. His parents felt more comfortable about their methods of handling Jamie and were continuing to set firm and consistent limits and to support each other. They both still rated him as well above the mean on measures of hyperactivity–distractibility and aggression–hostility. Jamie was also active during free play in the laboratory, although he was able to control himself better on structured tasks, such as the cookie delay task.

In terms of the issues delineated earlier in this chapter, Jamie's behavior seems to be more than just annoying; he is not merely showing age-appropriate behavior that is misconstrued by intolerant parents. Indeed, his parents appear especially sensitive and supportive of him. Noteworthy are the severity and patterning of Jamie's problem behaviors, a mixture of high levels of hyperactivity, aggression with peers, and noncompliance. Furthermore, his difficulties are apparent across situations: home, school, and laboratory and persistent from ages 3 to 4.

It is difficult to arrive at a satisfactory etiological formulation of this case, except by exclusion. Family disruption, poor child rearing, or other environmental explanations appear inaccurate and inappropriate. Although Jamie appears to have been active, irregular, and difficult to console from early infancy, the notion of a poor match between child temperament and family environment (Thomas et al., 1968) does not seem to apply. Indeed, we were struck by the incredible patience of

Jamie's parents and their ability to be firm but loving. It is hard to imagine what Jamie's behavior would have been like if, indeed, he had been born into a less stable, adaptive, and concerned family. There is a good deal of debate within the child development field about definitions of temperament and the relative contributions of constitutional factors and family environment to difficult child behavior (e.g., Bates, 1987; Campos et al., 1983; Kagan, 1984; Maccoby et al., 1984; Plomin, 1982). In this instance, it is hard to come up with predisposing factors except those reflected in Jamie's early problems with sleeping and consolability and the continuity noted over time in his excitability and problems with self-regulation, which may be indicative of a constitutional basis for his problems (Douglas, 1983; Ross & Ross, 1982).

Jamie continued to have difficulties at home, at school, and with peers despite his parents concerted efforts to deal constructively and sensitively with his problem.

Case 2: Annie J

Annie was also introduced at the beginning of this book. Her mother called the project when Annie was 2½ years old after seeing our poster in her pediatrician's office. Mrs. J expressed concerns about Annie's high energy level, tantrums, sleep problems, and fearfulness. She found Annie particularly difficult to discipline and seemed at a loss about how to handle her 2-year-old daughter's behavior. At the initial interview, Mrs. J complained about Annie's impatience, low frustration tolerance, difficulty playing alone, lack of concentration, and fussiness. However, she also reported that Annie could amuse herself for up to 20 minutes at a stretch and enjoyed watching "Sesame Street," suggesting that her attention span and ability to play alone were well within the typical range for a child her age. Mrs. J was a highly anxious woman with doubts about her own competence. She questioned her own ability to manage Annie and noted that she and her husband disagreed on the best approach to child rearing. Mrs. J had tried a number of different disciplinary approaches by the time she called the project, including reasoning, smacking, and time out. When interviewed, her current approach was "threatening" to spank Annie with a wooden spoon and "screaming" at her when she misbehaved. Annie in turn was fighting back by screaming and smacking her mother and by throwing things. Despite this negative approach, Mrs. J seemed unable to enforce limits, so that when a battle ensued between Annie and Mrs. J, Annie often won. Her tantrum behavior was clearly paying off. Annie's father appeared to be calmer, firmer, and less negative with her, as well as less easily manipulated; consequently, he did not elicit this explosive behavior from her. Mrs. J also reported that she perceived Annie's difficult behavior as purposely provocative. When first seen, Annie was not yet toilet trained and was still in diapers; she was still drinking from a bottle and she was sitting in a high chair for meals to keep her under control. Questionnaires completed by mother placed Annie above the mean on scales assessing overactivity and anxiety, but not aggression. Because she was not yet in preschool and had only limited peer experiences, it was not possible to assess this aspect of Annie's social behavior. Annie's father's ratings were also elevated, but he saw Annie as less overactive than his wife did.

According to maternal report, Annie was born full-term after a long and difficult delivery. Mrs. J also reported pregnancy complications. She noted that she had been concerned about behavior problems from early infancy because Annie never slept as much as she expected her to (although she also reported that Annie slept through the night for 6 or 7 hours from about 6 weeks on). She also reported feeding problems, a high activity level, and difficulty soothing Annie who did not like to be held or cuddled. However, further inquiry did not clearly substantiate these patterns.

Annie was then the only child of college-educated parents in their late 20s. Mr. J worked in a managerial position; the mother had stopped working just prior to Annie's birth and was home with her full time. The marriage was stable on the surface with the exception of parental disagreements over Annie. No marital problems were acknowledged. However, Mrs. J's high anxiety level, anger and frustration with her daughter, intense concern, excessively negative perceptions, and low self-esteem caused us to wonder about maternal depression and about the marital relationship as well.

Annie was an attractive little girl with blond hair and blue eyes. She was fussy and clinging during the home visit, demonstrating separation distress prior to the administration of the Stanford–Binet and insisting that her mother remain with her. The examiner noted that Annie was frequently out of her seat, was distractible, and refused to attempt several items. The test, although incomplete, revealed that she was functioning at least at the upper end of the bright normal level, and probably higher. During the visit to the laboratory, Annie was frequently out of her seat and off-task during structured activities; she was impulsive on a delay task; and she shifted activities frequently during free play, showing relatively limited involvement with toys and somewhat disorganized play. When asked to play with her mother, Annie was active, demanding, irritable, and noncompliant; her mother was seen as controlling and directive, as intruding inappropriately into Annie's play, as tending to nag, and as lacking in warmth. Overall, the quality of the interaction was fraught with tension and conflict over who was in control.

Although Mrs. J described Annie as a difficult infant and we did observe the overactivity and noncompliance she reported, it is hard to determine exactly what was going on here. The inconsistencies in Mrs. J's reports of Annie's behavior and her inability to set firm limits or provide opportunities to facilitate Annie's development were all indications of problems with mothering. Annie may have started out as somewhat difficult to care for as an infant or she may have been a relatively easy baby with an overanxious, unsure mother who was insensitive to her signals and unable to meet her needs early on. It was clear from the interview material that Mrs. J was not well informed about what to expect from a young infant; her expectations were at times unrealistically high (sleeping, attention span), at others unrealistically low (toilet training, weaning, experiences with peers). It was also apparent that Mrs. J was ineffective, inconsistent, and harsh in setting limits. Although she was intensely concerned about her daughter, she was not warm or affectionate. Indeed, project staff had the impression that Mrs. J really did not like Annie much, an impression that has persisted over the years. The early history paired with Annie's separation problems and her mother's high level of anxiety and tendency to infantilize her daughter clearly suggest problems in attachment, which appear to stem from overly intense, but insensitive and unresponsive maternal behavior (Ainsworth et al., 1978) at least as much as from any characteristics of Annie. By age 2½, Annie was locked in an ambivalent struggle with her mother over her needs for autonomy and independence, which were in conflict with her unmet needs for nurturance and support.

This impaired mother–daughter relationship was not helped by the fact that Mr. J had a much easier time with Annie. He was warmer with her and less negative and controlling, and she responded by being more affectionate and agreeable. At the completion of the assessment, we recommended that Mr. and Mrs. J attend our parent training group, which focused on normal developmental expectations for toddlers and preschoolers and on setting firm, loving, positive, and consistent limits. We also suggested that Annie be given the opportunity to play with other children. We also worked with Mr. and Mrs. J on toilet training because this area had become the focus of considerable parent–child conflict. Annie's parents eagerly followed our suggestions, but they had a difficult time thinking in developmental or psychological terms. They were not willing to accept a referral for additional help outside the project, although Mrs. J has continued to seek advice from the project staff from time to time.

When Annie was followed up 1 year later, she had improved somewhat according to the maternal report. Ratings were only slightly elevated relative to controls. Similarly, observational measures suggested some improvement, although Annie was still less focused in her play than many other children in the sample. The maternal report indicated that Annie was toilet trained and not drinking from a bottle any longer. She had been enrolled in a preschool program two mornings a week. There she reportedly was doing well with her peers and she loved going. The teacher saw no problems with her. However, the interview revealed that Mrs. J still saw Annie as requiring a good deal of structure, as defiant, and as difficult to control. Mrs. J complained of having particular difficulty when she took Annie shopping, expecting her to wait patiently and not to touch things, another example of inappropriate expectations. In addition, sleep problems were reported, with Annie going into her parents' bed several times a week; eating had also become an area of conflict, with Annie refusing certain foods and her mother trying to coax her to eat and at times feeding her. In addition, Mrs. J had been briefly hospitalized during the interim for a medical problem and Annie had begun to wet her bed in response to her mother's departure.

Thus, problems around developmental tasks continued to be in evidence, clearly fueled by parental difficulties conceptualizing their youngster's psychological needs or helping her to negotiate issues of separation–individuation and the establishment of autonomy and independence. It is particularly significant that Annie was able to separate successfully enough to attend a preschool program and that her teacher found her eager to play with other children and to participate in structured activities. With the appropriate emotional support provided by the preschool teacher, Annie was able to begin to reach out to others and to develop appropriately in certain areas.

It is significant that, although Annie appeared to have relatively severe difficulties at age 3, and according to maternal report, earlier behavior was problematic, she had made notable gains by age 4. Despite these gains, Mrs. J still complained about a range of difficulties with Annie, although it is also clear that these difficulties were specific to her relationship with her mother and did not spill over to affect her school adjustment. Thus, her problems were not cross-situational. Furthermore, the pattern of her symptoms suggests a mixture of anxiety and high activity level, rather than aggressive behavior. Her activity level may well reflect her high level of anxiety, and maternal reports of defiance and oppositional behavior may reflect inappropriate expectations or Annie's attempts to separate and gain control. Annie's problems would appear to stem primarily from insensitive parenting reflected in skewed expectations, an inability to respond to and meet her emotional needs, failure to recognize and appreciate her many strengths, and a lack of genuine warmth, acceptance, and affection. This pattern of mother–daughter conflict and negative maternal perceptions has persisted, although Annie also continues to function well at school and with peers.

Case 3: Robbie S

Mrs. S called the project when Robbie was just 3 years old, reporting that she was "at her wits' end" and no longer knew how to deal with her son's high activity level. She reported that he could not sit still, was up at 6 A.M. "running the halls," that he was moving all the time, and that he had an attention span of "less than 20 seconds." She also noted that he was unable to entertain himself, except in the bathtub.

During the intake interview, Mrs. S reported that she had first become concerned about Robbie's high activity level and sleep difficulties when he was 9 months old but was reassured by her pediatrician that his behavior was not that atypical and would be outgrown. She noted that he was still a restless sleeper who moved around a lot during sleep and that he slept for relatively brief periods. By age 3, he was no longer taking afternoon naps. She described Robbie as unable to relax and unable to focus on one toy for more than a few seconds, tending instead to move rapidly from one toy to another during play. He was also uninterested in stories or other sedentary activities. Mrs. S described relatively violent temper tantrums, which included throwing things, hitting, kicking, screaming, and crying, but she noted that Robbie was not aggressive around other children. Mrs. S was firm but patient with him; she set clear guidelines for acceptable behavior and did not give in to his tantrums. She was also quick to praise his good behavior and to provide rational reasons for limits and prohibitions. Mr. S, in contrast, was inconsistent, sometimes giving in to Robbie's tantrums, sometimes becoming angry and harsh with him.

Robbie was born full-term after a long and difficult labor, but there were no indications of fetal distress. Despite sleep problems and a high activity level, he was described as a cuddly infant without feeding or other difficulties. Robbie is the younger of two children. His 6-year-old sister was reported to be developing normally. Both parents graduated from high school and were employed in managerial positions. Robbie's mother returned to work when he was 6 weeks old, placing him in family day-care. He was still in the same day-care setting when he was first seen in the project.

At the time of the home visit, Robbie greeted the tester with an impish grin and proceeded to show her his trucks. Robbie was an extremely outgoing and engaging child with curly, blond hair and green eyes. He readily separated from his mother but left the test session from time to time to check in with her and tell her what he was doing. His language was somewhat immature and difficult to understand, but Robbie was a bright youngster and caught on quickly to task demands, performing in the bright normal range. He was frequently out of his seat during testing, but he was relatively easy to redirect with the introduction of a new task.

On parent questionnaires, Robbie was rated well above the mean on measures of activity level and noncompliance. During the observation of free play in the laboratory, he shifted activities frequently, playing only briefly with any one toy. Instead, Robbie was more interested in manipulating forbidden objects (e.g., video camera, microphone, locked cabinets) and climbing into the sink. He was at the extremes on measures of activity and inattention derived from these observations. In addition, on a delay task requiring him to wait for a signal from the experimenter before finding and eating a piece of cookie, Robbie made several impulsive responses. He was frequently out of his seat and off-task during structured tasks. Thus, during a laboratory assessment of activity level, attention, and impulse control, Robbie confirmed his mother's reports of problematic behavior.

During the mother–child play interaction, Robbie was able to focus attention on toys for much longer and even to complete several tasks. Mrs. S provided him with a good deal of structure, support, and positive feedback while firmly and consistently enforcing limits. The relationship between Robbie and his mother seemed warm and positive.

There was little doubt from Robbie's history and behavior at initial intake that he was showing early signs of problems that might well reflect hyperactivity–attention deficit disorder. However, several issues complicate the formulation of this case. First, Robbie had been in day-care from 6 weeks of age until 3 years in a setting that appeared to provide adequate physical and emotional care but inadequate cognitive stimulation or organized activities with age-mates. Second, there was a significant family history of antisocial behavior and what appeared to be manic–depressive illness in first-degree relatives of both parents. Third, Robbie's parents had an extremely poor marital relationship, with frequent arguments and much tension. Finally, Robbie's father was inconsistently and intermittently involved with him. Mr. S showed brief periods of great interest and concern but would then withdraw and ignore Robbie, rebuffing his overtures.

Mrs. S was eager for help and support. She attended the parent training groups faithfully and completed all homework assignments with incredible thoroughness. She was already utilizing most of the disciplinary approaches discussed in the group but seemed to derive a good deal of satisfaction and comfort from discussing Robbie with the other parents. She also felt vindicated by the support of the group leaders. Mr. S blamed Robbie's problems on his wife's "laxness" (i.e., her use of reasoning and time out rather than physical punishment) and Mrs. S was clearly concerned about whether or not she might be the cause of his difficult behavior. Mr. S refused to accompany his wife to any of these sessions.

Robbie was removed from the family day-care setting several months after entering the project. Instead, he attended a well-run, center-based day-care program with structured activities and a good staff:child ratio, where he could play with other children his own age. Robbie adjusted well to this new setting, got along well with other children, and became more manageable at home. For example, he would come home exhausted from day-care and began to sleep through the night. Bedtime was no longer a struggle.

At the age 4 follow-up, Mrs. S reported that Robbie's behavior continued to improve. His mother saw him as much more manageable and as able to entertain himself for brief periods of time. She reported that he got along well with the other children in his day-care program and enjoyed going. Although he still had relatively regular temper tantrums, Mrs. S felt much more in control of the situation. She was explicit and consistent in setting limits and able to ignore tantrum behavior. Laboratory observations likewise suggested some improvement in Robbie's self-control as reflected in more focused play and less impulsivity.

Despite these apparent improvements, there had been a number of significant changes in Robbie's life. The marital situation further deteriorated and his parents separated just prior to his fourth birthday. Robbie was, not surprisingly, confused about the situation; unfortunately, the conflict between the parents became increasingly intense and Robbie became the focus of their anger and resentment.

This situation has steadily worsened. In particular, Mr. S threatened Mrs. S with a custody dispute. When Robbie was 5, Mrs. S called asking for a referral for Robbie who was wetting his bed, having nightmares, and wanting to sleep with her. He was also having angry outbursts at home and getting into fights with his sister, as well as with other children at school. He and his sister had unfortunately been put into the position of message carriers between their warring parents. Robbie was seen in play therapy for a number of months in an attempt to help him deal with his confused and intense feelings of anger and betrayal, as well as his concerns about being abandoned. Like many youngsters his age facing parental separation, his ambivalence about his absent father was intense (Wallerstein & Kelly, 1980); he longed for and worried about his father and fantasized about reunion but was often reluctant to visit and adamantly refused to leave his mother on several occasions.

It appears that we are dealing with a youngster whose initial difficulties reflected a combination of temperamental difficultness (constitutional) and family tensions (environmental). His problems appear to have been exacerbated by the continuing instability in his life. Initial problems appeared relatively severe and apparent across situations, although his good adjustment to preschool and his lack of aggression with peers are noteworthy. The nature and severity of Robbie's problems appear to wax and wane in tandem with environmental stress and instability, factors that are likely to predict later outcome. Continued follow-up has revealed persistent problems that appear to worsen when family stress intensifies; Robbie has also had a good deal of difficulty coping with the demands for conformity, achievement, and compliance required in school.

Case 4: Teddy M

When Teddy was just under 2¹/₂ years old, Mrs. M called the project to seek help. She was concerned particularly about Teddy's high activity level, short attention span, excitability with peers, and difficulty amusing himself. He was not, however, described as either aggressive with peers or difficult to discipline. During the interview Mrs. M also noted concerns about Teddy's low frustration tolerance and his lack of sustained involvement in play. Although she described him as able to play alone for as long as 30 minutes on some construction activities, she was concerned about his tendency to move quickly from one activity to another and to show little interest in many of his toys. On parent questionnaires, both Mrs. M and her husband rated Teddy high on symptoms of overactivity and inattention; however, consistent with interview data, neither parent saw him as difficult to manage or as having problems getting along with other children.

Teddy was described as a somewhat irritable infant who cried a lot when tired and required more than an average amount of sleep. He was not a cuddly baby and, when upset, was described as difficult to console, sometimes crying for 30 minutes at a time. When distressed, Teddy did not like to be held and he generally resisted physical restraint. He was also active as an infant and walked early. Feeding was not, however, a problem. Teddy was a full-term infant, delivered without complications. There is nothing remarkable in his developmental or family history.

Mr. and Mrs. M were both college-educated and Mr. M was employed at a managerial level in a local business. Mrs. M, a former nurse, remained home full time with Teddy and his 5-year-old brother. She reported that she was able to discipline Teddy effectively, relying primarily on reasoning and sitting him on a chair in time out. The marriage appeared to be stable and Mr. M was involved with the children. There were no problems noted with their older child who was described as much easier to care for as an infant and much less active than Teddy as a toddler and preschooler. Since Teddy was only 28 months old when first seen in the project, he was not attending any organized preschool.

Teddy was a cute youngster with brown hair and brown eyes. At first he was somewhat shy with the tester, but after a few minutes of play and conversation with his mother present, he warmed up and showed interest in the "games" she had brought. Teddy was cooperative during the administration of the Stanford–Binet and he performed at the bright normal level. The examiner did not find him particularly fidgety or inattentive and he remained seated for the entire 30-minute testing session. During the laboratory assessment of free play, Teddy showed interest in the toys and became particularly involved with a family of dolls and a pounding toy, spending most of his time with one or the other of these. He did explore other toys and the room in general but was much more focused on specific toys than the other children described so far. Although Teddy was impulsive on the cookie delay task, he was neither fidgety nor inattentive during structured tasks. During the mother–child play interaction, Teddy was engrossed with a toy work bench and he played relatively independently. His mother, although warm and supportive, was directive. Based on the laboratory assessment and our observations of Teddy during the home visit, we did not see him as more active or distractible than the average 28-month-old. Both parents attended one of our parent training groups, where we hoped that exposure to other parents of children with more severe problems would place Teddy's behavior in a more appropriate developmental perspective.

When seen for follow-up 1 year later, Teddy was still described by his mother as somewhat restless and inattentive on interview, although questionnaire ratings were only slightly elevated above the comparison group mean; she also expressed some concern about his difficulty sharing toys and his emerging verbal defiance. However, she saw these as only mild problems. The laboratory assessment did not suggest that Teddy was particularly active, inattentive, or impulsive. Although he changed activities fairly often during free play, he was not impulsive on the cookie task and he was attentive and organized on other structured tasks.

Teddy seems to be a good example of a child who was developing normally, although he may have been somewhat more difficult than average in infancy. Alternatively, he may have been merely more active and less cuddly in infancy than his brother, something for which his parents were not prepared. In either event, it appears that Mr. and Mrs. M had very high expectations and they tended to misinterpret Teddy's age-appropriate activity level, relatively short bouts of sustained play, and limited ability to share toys as problems. Mrs. and Mrs. M were seen as somewhat perfectionistic, although they were also warm and loving. This type of early parent–child mismatch has the potential to lead to overly harsh discipline or to parent–child conflict that escalates and leads to more serious later problems. However, Teddy's family was a stable, caring, and concerned one, and his parents were firm but not overbearing in their approach to child rearing.

The pattern of Teddy's behavior is also worth considering. Not only were his symptoms relatively mild but also parental complaints of hyperactivity and inattention were not combined with concerns about aggression toward peers or high levels of oppositional or impulsive behavior. His behavior was also not problematic in many situations, and he did not become more difficult to manage with development. Rather, parental concerns at age 4 were somewhat different from their initial complaints and focused on age-appropriate manifestations of development. Thus, from the start, Teddy looked more like a comparison youngster than a child with a clinically significant problem that was likely to persist and/or escalate in severity. Continued follow-up was consistent with this interpretation.

Summary

In this chapter several clinical issues were discussed. Differences between age-specific problems and signs of more serious, potentially persistent problems were addressed. In particular, drawing on data from epidemiological studies, it was concluded that problem behaviors are common in the general population of nonreferred children and that many troublesome behaviors also show age-related developmental change. The social and developmental context in which problem behavior occurs was seen as crucial in determining whether an annoying or worrisome behavior should be considered merely typical, an indicator of a difficult developmental transition, or a sign of a potentially significant problem. It was concluded that symptoms that clustered together and appeared to interfere with developmental progress were particularly worthy of concern. Several factors influencing referral were also noted and patterns of behavioral disturbance in young children were described.

Diagnostic issues were also addressed. It was concluded that the developmental guidelines contained in DSM-III and DSM-III-R are inadequate and that most of the diagnostic categories described are inappropriate for children younger than 5 years, except in rare cases. Closer examination of the diagnostic criteria for attention deficit disorder, oppositional disorder, and separation anxiety disorder indicate that many of the behaviors that define these disorders may be age-appropriate behaviors or typical ways of reacting to stress in young children. Therefore, the use of these diagnostic labels was seen as likely to overpathologize typical behaviors in young children and possibly to be misleading and unnecessarily upsetting to parents.

An attempt was then made to illustrate these issues by describing our ongoing longitudinal study of parent-identified hard-to-manage preschoolers. Comparisons between problem youngsters and comparison children at intake and after a 1-year interval indicated that parental concerns were likely to be confirmed by data obtained from other sources and that problems persisted in some children. Four children from the study were then described in more detail to provide illustrations of the nature of early symptomatology in young children whose parents found them difficult to manage in toddlerhood and the early preschool period. In each instance, problems of one sort or another appeared early, at least by the child's first birthday; some relatively significant problems were also found to persist at the age 4 follow-up. In particular, the constellation of hyperactivity, impulsivity, inattention, and peer aggression was associated with continued externalizing problems. The relative contributions of child characteristics, parental expectations and management strategies, and ongoing family stresses to problem identification and persistence appeared to vary somewhat from one child to the next, illustrating different patterns of symptoms as well as different pathways to early difficulties.

In one instance, child problems appeared to be rather isolated symptoms in a well-functioning family. Unrealistic parental expectations, possibly paired with a somewhat difficult infancy, appeared to lead to perceptions of problems in youngsters who were not clearly atypical initially. In one instance, poor parenting and a negative mother–child relationship were associated with an uncertain outcome at age 4. In another instance, parental expectations, although high, were associated with positive parenting and a good mother–child relationship. The outlook for this child appeared to be good. In yet another case, the relative contributions of endogenous child characteristics and family dysfunction were more difficult to disentangle, although severe family disruption lead to the appearance of new symptoms. Symptoms of anxiety and sadness were especially apparent in association either with severe mother–child conflict or marked family disruption, although in most instances both externalizing and internalizing symptoms occurred together.

These case vignettes also illustrate the observation that particular symptoms appear to become salient at different stages of development, sometimes as exaggerations of normal developmental tasks. Thus, sleeping and feeding problems and consolability appear especially noticeable in infancy; activity level becomes particularly important as children become mobile and exploratory around the first birthday. By around age 2, compliance with requests and ability to play alone also come to the fore, as parental expectations change with the child's growing cognitive and self-regulatory abilities. Peer relations, the ability to play cooperatively with other children and to share toys without eruptions of excessive aggression, become noteworthy at about age 3 as children begin to enter the peer group in more formalized preschool and day-care programs. By age 4, children seem to be able to cooperate better within the peer group and to function more independently at home, although issues of noncompliance and self-regulation are still primary parental concerns.

CHAPTER FOUR

Family Factors

It is obvious that a variety of factors within the family have a major impact on children's development. Family influences include (1) child-rearing practices and parental expectations, which determine the nature and quality of the child's socialization experiences; (2) aspects of family structure and family relations, which influence the child both directly, through their impact on the climate of the home, and indirectly, via their effects on childrearing and parental availability and support; and (3) the family's social context, which also affects the child both directly and indirectly via its influence on the parents. Each of these factors will be addressed in turn. Where appropriate, clinical vignettes will be used to illustrate significant interactions among family, child, and parenting factors.

The Role of the Parents in Socialization and Social Development

Clinical wisdom, empirical data, and common sense converge to emphasize the crucial role that parents play in children's socialization and social development. From the earliest days of life, parents are responsible for meeting the infant's needs for protection, nurturance, and physical caretaking. They must help the newborn infant adapt to life outside the womb, for example, by establishing smooth caretaking routines, facilitating state control, and protecting the young infant from overstimulation (e.g., Campos et al., 1983; Sroufe, 1979). Over the course of the first year, parents must function primarily as caretakers and nurturers with the goals of protecting their young infants from harm, providing for their physical needs, and fulfilling their needs for social, affective, and cognitive stimulation. By the end of the first year, as children begin to develop language, symbolic thinking, a sense of self, and the ability to act on their environment in effective ways, the responsibilities of parents shift from one of primarily providing nurturance and protection to one in which caretaking must be balanced by limit-setting and the use of effective control strategies. At this developmental stage, parents must confront the difficult but rewarding tasks of teaching children the rules of appropriate social behavior, helping them to master the rules of social exchange and of the physical world, and facilitating the internalization of values and morals.

It seems obvious that some children are easier to socialize than others (Maccoby & Martin, 1983). For example, individual differences in infant characteristics, such as irritability and consolability, or in activity level will make some children more difficult to satisfy or to control than others. Similarly, some parents seem to have an intuitive sense of how to gain their child's cooperation, whereas others go about it in ways that limit their success from the start. There is a growing body of evidence linking qualitative features of the early mother–infant relationship to later social and cognitive competence (e.g., Matas et al., 1978; Pastor, 1981; Sroufe, 1983). this work dramatizes the importance of parental responsiveness and availability as well as warmth and sensitivity. Research on child rearing practices also indicates that positive, nonconfrontative approaches that are basically educative tend to be more effective than controls that are inflexible and harsh (e.g., Londerville & Main, 1981 Zahn-Waxler et al., 1979). In addition, children learn from observation and imitation. Thus, parental actions and affect will have a major impact on how the children respond to attempts at parental control, what values and goals they internalize, and how they behave with others in their social network.

The Quality of Parenting and Infant–Parent Attachment

As noted in Chapter One, attachment theorists (Ainsworth et al., 1978; Bowlby, 1969; Sroufe, 1985) see the quality of the early mother–infant relationship as the prototype of all later relationships and as forming the groundwork for later cognitive and social development. In addition, maternal sensitivity to infant signals is hypothesized to be a central determinant of early mother–infant interaction, which will influence the quality of the attachment relationship that develops over the course of the first year. Thus, mothers who are able to read their infants' social and distress signals and are then available to respond promptly and appropriately will be more likely to raise infants who are securely attached. Because securely attached infants have a history of positive interactions with mothers who are accessible and responsive, they have learned that the world is predictable and supportive, and they are also able to reach out to explore, secure in the expectation that they will be protected. This feeling is akin to what Erikson (1963) terms a sense of basic trust. In addition, such infants have learned that their communications lead to responses in others, fostering a sense of self-efficacy, what some theorists see as the underpinnings of basic motivation (Hunt, 1961; White, 1959).

Yet, when parents are insensitive and unresponsive, infants learn to expect that their needs will not be met, that the world is neither predictable nor supportive. Such infants will develop insecure patterns of attachment, reflected either in avoidant and socially withdrawn behavior or in angry, resistant behavior. Some insecurely attached infants are less likely to venture out to explore the environment because their parents have not provided them with consistent protection from harm or with comfort when they are frightened or upset, what Ainsworth and others (Ainsworth et al., 1978; Bowlby, 1969) have termed a secure base for exploration. Other insecure infants may focus their attention on objects that seem more predictable and under their control rather than on social interactions with people, which have been frustrating, unpredictable, and/or unsatisfying for them. Because they do not expect to be comforted when distressed, insecurely attached infants ultimately learn to avoid or resist contact with unavailable or frustrating parents, especially when under stress.

Studies indicate that insecurely attached infants tend to be more noncompliant with maternal requests and prohibitions than securely attached infants. They also exhibit less interest and flexibility in problem-solving situations, are less adept at eliciting help and support from their mothers when confronted with difficult problems to solve, and are less socially competent with peers. Bretherton (1985) and Sroufe (1983), among others, argue that the lack of a secure attachment, which stems initially from inept maternal behavior, has profound ramifications for the infant's social development and ability to cope with developmental challenges, such as environmental mastery, independence, autonomy, and the ability to function well with other children. Thus, according to attachment theorists, maternal responsiveness, availability, and sensitivity in the first year of life are crucial components of social adaptation and socialization.

There is some debate in the literature about the role of infant characteristics in the establishment of a secure attachment. It seems logical that infants who are extremely difficult to care for will be less likely to elicit sensitive and responsive caretaking. Furthermore, with some especially difficult infants, event the most sensitive caretakers may prove ineffective. Research findings linking infant irritability to the quality of later attachment have been equivocal, with some studies (e.g., Crockenberg, 1981) finding a relationship between infant difficultness and insecure attachment and others supporting Sroufe's (1985) argument that caretaking sensitivity overrides infant characteristics in determining the quality of the attachment that develops (e.g., Bates et al., 1985). Quality of caretaking and child characteristics are both significant in determining outcome, although with either very inept caretaking or extreme infant irritability, problems are likely to be in evidence.

Several studies have examined the relationship between insecure attachment in infancy and later psychosocial outcomes in an attempt to clarify the link between attachment security and later behavior problems. Sroufe (1983) studied an inner city, poverty sample and reported that insecure attachment was associated with a variety of internalizing and externalizing problems in preschool. Lewis et al. (1984) followed a sample of middle-class infants until age 6. Insecure attachment predicted behavior problems, but only in boys and only in the context of ongoing family stress and disruption. The third study to examine the relationship between quality of attachment and development of behavior problems was conducted by Bates and associates (Bates et al., 1985; Bates & Bayles, 1988) who found a relationship between infant difficultness and problem behaviors at ages 3 and 6 but no relationship between attachment security and behavior problems at either age. Thus, the findings to date are equivocal on the hypothesized link between attachment security and later social development and behavior problems. This is not surprising when one considers the complexity of the issues under study.

In line with the transactional and ecological perspective, early relationship problems in some mother–infant dyads probably do persist and continue to cause difficulties as the child grows older, especially if mothers are inflexible and rejecting and their children are angry and uncooperative. Other mother–child dyads probably overcome early difficulties as the child's needs change and the parents become more able to respond appropriately, either because they are better able to cope with an older child or because of decreases in external stresses that had taxed their limited resources. In still other instances, the negative impact of a poor mother–child relationship may be ameliorated in part by a warm affective bond and positive experiences with other adults: father, grandparents, or a caring baby-sitter. Thus, an insecure attachment is likely to be one ingredient in the mix of factors leading to behavior problems in young children. However, behavior problems do not inevitably signal an insecure attachment; conversely, an insecure attachment need not produce behavior problems.

Child-Rearing Practices and Socialization

Much of the work on parent–child relations has focused on child-rearing practices and their impact on children's development. Whereas the focus in infancy is on the quality of caregiving, by toddlerhood the focus shifts to include parents' ability to set limits and provide guidelines for acceptable behavior. Studies generally find that children tend to be compliant most of the time, although the relationship between child compliance and parental behavior is clearly a transactional one, with children's past behavior influencing the nature of future parental prohibitions and with parenting behavior contributing to children's willingness to cooperate. Thus, the quality of the ongoing mother–child relationship appears to play a role. As noted earlier, several studies have found that toddlers who are securely attached to their mothers are also more compliant with maternal requests and less likely to refuse to cooperate with restrictions. However, their mothers in turn are less restrictive and less likely to set arbitrary or punitive limits. That does not mean that these mothers never get angry and that their children are always well behaved. Rather, studies suggest that mothers who have harmonious relationships with relatively cooperative toddlers and preschoolers have not only a history of positive interaction but also a hierarchy of behavioral control strategies that they apply, based on the situation. For most situations they can obtain compliance with a request and an explanation.

There are a range of positive control strategies that mothers use with good effect, including anticipating trouble, diverting or redirecting attention, providing choices and explanations, enlisting cooperation, and suggesting rather than demanding. Numerous studies indicate that these approaches are associated with child compliance, whereas physical restraints, threats, and negative prohibitions are more likely to elicit both immediate noncompliance and ongoing power struggles. Furthermore, mothers who are able to set priorities appear to have an easier time. Thus, it appears important to childproof the house and to ignore minor infractions of household rules in favor of more serious violations that involve safety hazards or impinge on the rights of others. In one study (Zahn-Waxler et al., 1979), mothers who had clear priorities about what was and was not a serious transgression and who responded selectively to misbehavior, with strong prohibitions paired with explanations, had toddlers who exhibited more prosocial behavior and were more likely to make reparations for harm caused to others. Mothers who used more frequent prohibitions and failed to pair them with explanations and reasons had toddlers who were more likely to ignore maternal commands and less likely to behave prosocially.

In general, then, studies indicate that limit setting is more effective when it occurs in the context of a positive mother–child relationship and provides educative guidance and clear expectations, rather than punitive and apparently arbitrary rules. This has been termed authoritative (as opposed to authoritarian) child rearing by Baumrind (1967), and it is characterized by respect for the child's rights and feelings along with clear guidelines and expectations for mature and socially appropriate behavior. The ability to set appropriate limits and to engage in authoritative patterns of child rearing undoubtedly depends upon parental personality style, the understanding of young children's developmental needs, and on age-appropriate expectations. In this context, it is worth noting that studies reveal that the "terrible 2's" are rarer than popular writings suggest (e.g., Minton, Kagan, & Levine, 1970) and extreme child noncompliance in the late toddler and early preschool periods often reflects inappropriate child-rearing practices or the failure of parents to establish firm, consistent, child-centered controls (Brazelton, 1974).

Although positive approaches to obtaining compliance and setting limits on child behavior may work with most children, mothers of children with behavior problems routinely complain that "nothing works!" By the time such children reach the clinician, the escalating, negative, and coercive cycle described by Patterson (1980) is well established, and it is difficult, if not impossible, to tease apart the direction of effects. Thus, these mothers may be utilizing harsh and negative disciplinary practices because their initial attempts at more low-key and subtle approaches proved ineffective with angry, defiant, or inattentive children or because their initially negative approaches may have inaugurated the cycle of child noncompliance. In either case, it is clear that patterns of child noncompliance and negative maternal control are highly intercorrelated and built up over time, reflecting a history of ongoing negative transactions.

Several studies have examined disciplinary encounters in children identified as difficult or highly active. For example, it has been reported that toddlers who had been rated as difficult to handle in infancy were more likely to initiate behaviors that were forbidden or troublesome and in general to test limits at age 2 (Lee & Bates, 1985). Their mothers were more likely to employ power-assertive disciplinary techniques in response to these provocations, leading to a cycle of coercive and conflicted interactions. Buss (1981) found that highly active pre-schoolers and their parents became engaged in more frequent power struggles during a laboratory teaching task than their less active peers; mothers of more active youngsters were also less responsive to their preschoolers' needs during task solution and less able to convey clearly the nature of the tasks. In our own work (Campbell, Breaux, Ewing, Szumowski, & Pierce, 1986), we observed mother–child interaction during an unstructured play situation. Mothers of hard-to-manage toddlers and preschoolers redirected play activities more often than control mothers and provided more negative control statements; problem youngsters were more active and engaged in more aggressive play than controls. Finally, studies comparing clinically diagnosed hyperactive preschoolers and their mothers with control dyads indicate that hyperactive children are more negative and noncompliant during both free play and more demanding structured situations, whereas their mothers are more directive and less rewarding of independent play and compliance (Barkley, 1985; Mash & Johnston, 1982). Patterson (1980) has conducted observations in the homes of families who sought help with management of aggressive preschoolers. His findings highlight the reciprocity inherent in these aversive interactions as well as the child's typical role as initiator.

Parents often report that hard-to-manage children comply more readily with fathers than mothers and that they are more likely to listen to their mothers when fathers are present. Both of these parental perceptions of child compliance patterns have been confirmed by observational studies conducted in the homes of young children (Lytton, 1980; Patterson, 1980). Patterson suggested that in normal families mothers are the principal caretakers, although fathers contribute to child rearing both directly and indirectly by supporting mothers in their child rearing and socialization efforts. However, in families with children who are difficult to control, mothers are more likely to function as "crisis managers" who must cope on a daily basis with a range of child-rearing dilemmas and conflicts. Often fathers in such families withdraw to avoid dealing with unpleasant situations. This exaggerated role differentiation vis-a-vis child rearing is consonant with the complaints of many mothers of children with behavior problems who report feeling isolated and demoralized by their lonely battles for compliance and control (Barkley, 1981; Mash & Johnston, 1983a).

When fathers severely curtail or ignore their child-rearing responsibilities, there are obviously numerous ramifications throughout the family system. Their wives are likely to feel unsupported and abandoned by their husbands, fueling feelings of anger, resentment, and frustration. Such feelings may well be expressed in inconsistent, lax, or overly harsh discipline, which further exacerbates the child's problems as well as the ongoing hostilities between mother and child. Lack of paternal involvement in child rearing not only leaves the mother as the sole and unsupported agent of socialization but also deprives the young child of crucial experiences with an alternative role model and source of nurturance. Thus, the psychological unavailability of some fathers of problem preschoolers, even in two-parent families, may contribute to the intensity and duration of mother–child conflict and to more general and persistent problems in socialization.

Recent work also emphasizes the important role played by fathers in helping children, especially young boys, establish sexual identity, internalize standards for behavior, and develop the capacity to regulate their own behavior (e.g., Lamb, 1981). In addition, as noted earlier, the nature of father involvement in child rearing can have an indirect impact on the mother–child relationship as well as on the quality of marital interaction (e.g., Belsky, 1984). Thus, fathers who spend time with their preschoolers are cementing the father–child relationship, and contributing to their children's sex role identity, cognitive and social development, and sense of self-worth. They also are indirectly supporting their wives in their child-rearing efforts, something that may also strengthen the quality of both the marital relationship and the mother–child relationship.

It should be emphasized in this context that these comments apply whether the family functions as a "traditional" one (in which the mother has the major responsibility for child rearing and sex role differentiation within the family is clear-cut) or a more "contemporary" arrangement (in which both parents share the child rearing, household chores, and career roles relatively equally). From the perspective of the child, the most important factor is whether both parents are involved in child rearing and whether they support each other in their child-rearing efforts. Children can adapt to a variety of family organizations and structures provided they have a strong relationship with one, or preferably both, parents.

CLINICAL IMPLICATIONS

Several cases discussed in Chapter Three illustrate the complex interactions between child characteristics and child-rearing practices in contributing to the possible onset and persistence of problems or to the amelioration of some difficulties. In all four cases, infant difficultness of varying severity was reported, as indexed by behaviors such as excessive crying and unconsolability, irregular sleep patterns, and feeding problems. These reported behavior patterns probably reflect some endogenous infant characteristics as well as parental expectations and interpretations of infant behavior (Bates, 1987). Parental approaches to dealing with these early difficulties appeared to set the stage either for the development of harmonious parent–child relations despite the problems or for the development of an extremely tense and troubled relationship. Parental philosophy of child rearing, flexibility, and the general affective tone of the relationship also were associated with the nature of mother–child disciplinary encounters later on during the preschool period. The nature and extent of paternal involvement in child rearing also seemed to contribute to the quality of the mother–child relationship as well as to general family climate.

For example, Jamie was described as an irritable and fussy infant who was difficult to calm and who required little sleep. However, his parents appear to have handled his early demandingness with sensitivity and patience. Although at age 3 when he was seen in our project, he was noncompliant, aggressive, inattentive, and impulsive, the quality of the mother–child relationship did not appear to be seriously impaired. We were impressed with his mother's patience and supportiveness and with the warmth of feeling that characterized their interaction during play.

Unlike other mother–child pairs in our study, Jamie and Mrs. L did not get into negative, conflicted, and escalating coercive cycles of behavior. Mrs. L realistically perceived Jamie as difficult to deal with, but she also recognized his intelligence and creativity and the positive affective bond between them was unmistakable. Mrs. L remained patient and calm in her disciplinary encounters with Jamie. She was able to set clear and firm limits while permitting him some degree of autonomy, for example, by providing alternatives and reasons. Mr. L was also involved in child rearing and provided his wife with needed time away from this difficult and demanding youngster. It appears that these parents were coping extremely well with Jamie's difficulties and that they provided an optimal environment for his growth and development, despite his problems with self-control and social interaction.

In contrast, Annie's difficulties appeared to stem from a troubled mother–child interaction that began in early infancy. In speculating about the early development of Annie's problems, it is tempting to hypothesize that, based on maternal report and observed behavior in toddlerhood, Annie had developed an insecure attachment to her mother. This troubled relationship was reflected in her excessive anxiety, clinging behavior, and separation distress, and the absence of warmth and reciprocity in the interaction. Furthermore, Mrs. J's lack of sensitivity to Annie's needs as a 2½-year-old and her ineffective management strategies make it likely that she was not particularly sensitive or tuned in to Annie when Annie was an infant. This hypothesis gains support form Mrs. J's inconsistent reports and distorted expectations. Annie's role in this situation is less clear. She may indeed have been somewhat difficult as Mrs. J described or she may have developed into a difficult youngster as her needs were constantly frustrated by a mother who was relatively inept at caretaking, highly anxious and insecure in her new role, and ignorant of the needs of young infants. This interpretation is consistent with the views of Greenberg and Speltz (1988) who suggested that behaviors labeled by mothers as discipline problems in early childhood may instead reflect the frustrated attempts of toddlers to gain attention and nurturance from unresponsive or inept caregivers.

By the time Annie was a toddler, she and her mother were locked in a daily struggle for control. Mrs. J, unable to set firm, consistent, and reasonable limits, tended to be inconsistent, unpredictable, and over-bearing, resorting to power-assertive disciplinary methods, such as threatening and shouting. However, these methods proved ineffective, only serving to fuel Annie's noncompliant behavior. Furthermore, in the absence of a close, positive mother–daughter relationship, Annie had little incentive to respond cooperatively to Mrs. J's requests and tended to vent her frustration and confusion by challenging her mother's authority. Mrs. J, in turn, anticipating a struggle, approached Annie in ways guaranteed to elicit anger and defiance. Interparental disagreement over child rearing and interparental inconsistency probably contributed to this troubled mother–child relationship. Finally, inappropriate developmental expectations appeared to exacerbate interactive problems as well. Mrs. J's beliefs about appropriate behavior and her negative perceptions of Annie seemed resistant to change. Although Mr. J was involved in some caretaking and he tended to see Annie in a more positive light than did his wife, it does not appear that his involvement was sufficient in either quantity or positivity to counteract the problems inherent in the mother–daughter relationship. Furthermore, there is some suggestion that marital tension contributed to maternal insensitivity, impatience, and anger that was directed primarily at Annie.

Although unrealistically high standards of behavior and inappropriate developmental expectations also characterized Teddy's parents, they were able to modify their perceptions and to gain greater understanding of his developmental needs. Their ability to change their expectations may well have averted the development of more serious problems. Furthermore, changes in both Teddy and his parents occurred in the context of a positive parent–child relationship and parental unity around child-rearing expectations and goals.

These case examples support suggestions from both our own work (Campbell, Breaux, Ewing, & Szumowski, 1986) and that of others (Richman et al., 1982) that high levels of ongoing parent–child conflict and negative maternal attitudes are associated with the onset and persistence of problems in young children. Alternatively, improvement in parental attitudes and expectations can ease parent–child conflicts. Yet some problems do persist despite optimal child-rearing efforts.

Family Climate

Not surprisingly, parent–child conflict rarely occurs in isolation from other factors. Numerous studies indicate a relationship between a disturbed family environment and children's problems (for recent reviews, see Emery, 1982; Hetherington & Martin, 1986). In general, childhood problems, especially externalizing problems in boys, are associated not only with parent–child discord but also with marital distress, separation and divorce, parental psychopathology, maternal depression and general malaise, and more general family stresses including unemployment and poor housing. The nature of these relationships is undoubtedly complex. Many of these indicators of family climate are highly intercorrelated with each other as well as with methods of child rearing. Thus, the impact of any one problem on the child can rarely be examined in isolation from other associated factors. In addition, as noted earlier, each of these factors will have complex ramifications throughout the family system, impinging directly on the child but also indirectly through their impact on parents and siblings.

Marital Distress and Disruption

A relationship between marital distress and childhood problems has been established in numerous case studies and empirical investigations (e.g., Cohen & Minde, 1983, Emery, 1982; McGee, Williams, & Silva, 1984; Richman et al., 1982). The specific nature of this relationship remains obscure, however, because few studies have examined the mechanisms that account for this association. In general, studies suggest that boys are more vulnerable to the impact of marital discord than girls and that the result is more likely to be acting out undercontrolled behavior characterized by noncompliance and aggression rather that overcontrolled behavior, characterized by social withdrawal and anxiety. This conclusion may be premature because overcontrolled behaviors are more likely to be overlooked and less likely to lead to clinic referral. In addition, as Emery (1982) has suggested, boys may be more readily upset by family conflict and may express this in a range of symptoms, with externalizing ones most easily identified. Longitudinal, prospective studies do indicate that both interparental disagreement over child rearing and marital discord are precursors of childhood problems (Block, Block, & Morrison, 1981; Richman et al., 1982) and that overt marital hostility and anger are more closely associated with children's externalizing behaviors than marital distress per se (Emery & O'Leary, 1982). Thus, it is well established that marital turmoil can lead to problems in children, and it is likely that a tension-ridden and conflicted home environment will have both direct and indirect effects on children. Furthermore, it is logical to suppose that preschoolers may be particularly vulnerable to the negative impact of family conflict.

For example, Cummings, Zahn-Waxler, and Radke-Yarrow (1981, 1984) studied young children's reactions to expressions of anger and affection in the home and noted that even very young children responded with anxiety, overt distress, and anger to expressions of anger by others, whether they themselves were involved in the conflict or were merely bystanders. Some toddlers attempted to comfort a distressed adult or to reconcile angry individuals. When older children (6 to 7 years) were witnesses to confrontations between adults or between adults and children, they were even more likely to attempt to protect one member of the dyad or to mediate the dispute. Thus, there is little doubt that young children are highly responsive to the intensity and quality of the affective exchanges that occur in their immediate environment.

When children witness frequent arguments and interparental strife, feelings of anxiety and insecurity are likely to result, children's perceptions of themselves and of their parents are likely to be affected, and the nature of family interaction patterns is likely to be changed. For example, children who attempt to intervene in parental disputes and are unsuccessful may feel both guilty and incompetent. If the child is the focus of the parental discord, as is often the case, the child may feel even worse. Even very young children may be enlisted as the ally of one parent against another, possibly also contributing to feelings of anger and guilt. Such feelings may be expressed in a variety of ways, including social withdrawal and tearfulness, aggression toward others, or anger and noncompliance. These responses may be mediated through the emotional contagion observed in very young children as well as through imitation and modeling. Because parents serve as the most important agents of socialization, parents' styles of solving interpersonal problems may be modeled by their children. Thus, hostility and anger may be imitated by children who learn that this is a usual and acceptable way to deal with interpersonal disputes. These constitute some of the direct effects of marital discord on children's behavior.

In addition, there are pervasive effects that are indirect, mediated by the impact of marital distress on the parents and their ability to fulfill parental roles. For example, conflict is often associated with the unavailability of one parent and with added burdens on the other. Richman et al. (1982) noted that mothers of problem preschoolers who complained of unsatisfying marriages discussed problems with their husbands less often and made more decisions alone than mothers of youngsters without problems. Chronic, ongoing marital dysfunction also leads to anger and hostility in one or both parents that may be directed at the children. This has been called scapegoating by family systems theorists (e.g., Minuchin, 1974). Parents, when they are engaged in constant bickering, may have little tolerance left for the typical behaviors of young children. They may also have less energy available to provide emotional and instrumental support to children, leaving the children feeling frustrated, unloved, or neglected. These feelings may trigger defiance, demandingness, and anger in some children or may lead to sadness, fearfulness, and withdrawal in others. Some distressed parents may unrealistically expect young children to meet some of their own emotional needs, those that would be more appropriately met by their spouses or other adults. Finally, parents, preoccupied with their own problems, may become ineffective and inconsistent disciplinarians, further contributing to the development of behavior problems in their children. Thus by draining parental resources, marital dysfunction may take its toll on the children by leaving them bereft of adequate parenting. Younger children are likely to be especially vulnerable because they are in need of more sustained caretaking and social stimulation from parents and because they are less able to separate themselves from parental squabbles by spending prolonged periods of time with peers away from home.

However, the relationship between marital discord and children's problems is frequently a bidirectional one. The association between parental reports of marital conflict and child behavior problems may reflect the fact that having a difficult child can increase tensions within a family. Thus, the child's problem behaviors may fuel latent marital conflicts, become the focus of marital disagreements, or exacerbate already existent marital dysfunction. For example, parents may engage in intense disagreements over how to handle a difficult child, with one parent advocating sterner discipline than the other. Conflict over child rearing may become the overt focus of anger and discord, masking other ongoing problems in communication that are more subtle or more threatening to confront. The child's difficulties may also bring other problems to the fore. For instance, conflicts over finances, in-laws, or the distribution of responsibilities may become more salient as children's problems worsen. Parents may also use a child's problems to dramatize other marital issues or to retaliate against the spouse. In clinical interviews, it is not uncommon to witness one parent assigning blame to the other for the child's difficulties or for parents to engage in mutual recriminations. A mother may attribute a child's problem behavior to lack of paternal involvement or a father may blame his wife's laxness or incompetence for his child's lack of control or problems with peers. Negative rather than supportive interactions between parents regarding a child's problems are a clear signal that marital stresses are relevant to an understanding of the child's difficulties, whether they appear to figure as an etiological factor or a factor contributing to environmental stresses that exacerbate and/or maintain ongoing problems within the family.

It has been suggested that children may fare better in a harmonious one-parent family than in a discordant two-parent family (Emery, 1982). Although this is undoubtedly the case when one parent is seriously disturbed or abusive (Wallerstein & Kelly, 1980), there is also accumulating evidence linking marital disruption to both short-term stress reactions and longer term adjustment difficulties in children. For example, studies confirm that separation and divorce are more common in the lives of young children with problems than controls or non-referred age-mates (e.g., McGee, Williams, & Silva, 1984; Cohen & Minde, 1983). It also appears that preschool children, especially boys, have a particularly difficult time adjusting to parental divorce (Hetherington, 1989; Hetherington et al., 1978; Wallerstein, 1983; Wallerstein & Kelly, 1980). Wallerstein and Kelly (1980) described the reactions of young children to marital separation. Preschoolers were particularly devastated by the experience, reacting with nightmares, regression, guilt, fear of abandonment, and intense longing for the absent parent.

The impact of marital separation on children partly reflects other life changes and losses that occur in tandem with the loss of the departed parent. Marital separation usually occurs in the context of a number of pervasive life changes, such as a decline in living standards, changes in living arrangements, a move to a new neighborhood, changes in relationships with both parents, and mother's return to work. Thus, the youngster may have to adapt to altered routines, a new baby-sitter, a new school, and the establishment of new friendships, while coping with the loss or partial loss of both parents. Both Hetherington et al. (1978) and Wallerstein and Kelly (1980) discuss the diminished ability of angry, depressed custodial mothers to provide adequate parenting in the immediate aftermath of the separation, the time when the preschooler is especially vulnerable to feelings of loss, rejection, and self-blame.

These changes in family structure and functioning are also associated with increased mother–child conflict (Hetherington, 1989;

Hetherington et al., 1978; Wallerstein & Kelly, 1980), especially between custodial mothers and their preschool sons. The combined impact of a distressed youngster, mourning for the absent father, and a depressed, angry, and overwhelmed mother results in heightened conflicts over discipline, and these negative interactions spill over to the preschool classroom, where young children from divorced or separated families are also more likely to get into conflicts with peers and to demonstrate a diminished capacity for independent and creative play. Preschoolers of both sexes show profound reactions to the initial separation, girls and their mothers are more likely to reestablish harmonious relationships by 18 to 24 months postdivorce, and mother–son conflict is more likely to persist.

There is some suggestive evidence (Santrock & Warshak, 1979) that boys raised by fathers do better than boys raised by mothers and that same-sex custody arrangements may be better under some circumstances. However, studies have not systematically compared the impact of maternal, paternal, and joint custody arrangements on samples of preschool boys and girls. It is clear from the extensive literature on the impact of divorce that young children show particularly dramatic reactions to family break-up, that reunion fantasies persist for many years, and that the capacity of young children from divorced families to adapt to change ultimately depends upon the ability of both parents to maintain strong, positive, and supportive relationships with their children, while shielding them from interparental conflict. When children are cut off from contact with the noncustodial parent, when they are enlisted as allies of one parent against the other, or when they are used as message carriers, the likelihood is high that problems will be both prolonged and severe.

CLINICAL IMPLICATIONS

Robbie, who was introduced in Chapter Three, illustrates a number of these themes. Despite a good relationship with a competent and devoted mother, Robbie became the focus of early marital conflict, with his unpredictable and often unavailable father blaming Mrs. S for Robbie's difficulties. Once his parents separated, Robbie became embroiled in their battles as a message carrier, and he contributed to the heightened tension by provoking both parents with stories of the other. Clinically, he exhibited all the symptoms described by Wallerstein and Kelly, including regression, self-blame, fear of abandonment, intense concern about the absent father, and elaborate reunion fantasies. These themes were apparent in his play and conversations. Furthermore, reunion fantasies appeared to spur him on to provoke his parents because their only communication consisted of mutual recriminations about who was to blame for Robbie's ongoing difficulties. As conflict between his parents intensified, Robbie's problems became more serious, spilling over to his once good relationship with peers and resulting in poor school achievement. Robbie's problems appear to have stabilized at a fairly severe level, clearly fueled by his troubled family situation and by his inability to adapt to parental divorce.

Parental Psychopathology

Numerous studies have demonstrated a link between psychological problems in parents and difficulties in their preschool children. These range from studies in which maternal self-reports of depressive symptomatology and somatic complaints have been correlated with maternal ratings of children's problems (e.g., Fergusson, Horwood, & Shannon, 1984; Panaccione & Wahler, 1986; Richman et al., 1982) to more detailed clinical studies employing careful diagnostic appraisal of parents (e.g., Gamer, Grunebaum, Cohler, & Gallant, 1977; Radke-Yarrow, Cummings, Kuczynski, & Chapman, 1985; Sameroff, Seifer, & Zax, 1982). Findings consistently indicate that mothers who report more symptoms of depression also are more likely to perceive their preschool children as hard to manage than are less distressed women. In addition, they are more likely to engage in conflicted and coercive interactions with their children than mothers who do not report feeling depressed. Mothers who report more depression and anxiety also arc more likely to seek pediatric (Wolkind, 1985) and mental health services (Shepherd et al., 1971) for their children. It appears that maternal mood influences both the quality of caretaking and a woman's interpretation of and tolerance for her preschooler's behavior. Women who feel fatigued, dispirited, and unsupported have less tolerance for the typical behavior of preschool-age children, which leads them to label even age-appropriate behavior as problematic and to seek help for problems that other parents would just ignore. Moreover, there is accumulating evidence that depressed women have less energy available to provide responsive and appropriately stimulating caregiving to their children (e.g., Panaccione & Wahler, 1986; Sameroff et al., 1982).

Several large-scale longitudinal studies of mentally ill parents document the profound impact of parental psychopathology on the early development and psychosocial adjustment of children (Sameroff et al., 1982; Zahn-Waxler, Cummings, McKnew, & Radke-Yarrow, 1984). In general, these studies indicate that infants, toddlers, and preschoolers with seriously disturbed parents show less adaptive behavior with parents and peers. Furthermore, there is some evidence that the severity and chronicity of the parental disturbance may be more important then the specific diagnosis in predicting problem behavior in children, although there is also evidence that children of mothers with major affective disturbances may fare more poorly than offspring of schizophrenic mothers. In one detailed longitudinal study (Zahn-Waxler, Cummings, et al., 1984), a small sample of children with one bipolar (manic–depressive) parent was compared with control children. Most of the spouses of the bipolar patients also met DSM-III criteria for a psychiatric disorder, mostly unipolar depression.

When studied at between 2 and 2½ years of age, the children of disturbed parents showed less ability to regulate emotional expression. At times they withdrew from social contacts and at other times they showed excessive expressions of anger and excitement in comparison with the controls, whose parents were functioning adequately. The offspring of disturbed parents also became more aggressive with peers; in particular, they tended to show displaced aggression after separation from mother and less ability to share and cooperate during play. They also became more distressed than controls after observing conflict between adults and were less able to use their mothers to help them cope with the distress.

When observed during a standard laboratory assessment of attachment, offspring of disturbed parents showed less secure attachments to their mothers. Their mothers in turn tended to express more negative affect toward their children and to exhibit more disorganization, tension, inactivity, and inconsistency when observed interacting at home (Davenport, Zahn-Waxler, Adland, & Mayfield, 1984). Home visitors also described these offspring as exhibiting a range of symptoms, including excessive shyness, dependency, inappropriate affect, tantrums, overactivity, and poor impulse control, suggesting that in young children severe parental pathology is associated with a variety of nonspecific externalizing and internalizing problems (Zahn-Waxler,

McKnew, Cummings, Davenport, & Radke-Yarrow, 1984). Similar findings of impaired mother–child relations and social incompetence have been obtained in other studies of young children and their disturbed mothers (Persson-Blenow, Naslund, McNeil, & Kaij, 1986; Sameroff et al., 1982).

Radke-Yarrow et al. (1985) also examined the attachment patterns of mothers and toddlers in a sample with a range of maternal affective disorder: bipolar disorder, major and minor affective disorder, and controls. There were much higher rates of maladaptive attachment patterns in the offspring of bipolar and seriously depressed women than in the offspring of women with minor affective disorder or no disorder. Both diagnosis and severity of disorder contributed independent variance to attachment classification, as did the presence of the father in the home. Father's presence, regardless of his mental status (depressed or not), appeared to buffer some toddlers from the effects of severe maternal mental illness.

Taken together, these studies clearly indicate a link between parental psychological distress, including psychiatric disturbance and young children's social-emotional development. As with the findings on marital discord, the nature of the causal mechanisms are unclear. It is generally accepted that the development of children's problems derives from a transactional process in which children with genetic vulnerabilities to disorder are raised in disturbed environments (e.g., Beardslee, Bemporad, Keller, & Klerman, 1983; Radke-Yarrow et al., 1985) in which a number of developmental needs are inadequately met. A variety of psychosocial environmental factors may partly explain this association. The studies cited above indicate that disturbed women are less effective in the mothering role than control women. Thus, they provide their young children with less appropriate cognitive, social, and emotional stimulation and are less sensitive and responsive to their children's needs and communications. They tend to be unpredictable and explosive or sad, withdrawn, and unresponsive, depending upon their diagnosis. Thus, they present poor role models to their children. The work of Cummings et al. (1984) cited earlier also suggests that disturbed parents would be expected to elicit a range of negative emotions in their children because young children tend to mirror the affective exchanges of those in their immediate environment. Finally, they may deprive their children of adequate mothering. Thus, their children are less empathic and prosocial with peers, and they are likely to develop lower self-esteem and feelings of self-efficacy. These direct effects of living with a disturbed parent are thought to interact with biological factors to produce disturbances in offspring.

In addition, however, parental mental illness is associated with more general factors, such as psychological disturbance in the spouse (Zahn-Waxler, Cummings, et al., 1984), more marital discord and divorce (Radke-Yarrow et al., 1985), and more social isolation (Pan-accione & Wahler, 1986), further compounding the impact of parental illness on the child. Thus, the young child with a severely disturbed parent is also more likely to be deprived of support from an intact and emotionally competent parent who could compensate for the inadequacies of the ill parent. There is some evidence that other adults can buffer young children from the negative impact of poor parenting. In addition, other adults can serve as role models and can provide sufficient support to poorly functioning parents to help them overcome some of their deficits. However, the increased social isolation and lack of support from significant adults experienced by disturbed families are also associated with poor parenting and inconsistent discipline. Thus, these more general factors also may be contributing to the association between parental psychiatric disturbance and poor child outcomes.

CLINICAL IMPLICATIONS

Both Robbie's and Annie's problems may have resulted in part from parental problems and/or biological vulnerabilities associated with problems in close relatives. Annie's mother did not acknowledge problems with herself or her marriage, although she appeared highly anxious and somewhat depressed. It is not inconceivable that her negative attitudes toward Annie and her poor tolerance for her daughter's behavior partly reflected her own feelings of anger, despair, and helplessness in the context of marital problems or her own depression. Robbie's family had a positive history of depression and antisocial behavior. In addition, his father appeared seriously impaired, although he did not have a history of psychiatric contacts. In our formulation of Robbie's problems, it was logical to consider the possibility that a biological vulnerability to disorder was interacting with the severe psychosocial stress he was under, thereby exacerbating and maintaining his symptoms.

Social Context

As noted in Chapter One, a variety of other environmental factors also have a direct impact on the child and an indirect influence mediated through the parents. These have been discussed in detail by Bronfenbrenner and Crouter (1983) in the context of an ecological model of development. Relevant factors that influence the quality of a preschooler's life, such as the availability of social support for the family and material resources, must be considered here. These include financial and material resources, nutrition, the quality and availability of health care, parental educational level, the nature of parental employment, and the presence in the community of extended family members or close friends.

The availability of social support from family members or friends appears to be especially important for the mental health of adults and for optimal child development (Brown & Harris, 1980; Cochran & Brassard, 1979). Women who feel supported by others are better able to cope with difficult and irritable infants (Crockenberg, 1981; Cutrona & Troutman, 1986). Women who consider their support adequate also are more responsive to their infants' communications (Crnic, Greenberg, Ragozin, Robinson, & Basham, 1983). Conversely, socially isolated women with limited social support and few friends are more likely to perceive their children negatively and to engage in coercive interactions that have the potential to become abusive (Wahler, 1980). Social support in the form of assistance with child care and advice and modeling of caretaking and limit setting, as well as more general emotional support should all have an effect on parental behavior.

In addition, Cochran and Brassard (1979) emphasize the role of extended family and adult family friends in facilitating cognitive and social development in young children by direct social interaction and by indirect modeling. Other familiar and caring adults in the child's environment may take over important caretaking functions when a parent is ill or otherwise incapacitated. Studies suggest that older adults in the child's social milieu may serve a buffering role, protecting children from the negative effects of parental unavailability occasioned by mental illness, divorce, or other environmental stresses.

As more mothers of infants and preschoolers juggle careers and family responsibilities, the importance of adequate, accessible, and affordable child care also becomes crucial to child and family well-being. The substitute caregiver becomes an integral member of the child's social network with an important role to play in providing nurturance and socialization experiences. The effect of day-care on the development of infants and toddlers has become a highly volatile and contentious issue recently in both the mass media and at scientific meetings. The debate has focused on the relative importance of such factors as age of entry into care, quality of care, parental behavior, and other family factors in determining or mediating the impact of day-care experiences on young children.

For example, Belsky has argued (Belsky, 1988; Belsky & Rovine, 1988) that infants placed in more than 20 hours per week of nonparental care during the first year are at risk to develop insecure attachments to parents, as well as a range of later difficulties including poor self-regulation, noncompliance, and aggression toward peers, possibly mediated by the insecure attachment to parents. In support of his argument, Belsky cites studies indicating that children placed in full-time care prior to 12 months of age are more likely than children not in care or in care only part-time to develop anxious attachments, reflected in avoidance of the parent when distressed. He also notes that several longitudinal studies have found that children who had been in early nonmaternal care were more aggressive with peers, more noncompliant with adults, and functioning more poorly at school when followed up in the early elementary school grades than children who had not experienced nonmaternal care in infancy (e.g., Vandell & Corasaniti, 1988). Others have countered (e.g., Clarke-Stewart, 1989; Phillips, 1988) that the data have been overinterpreted by Belsky. For example, avoidance of parents in a laboratory assessment of attachment security may reflect precocious independence as a result of day-care experiences rather than insecurity.

Furthermore, any purported negative effects from day-care attendance must take into account issues of quality of care (e.g., child:caregiver ratio, caregiver training, staff turnover, and caregiver responsiveness and sensitivity) because these factors have been shown to influence the impact of child care. In addition, family factors must be considered. Factors such as social class and educational level, parental involvement, and marital status influence the nature of the care parents seek for their children and interact with child care quality to determine outcome (e.g., Howes & Olenick, 1986). Furthermore, whereas Belsky has emphasized the potential negative effects of day-care, others have noted that there are positive benefits when children are in high quality programs (Clarke-Stewart & Fein, 1983). These include greater competence with peers, for example, sociability and prosocial behavior, and enhanced language development. In addition, the relative effects of center care, family day-care, and home care remain to be determined because the ecologies of these settings differ greatly and they may have different effects, either positive or negative, at different stages in a young child's development.

This important debate is far from settled because the appropriate studies have not yet been conducted. Child care, whether in home or center, must provide children with adequate numbers of familiar, consistent, warm, and responsive caregivers who have both a genuine concern for children and some basic knowledge of child development. Unfortunately, there is a serious shortage of child care, even care of low quality. Furthermore, the lack of uniform federal standards for day-care centers and the limited controls on family day-care mean that many settings are understaffed, must rely on untrained workers, and are plagued by high staff turnover, all of which have been shown to be detrimental to young children. The result of this child care crisis is that those children most in need of high quality substitute care are often those who are least likely to receive it. Rather, children from distressed or disorganized families are most likely to receive custodial care in substandard facilities rather than stimulating and nurturing care that might help them to overcome problems. However, the relationship between inadequate or unstable child care arrangements and the development of behavior problems in preschoolers has not yet been examined in appropriately controlled studies.

Cultural beliefs and values about child rearing, children's roles in the family, and children's rights and responsibilities will also influence parental behavior toward children and the nature of parent–child relationships. Subgroups within North American society differ widely in beliefs about such questions as what constitutes effective and appropriate disciplinary practices. Some groups value reasoning and explanation, whereas others consider physical punishment not only acceptable but necessary. Cultural pressures to excel intellectually differ, as do expectations for mature behavior within the family setting. The limits of acceptable behavior at different ages also vary with cultural values, for example, with regard to the expression of aggression within the family and the peer group. These and other cultural variables have an important impact on family organization, role assignments, communication patterns, child-rearing strategies, and affect expression, all of which ultimately influence family climate and child development.

CLINICAL IMPLICATIONS

Several parents have called our project recently to complain about their children's difficulties in day-care and at home. The similarity among the cases was striking in terms of presenting complaints, although the cases differed in complexity. In each instance, parents called the project after their preschool-age son was threatened with expulsion from a day-care center; complaints focused on marked aggression toward peers (including biting), noncompliance with staff, tantrums and noncompliance at home, and intense sibling conflict and jealousy over parental attention. In one case, a 3-year-old boy was adjusting to a younger sibling who was becoming mobile and sociable. He and his younger sister were in a high quality center for less than 20 hours per week. The family situation appeared stable, although his parents were confused and baffled about how to deal with his aggression toward his sister and toward other children. It is noteworthy that this child was solicitous of his sister while at the center; his aggression toward her was evident only when he had to share his parents with her. In this case, it appeared that the combined stress of coping with an appealing younger sibling and adjusting to a day-care setting was more than this youngster could handle, and he was expressing his upset and confusion by lashing out. He may not have been ready for out-of-home care; as well, the combination of fewer hours with his mother and then having to share her time and attention may have been too much for him. Suggestions were made about increasing his individual, special time with each parent and about handling the aggression and tantrums firmly and consistently.

In several other cases, however, the issues were more complex. Children's difficulties occurred in the context of high levels of family stress, including financial pressures, job stresses, marital discord, and difficulties with extended family. The quality of the mother–child relationships in these cases was very poor, with mothers appearing abrupt, uninvolved, depressed, and drained. These mothers were so immersed in and overwhelmed by their own problems that they appeared unable to take their child's perspective or to recognize that 3- and 4-year-olds require individual attention, nurturance, warmth, and support from a consistent adult. These parents worked long hours in high pressure jobs, and their preschoolers spent from 50 to 60 hours a week in center care. Despite the pressures on these mothers, their husbands were less involved than they in child care.

When we visited these homes and observed these youngsters in our laboratory playroom as well as in their day-care setting, we were struck by their neediness. These were young children who cooperated readily with us and their mothers during our home visit and playroom observations. They blossomed during the testing portions of the sessions when they received the undivided attention of a friendly, supportive adult; they also reveled in the opportunity to come alone with their mothers to our playroom and even willingly cleaned up the toys at the end of the play period, something they would never willingly do at home. However, observations in their child care settings revealed socially isolated children who were relatively ignored by peers and caregivers. In one instance, the staff at the center was clearly mishandling the child's problems, possibly exacerbating his difficulties and also indicating an extremely poor understanding of young children's emotional needs and level of cognitive development. This 3-year-old was isolated often and threatened with expulsion. Center staff were abrupt and irritated with him, even when he was behaving appropriately (and even with our observer in the center). The director suggested to this child's parents that he be banished to his room as soon as he arrived at home. This was just what this very needy and anxious youngster, who was obviously starved for quality attention from his parents, did not require. These cases certainly do not indict all child care settings, but they highlight the complex interactions among parenting skills and resources, family stresses, and the nature of the child care setting. In particular, they underline the importance of well-trained, psychologically minded child care staff who are sensitive to the meaning of young children's behavior and able to recognize that behavior problems are often a signal of unhappiness, anxiety, and distress.

Summary

A number of variables associated with the development of problems in preschoolers have been reviewed in this chapter and the preceding ones. These include child characteristics, parenting behaviors, family composition and interaction patterns, and factors in the family's wider social environment. The complex direct and indirect relationships among relevant factors was depicted in Chapter One, Figure 1.1. In general, the transactions over time between child characteristics (including possible biological vulnerability, personality and temperamental dispositions, and developmental needs and competencies) and parenting factors (primarily the quality of parental affective involvement with the child and child-rearing approaches) have the greatest impact on child outcomes. However, family climate, as indexed by the quality of the marital relationship , family composition, and parental personality and psychological well-being, also has a profound affect on the child's psychosocial adaptation. Family climate has both a direct impact on children as well as an indirect one, mediated through the effects of the family environment on parental availability, sensitivity, and child-rearing strategies. Finally, more general aspects of the psychosocial environment including the quality and availability of social support for parents, the nature and availability of institutional supports, and the availability of material resources influence the child both directly and indirectly. Such factors, however, have their greatest impact on the child in terms of their effects on parental well-being, the level of stresses within the family, and the ability of parents to carry out their parenting functions. In this context, the issue of day-care was highlighted because it has particular relevance for parents and young children.

Although all these factors appear important when problems are conceptualized in general or abstract terms, particular factors appear more relevant than others when individual cases are considered. Although various factors converge to produce problems, the mix of relevant factors probably varies from child to child. Thus, in the cases discussed earlier, different aspects of child family transactions seemed salient. For example, in considering Jamie's difficulties, biological vulnerabilities or personality dispositions (i.e., within-child factors) appeared most relevant because other obvious family contributors to childhood problems were not in evidence. Moreover, it was my clinical impression that Jamie's problems were mitigated by a stable and supportive family environment in which stresses were minimal and his unique needs were respected and responded to by caring and concerned parents. Teddy's family environment was likewise positive, characterized by parental unity and mutual support. The early conflicted and negative transactions between Teddy and his parents, especially in view of their high standards and expectations for maturity and compliance, had the potential to escalate into more serious difficulties. However, it appears that parental flexibility in tandem with developmental changes in Teddy's social understanding and behavioral control ultimately led to the resolution of early difficulties.

Annie's continued problems may be interpreted to illustrate the importance of early mother infant reciprocity and positive affective engagement as well as the escalation of mother–child conflict over time. These problems occurred in the context of unrealistic maternal expectations and inflexible child-rearing strategies that failed to accommodate to the child's emotional or developmental needs. These difficulties were compounded by limited paternal support and the possibility that there were additional problems within the family system. Finally, Robbie's case illustrates the complex interactions among possible biological vulnerability, parental personality problems, and chronic ongoing family disruption and turmoil. Furthermore, his problems worsened despite an apparently warm and positive mother child relationship.

In summary, then, multiple factors within the family and the wider social environment interact with child characteristics, and together they converge to lead to problems in children. However, problems in individual children probably develop from different combinations of factors with different implications for treatment and for long-term outcome. These issues will be addressed in later chapters.

Sibling Relationships

Sibling relations figure prominently in any consideration of the development of preschoolers because many preschool-age children have to cope with the birth of a sibling and many others must adjust to the role of being the younger brother or sister. Developmental psychologists have only recently begun to examine the development of complex and affectively laden sibling relationships. The interested reader is referred to several recent review articles and books (Dunn, 1983, 1985; Dunn & Kendrick, 1982) and much of what follows is based on these sources. Although it is widely recognized that peer relationships play a central role in children's social development (see Chapter Six), surprisingly little attention has been focused on the role that siblings play in children's socialization. Whereas relationships with peers are, by definition, relationships between relative equals, sibling interactions are characterized by complementary roles and role asymmetries, including differences in dominance and submission, that derive from the necessary age differences between nontwin sibling pairs (Hartup, 1983; Stoneman, Brody, & MacKinnon, 1984). Older siblings serve as companions, attachment figures, role models, and teachers; younger siblings are help-seekers, pupils, imitators, and playmates. The emotional bond between siblings is almost always intense, with conflict between siblings the more salient aspect in the minds of many parents, despite the many positive features of most sibling relationships. Developmentalists are beginning to delineate the important role played by siblings and have suggested that sibling relationships provide children with different social experiences and serve different functions in their socialization than do relationships with peers (Hartup, 1983; Stoneman et al., 1984).

In our own study of parent-referred problem preschoolers, parental concerns about sibling conflicts were among the main factors leading parents to seek help. Indeed, there was a significantly higher proportion of first-born children with younger siblings in the problem group than in the comparison group, and the presence of a sibling was associated with higher ratings of aggression at age 3. Thus, in our sample of hard-to-manage preschoolers, the presence of a sibling appeared to exacerbate already extant parent–child conflict or to sensitize parents to concerns about their preschooler's aggressive and demanding behavior. Parents invariably described aggressive and provocative behavior toward the sibling that ranged from relatively typical and age-appropriate squabbles over toys to more premeditated and serious attempts to harm the younger child. In some instances, parents seemed to be overly fearful of their child hurting the infant, whereas in others the older child's resentment of the sibling was angry and overt. Hard-to-manage children who were the younger of two or more siblings were also involved in sibling conflicts, although parents seemed less concerned about these confrontations, feeling that the older child could take care of himself/herself.

In this chapter, the typical reactions of toddlers and preschoolers to the birth of a sibling are described and the nature of the relationship that develops between siblings over the first few years of life is discussed. Sibling relationships are seen as having an important influence on social cognitive development and general socialization. The role of parents will be addressed as will the impact of the birth of a second child on the family system. Finally, the discussion will focus on sibling relationships in families in which one child has been identified as a problem.

Reactions to the Birth of a Sibling

Rutter (1981) has suggested that the birth of a sibling is among the major stressors that young children must learn to deal with routinely. Indeed, many of the behavioral changes that parents describe following the birth of a sibling appear to reflect the typical ways young children respond to stress. The popular focus on sibling rivalry is based on the view that "dethronement" (Stewart, Mobley, Van Tuyl, & Salvador, 1987) and jealousy are the most salient aspects of the sibling relationship and that the major impact of the birth of a sibling is its effect on the mother–child relationship. Thus, it is assumed that young children feel displaced and resentful and that the need to share parental attention and affection with the sibling is the primary issue to be addressed. This is undoubtedly important, as illustrated by the comments of one very bright and verbal 3-year-old. Shortly after his sister's birth he poignantly expressed his fear that his sister was going to take all his mother's love and that there would not be enough left for him. However, Dunn and Kendrick (1982) and others (e.g., Abramovitch, Corter, & Pepler, 1980; Stewart et al., 1987) have noted the complexities inherent in sibling relationships, which can best be characterized as ambivalent. Although rivalry and jealousy are often apparent, many children also show increased maturity, concern for others, and independence after the birth of a sibling.

Several recent studies have documented the nature and extent of initial reactions to the birth of a sibling and their development over time (Dunn & Kendrick, 1982; Stewart et al., 1987). These authors have argued that both the initial reaction to the birth of a sibling and the sibling relationship that develops over the first few years of life are especially complex, with both positive and negative aspects. They maintain that emphasis only on the rivalry for parental love and competition for adult attention leaves out many important features with an impact on children's social-emotional development and on the family system. Thus, they maintain that in addition to resentment, strong bonds of friendship, companionship, and affection develop between young siblings and that siblings learn a lot from each other about feelings, handling competition constructively, and acceptable patterns of social behavior.

There is general agreement from several studies that have examined the initial response of toddlers and preschoolers to the birth of a sibling that children show a mix of reactions, positive, negative, and anxiety-laden (Dunn & Kendrick, 1982; Field & Reite, 1984; Stewart et al., 1987). These include regressive behavior, such as increased clinging and separation distress, toileting accidents, the desire to drink from a bottle, feeding problems, and crying. Children are also likely to become more angry, aggressive, and noncompliant, although contrary to popular belief, aggression and confrontation are usually directed at parents, not at the infant sibling. Dunn and Kendrick noted a dramatic increase in mother–child conflict and confrontation in the immediate postpartum period, especially during the times when the mother was involved in feeding and otherwise caring for the new baby. In general, the incidents they describe suggest intense anger toward the mother and a desperate attempt to gain attention from her. In addition, expressions of anxiety and social withdrawal are often apparent. Thus, a mixture of regression, anxiety, and defiance characterizes the reactions of young children to the birth of a sibling.

In addition to these negative behaviors, however, observers have noted increased maturity and independence, often in the same children who are showing regression or confrontation in other domains of functioning. Children may react with increased anger and noncompliance, but at the same time show increased independence in self-help skills or a surge in language development. This underlines the complexity of children's reactions as well as the exacerbation of typical, developmentally related conflicts within the child, such as confusion over mastery and autonomy. Young children confronted with the birth of a sibling are particularly ambivalent about whether they want to maintain their dependence or become more independent. Almost all the children observed by Dunn and Kendrick (1982), who were between 18 months and 4 years old at the birth of the sibling, reacted with some combination of behaviors reflecting this ambivalence, with younger children having more frequent toileting accidents and older children becoming more clinging. Thus, there is strong evidence that toddlers and preschoolers react intensely to the birth of a sibling and that overtly negative reactions are directed primarily at parents rather than at the new infant.

Dunn and Kendrick (1982) also note that toddlers and preschoolers are extremely interested in and curious about the new infant; they ask questions, want to help with caretaking, express affection, and often imitate the infant's behavior. Children as young as 18 months are interested in holding the baby or helping their mother, although these same children may express their hostility openly, for example, by suggesting that mother return the infant to the hospital. Thus, ambivalence is more characteristic of the feelings children have for the newborn than outright and unmitigated dislike. This initial ambivalence appears to reflect a complex process of adjustment to the reality of sharing parents and grandparents with another person who is helpless and fascinating as well as extremely demanding of adult time, attention, and affection.

The Development of Sibling Relationships

Once older children have gotten over the initial stress of the arrival of the younger sibling, they begin to adapt to the complexities that are a natural consequence of integrating a new member into the family circle. Two longitudinal studies of adaptation to the birth of a sibling have been conducted recently (Dunn & Kendrick, 1982; Stewart et al., 1987). In both studies stable, two-parent families were studied prospectively from the third trimester of the mother's pregnancy with her second child through at least the first year postpartum. In both studies first-born children ranged in age from just under 2 years to 4 years at the time of the sibling birth. A combination of observational and interview data were collected during home visits. Dunn and Kendrick obtained particularly detailed narrative accounts of ongoing natural interactions in the home, and these provide an especially rich source of information on developmental change in parent–child and sibling relations. Their data indicate that although relationships between siblings remain complex and ambivalent, the intense reactions that were apparent initially had waned considerably by the end of the first month or so and represented transient stress reactions rather than a long-term pattern of adaptation. The intensity of the initial reaction was not predictive of more serious problems in adjustment to the sibling. Rather, children who responded more explosively were more likely to learn to get along with their sibling than were children who became seriously withdrawn. In addition, children who expressed interest in and affection toward their infant siblings early on were more likely to have positive relations with them in toddlerhood. Stewart et al. also report that children initially showed high rates of regression and confrontative behavior but that these reactions had waned considerably by 4 months postpartum. In addition, most first-born children expressed interest in the newborn and assisted their mothers with caretaking in some way, by holding the baby, fetching diapers or other objects, and amusing the baby. These studies document the fact that children's reactions to a sibling's birth are multifaceted.

Toddlers and preschoolers appear to use complex strategies to help them adjust to the presence of a younger sibling. Both Dunn and Kendrick and Stewart and colleagues emphasize the importance of imitation or "regression" as an adaptive strategy. They argue that asking for a bottle, reverting to baby talk, or having toileting accidents, for example, may be the child's way of maintaining or regaining parental attention. Imitation of the baby's behavior may also allow the child to work through conflicts using fantasy and role playing. Field and Reite (1984) also noted that young children increased their use of fantasy after the birth of a sibling, and they suggest that this helped the children to cope with both the temporary separation from mother and the marked changes going on in the family. Most of the children in this study, when observed during free play, engaged in fantasy play with aggressive themes. Fantasy aggression was directed both toward the mother and the new baby, with aggression toward the baby more common. These findings may suggest that children use fantasy to express their anger and ambivalence toward the infant, but they are more likely to act out their anger and confusion about parental love and attention more directly toward their parents by becoming confrontational and showing more immature behavior. The longitudinal data also suggest that parents need not be concerned that children are reverting to earlier, more primitive forms of behavior. Rather, children may be using earlier, more familiar forms of behavior as a bridge to higher level functioning (Dunn & Kendrick, 1982). In most instances, regressive behaviors were relatively short-lived initial reactions to the sibling's birth. As younger siblings developed, the sibling relationship changed as well.

The nature of sibling relationships obviously becomes even more complex as the younger child develops mobility and begins to explore the world of objects actively. At this point the younger child is a much more serious threat to the older child, and it is at this time that more overt physical conflict is likely to develop. As the younger child becomes more independent and more of a social being, the competition for adult attention intensifies. Squabbles over toys and territory become more intense as both members of the dyad participate in play (Dunn & Kendrick, 1982). Stewart et al. (1987) reported that while confrontations with parents were common during the first few months after the siblings' birth, by the end of the first year, preschool-age children were engaging in more frequent conflict with younger siblings. As younger siblings reach toddlerhood, the older children are likely to complain about intrusions into their toys and games; this seems to be a particular source of stress among same-sex dyads. In this context, the older siblings are likely to rely on their superior cognitive and linguistic skills and physical coordination in settling squabbles, thus asserting their dominance in the relationship. In response to the power tactics of their older siblings, young toddlers seek parental assistance, and usually get it. By the end of the second year, however, the younger sibling is capable of retaliating with physical aggression, which often serves to escalate the encounter. Younger siblings are also able to initiate conflict by age 2 or somewhat earlier by teasing or otherwise provoking the older preschooler. These interactions, although upsetting to parents, teach children about dominance and power, indicate some appreciation of the other child's vulnerabilities, and ultimately lead to the development of skills in the negotiation and resolution of disputes (Dunn & Kendrick, 1982).

At the same time that conflict and confrontation may be more evident in the sibling relationship, the younger sibling is also becoming more of a companion and playmate for the older child. Thus, the positive bond between them may likewise become stronger. Despite frequent conflicts over possessions, young siblings may spend much of their time in cooperative play. Dunn and Kendrick comment on the important role sibling interactions play in facilitating socialization of both younger and older children. Children as young as 3 years are capable of adjusting their speech to make it simple enough for their younger siblings to understand. They also show empathy and concern for their sibling's distress, indicating early signs of social perspective taking and prosocial behavior. Younger siblings, likewise, may comfort an older one or express concern about their distress. In general, the mutual regulation of social behavior occurs often in the interchanges between very young sibling pairs. Pretend play, turn taking, and sharing are all facilitated by the social interaction occurring within the sibling dyad. Children also learn to negotiate to solve disputes in interaction with siblings. Finally, older children serve as models for their younger siblings who in turn serve as pupils for their older sibling's teaching. Dunn and Kendrick found that social perspective taking and empathy on the part of the older child were influenced in part by maternal behavior. The older child's social development and ability to engage in positive interactions with the younger sibling were enhanced if the mother frequently discussed the new baby as a person with reference to feelings, wishes, and moods and if she included the older child in caretaking and other activities.

The importance of the sibling relationship, as well as its relationship to both maternal behavior and social-cognitive development, is highlighted in a recent study of sibling attachment and caregiving. Stewart and Marvin (1984) reported that when 3- and 4-year-olds were left alone with their younger siblings in a waiting room, over one half responded to their younger sibling's distress by providing reassurance and comfort, for example, by hugging the infant and explaining that their mother would eventually return. In addition, the younger siblings displayed attachment behaviors toward their older siblings, seeking proximity and contact with them and then using them as a secure base for play.

However, not all preschoolers sought to comfort their distressed younger siblings and not all younger siblings reached out toward their older brothers or sisters. Older siblings who showed more advanced social cognitive development, as reflected in their ability to take the perspective of another, were more likely to comfort and reassure younger siblings; those younger siblings who had experienced nurturance and caregiving from more cognitively mature siblings were more likely to seek comfort from them when distressed, suggesting that these mutually regulated attachment and caregiving behaviors were part of their ongoing relationship. Finally, it is interesting to note that mothers were more likely to ask the more cognitively mature older siblings to take care of the younger sibling in their absence than was the case with non-perspective-taking older siblings. This may suggest that maternal socialization played a role in the development of children's sensitivity to the needs of their younger siblings or that mothers were more likely to make such requests of more socially mature children. In either case, this study depicts an important aspect of the positive and supportive relationship between young siblings, as well as the interrelationships among child, sibling, and maternal behaviors and expectations.

Dunn and Kendrick (1982) observed wide individual differences in the character of ongoing sibling relationships. Some dyads were characterized primarily by positive interactions and cooperative play, despite the occasional squabble; others showed a mixture of positive and negative interactions; still others engaged in severe and continuous conflict with few instances of cooperative play. Several variables have been examined to explain some of these variations in the quality of sibling relationships, including the gender composition of the sibling pair, the age differences between them, and their temperamental characteristics.

Gender Composition

The gender composition of sibling pairs has been examined as one possible determinant of the character of sibling relationships in several studies. When this is evaluated in terms of the gender of the older sibling, the data on this issue are contradictory. Dunn (1983) reviewed evidence suggesting that girls are more nurturant toward their younger siblings than boys are and that younger siblings seek more help and comfort from their older sisters. Some studies indicate that these sex differences in nurturance and caregiving depend upon the specific behaviors observed and upon the age of the children at the time of the observation. Similarly, some studies suggest that girls are more involved as teachers of younger siblings, whereas boys are more likely to become aggressive. Yet, both Dunn and Kendrick (1982) and Pepler, Corter, and Abramovitch (1982), who studied preschool- and school-age sibling pairs, reported relatively few sex differences in prosocial behavior, imitation, or aggression when children were studied over time.

In addition to considering the impact of the gender of the older sibling, studies have compared the interactions of same-sex and opposite-sex sibling pairs. Again, the findings are not consistent. There are some data suggesting more conflict among same-sex dyads (Stewart et al., 1987), as well as studies suggesting that more imitation and prosocial behavior occur in same-sex dyads (Dunn, 1983; Pepler et al., 1982). Dunn and Kendrick (1981) examined changes in the social behavior of same-sex and opposite-sex dyads that occurred when infants were between 8 and 14 months old. In same-sex pairs, both children increased the amount of positive interaction, including vocalization, smiling, and joint play; younger siblings also became more negative, a reflection of their increased autonomy and more advanced social skills, which permitted them to stand up for themselves as they entered toddlerhood. In opposite-sex pairs, both children became more negative over time, as reflected in increased fighting, toy taking, and protests; neither member of the dyad became more positive, suggesting that older opposite-sex siblings were not making allowances for their younger siblings' behavior. These differential results also indicate that developmental changes do not reflect merely an increase in interaction with development. Dunn and Kendrick (1981) suggest that same-sex pairs may begin to become more aware of gender similarity and identify with one another, whereas opposite-sex dyads may become more aware of the differences between them. Furthermore, this may be fueled somewhat by differences in maternal behavior. The researchers noted that mothers paid more attention to younger children who were opposite in sex from their first-borns. Because only a handful of studies have addressed questions about the impact of gender composition on the interactions among siblings and the few extant studies differ widely in terms of study methodology and age of subjects, it is not yet possible to draw any firm conclusions about how the gender composition of sibling dyads influences the nature of interaction at one point in time or over the course of early development. The age spacing of siblings also was thought to be important, although studies find little support for this view (Dunn, 1983).

Temperament

The impact of child temperament on the development of sibling relationships has begun to receive some attention recently. The issue of child temperament is especially relevant to a consideration of the sibling relationships of hard-to-manage preschoolers. According to Dunn and Kendrick's findings, children who were reported by their mothers to be difficult to manage, as indexed by negative mood and intense emotional reactions to upset, were more likely to withdraw at the time of the sibling's birth, becoming tearful, sullen, and dependent upon transitional objects for comfort. Difficult boys were especially likely to show this initial reaction, and it was likely to persist. By 8 months after the sibling birth, many of these children were worried, fearful, demanding, and irritable and had sleeping and feeding problems. Thus, these findings suggest that children who are difficult to handle have a harder time adapting to the birth of a second child and establishing a positive relationship with the younger sibling.

Similar findings are reported by Brody, Stoneman, and Burke (1987a) in a study of school-age children and their same-sex, preschool-aged siblings observed in a semistructured play interaction at home. Maternal ratings of high activity and intense emotionality were associated with high levels of conflict and quarreling between sisters, regardless of whether the younger or the older sister was seen as more active and/or intense. High levels of activity among younger brothers was associated with high levels of conflict but also with high levels of prosocial behavior, suggesting that active younger brothers engaged in more interaction, both positive and negative, with their older brothers. Older brothers' activity level did not predict the quality of sibling interaction. However, when older brothers were more emotionally intense, their younger brothers engaged in more aggressive and argumentative behavior. These two studies highlight the importance of considering children's personality characteristics as potential contributers to individual differences in sibling relationships. These studies do raise questions about the direction of effects. The nature of sibling relationships also undoubtedly influences the development of personality. These are clearly fruitful areas requiring further study.

Parenting and Sibling Relationships

It seems obvious that the way parents behave toward both younger and older siblings, as well as their expectations about children's behavior toward one another, will have a major impact on the interaction between siblings. Parents' initial reactions to the second child's birth and their ability to include the older child in the process of family adaptation appear to set the stage for later sibling relationships. In addition to establishing a relationship with a younger sibling, the older child must respond to decreased parental attention and modified parental expectations. Dunn and Kendrick document the marked change in mother–child interaction after the birth of a sibling. Mothers spend less time in playful interaction and in conversation with the older child and considerably more time in confrontation. Moreover, when interactions between mother and first-born do occur, the child is more likely than before to initiate the exchange, be it playful, conversational, or confrontative. This may account for the angry responses of first-borns who had experienced a warm and positive relationship prior to the birth of the sibling. In addition, parents often expect more mature behavior from the older sibling, just when the child is particularly vulnerable and ambivalent. This pressure for greater maturity may be paired with increased time spent with substitute caregivers or with fathers, further confusing and stressing the child. Increased father involvement in child care may ultimately strengthen the father–child relationship, or the father may become involved in daily struggles for compliance that lead to increased conflict.

Initial reactions to the birth of a sibling and the quality of later sibling relationships are also related to other aspects of family functioning and the earlier parent–child relationship. In Dunn and Kendrick's (1982) study, maternal fatigue and depression were associated with more withdrawal, sadness, and anxiety on the part of the first-born, presumably in response to depressed maternal mood and consequent decreases in caretaking and sensitivity to the other child's emotional needs. When mothers and their first-borns had previously had a positive relationship characterized by much joint play and cooperation, the negative reaction to the birth of the sibling tended to be particularly intense and the first-born child, especially a first-born girl, was likely to be more hostile and aggressive toward the sibling 14 months later. This probably reflects the older child's resentment and jealousy of the sibling and the yearning for undivided maternal attention. Furthermore, Dunn and Kendrick (1981) reported that mothers spent more time playing with second-born children who were opposite in gender from their first borns. As already noted, this may account, in part, for the increased conflict that developed between opposite-sex sibling pairs between 8 and 14 months.

However, maternal behavior toward both the first-born and the younger sibling can also have a positive impact on the quality of the sibling relationship. Older siblings in the Dunn and Kendrick study appeared to develop more empathy toward and engage in more positive interaction with their younger siblings if mothers involved them in caretaking from very early on, making it a shared experience, and also discussed and modeled respect for the baby as a person with distinct needs and feelings. This approach seems to encourage prosocial behavior and greater understanding of the infant, facilitating the development of empathy, at the same time that it minimizes feelings of being shut out by the close mother–infant bond. In addition, high levels of paternal involvement with the child often served to ameliorate the negative reaction to the sibling birth. This probably is best interpreted as both a direct effect of increased father–child contact on the first-born child as well as an indirect effect of the quality of the marital relationship on the older sibling and on the mother's ability to provide nurturance to both children.

It is also logical to suppose that the nature of parental child-rearing strategies will influence the quality of the sibling relationship. Families that are child-centered and warm are more likely to foster both positive parent–child and sibling relationships. Brody et al. (1987a) suggest that consistent use of nonpunitive child-rearing strategies and responsiveness to children's needs are associated with less aggressive and conflicted sibling interaction and a more positive relationship. This is consistent with the general view of child rearing and socialization espoused in Chapter Four. Other aspects of parenting have also been hypothesized to relate to the nature of sibling relations. For example, differential maternal behavior that unfairly favors one child over another has been hypothesized to lead to problems between siblings, particularly to more aggressive and conflicted interactions (Brody et al., 1987a; Dunn, 1983). Brody et al. specifically examined this issue in their sample of same-sex sibling pairs. Mothers and siblings were observed in a semistructured play interaction at home that included a construction activity and a board game. Mothers directed significantly more prosocial behavior, as well as negative and controlling behavior, toward the younger siblings, but differential maternal behavior was unrelated to the quality of the sibling interactions observed in a similar situation on a different occasion. Brody et al. suggest that the older siblings understood that their younger siblings required more help and direction completing the play activities. In addition, it is worth noting that mothers addressed both more positive and more negative comments to the younger children; consequently, the differential behavior was not only in the direction of more positive or affectionate interactions. Whereas several other studies have suggested that mothers behave differently with first-borns versus second-borns, other studies do not document clear differential treatment (see Dunn, 1983). Moreover, findings depend upon context and the age of the children. For instance, there is evidence that mothers attend more to younger children when both children are present but that first-borns receive more individual attention. However, few studies have actually examined the relationship between differential treatment and sibling interaction, making this an important issue for further research.

The studies that have examined differential maternal behavior, by necessity, confound maternal behavior with age differences between siblings. Thus, maternal behavior toward siblings might be similar at various developmental points, although differences are apparent when mothers are observed interacting with two children who are at different developmental stages. Dunn, Plomin, and Nettles (1985) examined this question as part of a longitudinal study of within-family environmental influences. Mothers and each of two siblings were observed at home during feeding and play when each infant was 12 months old. Measures of maternal positive affection, verbal interaction, and negative control showed surprisingly high consistency from the first baby to the second, and consistency held for both same-sex and opposite-sex sibling pairs. These data suggest a relatively enduring maternal behavioral style that is fairly independent of the specific eliciting characteristics of the infant. Additional work will need to be conducted to replicate and extend these interesting findings.

Other contextual factors also appear to influence the quality of sibling interactions. Both Brody et al. (1987a) and Corter, Abramovitch, and Pepler (1983) assessed the influence of maternal presence versus absence on the nature of sibling interactions. In the Brody et al. study, siblings and their mothers were observed at home during a semistructured play session with the experimenter providing the materials. Corter et al. observed naturally occurring interaction in the home.

Despite these differences in procedure, both studies revealed a marked decrease in sibling interaction when mothers were present, with a particularly dramatic drop in cooperative and prosocial behavior. Although the absolute amount of aggressive behavior also dropped in mothers' presence, the relative proportion of aggressive acts increased in the Corter et al. study. This may reflect attention-seeking behavior or, because this was an unstructured home observation, the fact that mothers may be more likely to make their presence known when they think a conflict is about to begin or to escalate. Parents frequently voice concerns about the ability of their children to cooperate. The findings from these two studies are interesting in that they indicate that children do well on their own and that prosocial interactions predominate. This may suggest that, at least with many school-age children and their preschool-age siblings, parents need not monitor their interactions too closely or feel the need to intervene whenever a conflict ensues. As is the case with peer relations, children need to learn to solve problems and resolve disputes on their own without too much adult intrusion.

Dunn and Munn (1985, 1986) specifically examined the nature of sibling conflicts and how children resolved them. They also assessed how mothers dealt with quarrels between the preschool- and toddler-age children in their sibling sample and what the consequences of maternal intervention were. It is worth noting that sibling pairs engaged in some form of conflict about eight times per hour. Preschool-age older siblings aggressed physically approximately 25% of the time, but they also used relatively mature means of conflict resolution, including distracting the younger child, justifying their actions with a reason or rule, and making conciliatory gestures or statements. By 24 months of age, a number of younger siblings were likewise using these more mature strategies on occasion, highlighting the important role that peer interaction can play in socialization. Furthermore, cross-age correlations suggest that younger siblings may learn specific strategies, such as justifying their actions and referring to rules, from their older brothers and sisters.

Mothers intervened in just over 50% of the disputes observed. Moreover, children sought maternal intervention when they were aggressed against, but not when they were the aggressors. Mothers responded differently to their younger and older children in the context of sibling quarrels. Although they were more likely to attempt to distract the younger child, they were more likely to prohibit the older one and then to teach explicit principles about social conventions and other peoples' feelings, not unlike the behavior described by Zahn-Waxler et al. (1979) in response to children's transgressions in other contexts. Thus, mothers referred to the younger child's feelings, explained the reasons for the younger child's actions, and suggested conciliatory behaviors to deescalate the conflict. When younger siblings were 24 months old, mothers stated social rules equally often to both children in response to disputes between them. Maternal interventions were associated with younger children's use of both more mature strategies and with physical aggression. For example, children whose mothers suggested conciliatory behaviors were both more likely to resolve some disputes peacefully but also to hit during others. Overall, maternal involvement in sibling quarrels was related both to more frequent conflict and physical aggression between siblings and to the use of more mature strategies of conflict resolution. Maternal involvement may provide young children with a larger repertoire of behaviors suitable for resolving disputes, or these findings may indicate that when children engage in more frequent conflict, mothers are more likely to intervene with an array of responses. Clearly, these maternal interventions involved teaching about appropriate rules and social behaviors, and children showed increased awareness of social rules and the impact of their behavior on their siblings as a result of this maternal teaching. It is noteworthy that although Dunn and Munn coded maternal strategies, such as punishment and physical intervention, they occurred too infrequently to be analyzed.

There is no doubt that the birth of a sibling leads to many changes within the family system that are likely to have an impact on the marital relationship and the relationship of each parent to the older child. Some of the many changes in the mother's relationship with the older child have been discussed. In addition, it has been suggested that paternal involvement in parenting can help ameliorate some of the stress on the mother, while his involvement with the older child may further cement their relationship and help the child to cope with the loss of undivided maternal attention. The nature of the marital relationship may also change with the additional responsibilities of a second child. Both parents may feel more stressed and have less time to devote to their own relationship, leading to increased strains in the marriage. This too will feed back to affect the older sibling's feelings of security and willingness to cooperate with parental wishes. In addition, marital distress and overt marital conflict witnessed by the children has been found to be associated with more sibling conflict (Brody, Stoneman, & Burke, 1987b). This may reflect the direct effects of modeling, the anxiety and upset caused by a tense family environment, and/or the indirect effects of marital distress on parenting, including the provision of inadequate guidelines for the resolution of conflict. However, if paternal involvement in family activities increases, this usually would be expected to have a positive effect on the family system.

Sibling Relationships in Families with Hard-to-Manage Children

Few studies have examined the sibling interactions of hard-to-manage preschoolers, although it is safe to assume that they are problematic. For example, Richman et al. (1982) found that sibling conflict at ages 3 and 4 was predictive of continuing problems at age 8. This may reflect the aggressive behavior of the target child and ongoing family discord and disruption. However, it is also possible that continuing conflict between siblings contributes to maternal concerns about aggressive and coercive behaviors that are reasonably typical. Mash and Johnston (1983b) examined the interactions of clinically diagnosed hyperactive boys and their brothers in comparison with nonclinical pairs of brothers of comparable age. Dyads were observed interacting during free play and structured tasks. Few significant differences were found within sibling pairs. However, hyperactive boys and their brothers engaged in more reciprocal conflict than comparison dyads. High rates of negative behavior in the hyperactive brother pairs were associated with maternal reports of less skill and knowledge of parenting, suggesting that sibling conflict might have contributed to mothers' negative self-evaluations or these mothers may have been less adept at helping their children resolve disputes. These observations are consistent with maternal reports of high rates of sibling conflict among children with externalizing problems. The role of the hyperactive child in initiating and maintaining the conflict is not clear from this study and probably varies with the relative age of the diagnosed child and his brother. For example, it is reasonable to suppose that older hyperactive boys are more aggressive and likely to bully their younger brothers, while younger hyperactive boys are more likely to irritate, provoke, and tease their older siblings. Patterson (1980) has noted that in families with aggressive children, both target children and their siblings initiate conflict and contribute to its escalation into high intensity encounters. Problem children, however, tend to function at higher levels of anger and aggression than their siblings.

The families in our study, with a hard-to-manage preschooler already creating conflicts in the marriage or taxing parental resources, were severely stressed by the birth of a second child. In addition, because many of the second children were born shortly after the first-borns' second birthdays, the older children were often about to start preschool just as the younger siblings were entering toddlerhood and becoming more active and demanding rivals for parental attention. Some children reacted to this dual threat to their relationship with their mothers by showing intense separation distress in nursery school and/or increased anger and defiance at home. In addition, many mothers in our study described conflict and ambivalence between their children.

In a typical case, Jamie L's younger brother was born when he was 30 months old. His mother described initial tantrum behavior and moodiness along with a tendency to ignore his baby brother. By the time his sibling was 10 months old, Jamie showed extreme shifts in behavior, showering his brother with love and attention 1 minute and becoming hostile and aggressive the next. When Jamie was followed up 1 year later, his mother commented on the frequent conflict between Jamie and his brother Jeffrey, who was nearing his second birthday. Although Jamie often became upset and angry when Jeffrey entered his room or wanted to play with his toys, Jeffrey also instigated fights by teasing and provoking Jamie and then crying when Jamie responded. Mrs. L noted that Jeffrey set Jamie up to get into trouble and vice versa. Nevertheless, the two were able to play together quietly from time to time and their relationship was not a totally negative one.

Several mothers of especially aggressive and noncompliant boys with younger sisters worried about leaving their children together out of sight. They felt the need to supervise their sons constantly for fear that they would intentionally harm their baby sisters. Indeed, one mother of a 42-month-old boy, among the most aggressive, angry, and noncompliant in our sample, expressed concern about his extreme jealousy and animosity toward his 18-month-old sister. As with Jamie, this youngster's problems were apparent from very early infancy, but they tended to escalate after his sibling's birth. Although he expressed some interest in his baby sister in early infancy, his handling of her tended to be rough, especially as she got older, and he became increasingly more aggressive, often expressing anger and annoyance at her social initiations. At the 6-year follow-up interview, this child's mother commented on her daughter's patience and devotion to her older brother, who either ignored her or harassed her, and was rarely pleasant or affectionate toward her.

Similarly, the mother of one 29-month-old boy called the project shortly after the birth of her daughter. Although her son, too, had been an extremely difficult child since early infancy, his intensely angry reaction to the birth of his baby sister precipitated her call. She described her relationship with her son as one of "constantly butting heads" and was at a loss about how to cope with the increase in noncompliance, tantrums, and separation distress that accompanied the sibling birth. Although tantrums had been frequent, occurring as often as three or four times weekly, they had risen to as many as five a day and were occurring in response to almost any request. He had also become exceedingly clingy, refused to visit peers, wanted to drink from a bottle, and requested a pacifier. Consistent with the descriptions presented by Dunn and Kendrick (1982), however, his relationship with his sister was characterized by ambivalence rather than by outright rejection. He did show some curiosity about her, was interested in holding her, and did express affection toward her, caressing and kissing her. However, the day before his mother called the project, he had spit on his sister and his mother was afraid that his caresses sometimes bordered on aggression, another rather explicit indication of his ambivalence.

These observations suggest that the initial reactions of hard-to-manage children are more extreme than usual, although similar in type to those described by Dunn and Kendrick. Furthermore, it appears that the problems that are exacerbated by the birth of a sibling are not as transient in children with preexisting problems. Rather, they appear to exaggerate a pattern of maladaptation that was apparent before the sibling birth and to fuel the mother–child conflict still further. Several of the mothers in the project expressed worry about rejecting their problem children in their efforts to curtail aggressive behavior and to protect the more vulnerable younger children. These mothers were intensely upset by the negative behavior their problem youngsters showed toward their siblings, and although they were sensitive to the needs of both children, they were uncertain about how best to handle this complex situation.

However, not all children identified as problems by their parents had troubled relationships with their siblings, although their initial reactions may have involved ambivalence. Annie J was nearly 5 years old when her sister was born, and she was extremely interested in helping her mother to care for the baby. She reacted initially with some bed-wetting. When the baby was 6 months old, Annie started kindergarten. Although Annie had loved going to nursery school, the transition to kindergarten was stressful for her and she had several episodes of school refusal. This may have partly reflected the excessive anxiety she felt at leaving her mother and sister home alone for prolonged periods of time at the stage when her sister was becoming more socially responsive and engaging. Given the intensely conflict-ridden relationship between Annie and her mother, the prospects of leaving home for several hours each day may have intensified her anxiety about additional displacement and rejection by her mother. However, as her baby sister got older, Annie was involved increasingly in caretaking and also in playing with her sister and keeping her amused. It appeared overall that her relationship with her sister was very positive and close, and this may have helped to fill the emotional void left by her relatively poor relationship with her mother. Dunn and Kendrick (1982) also note that especially warm sibling relationships may sometimes compensate for confrontational mother–child relationships.

Problem children with older siblings were less likely to become engaged in constant battles, or at least in battles that were as serious a concern to parents. Both Teddy M and Robbie S had older siblings who, by the time we saw them, were able to cope with their little brothers' annoying and intrusive behavior. Arguments and tattling were more frequent than overt physical confrontations, and as the older siblings entered elementary school, they more easily escaped to their rooms or the homes of peers, thus avoiding conflicts some of the time. Robbie's older sister was basically positive and supportive of her difficult younger brother, although she also resented the attention that he demanded from their mother and the fact that family outings were sometimes spoiled or curtailed because of his uncooperative or provocative behavior. Teddy often tagged along after his older brother, but they played well together and their parents considered them good friends.

However, older siblings did not always cope this well. In another family in which the younger brother was a behavior problem and the baby sister had a chronic physical illness, the 7-year-old sister became depressed and withdrawn. She was defiant at home and her school performance deteriorated. It seemed clear that she was feeling neglected by her parents who were preoccupied with the problems presented by their younger children and did not have the time or resources left to meet her needs adequately. Other older sisters were confused by their younger brothers' annoying behavior and the attention it elicited from those around them. One 5-year-old sister of a problem youngster commented wistfully to the home visitor, "My brother is weird; he always takes my toys." It is also worth noting in this context that most of the siblings of the hard-to-manage children were doing reasonably well, despite the difficulties evident with the target child and/or more generally in patterns of interaction within the family.

Summary

In summary, preschoolers typically react with a range of problem behaviors when they must adapt to the birth of a sibling. In most families these behaviors represent relatively brief and transient stress reactions rather than long-term patterns of maladjustment. In children not identified as having behavior problems, sibling relationships appear to range from positive and warm to hostile, although most sibling relationships reflect a blend of positive and negative features. The ability of children to adapt to the birth of a sibling is partly related to aspects of parenting and the family climate as well as to the children's more typical style of responding to stress and environmental change. Not surprisingly, children considered to be difficult before the birth of a second child have a particularly hard time dealing with the sibling birth and adapting to the attendant changes in the family system. This may be ameliorated by parental sensitivity to the older child's feelings and by continued involvement with him or her, both alone and as a helper in taking care of the younger child. However, the older child's hostility and frustration, whether directed at the parent or the younger sibling, may also serve to exacerbate mother–child conflict as the mother seeks to rebuke the older child and protect the younger one from harm. Fathers may play a central role here in easing these conflicts. As younger siblings mature, relations between older and younger children become more complex. Although conflicts over toys and attention are often salient, siblings also socialize with each other, and a sibling may help to fill the void created by a troubled or rejecting mother–child relationship. Over time, siblings may become not only rivals but companions and friends.

CHAPTER SIX

Peer Relationships

The Developmental Importance of Peers

It is widely recognized that peer relations, like relations with parents, siblings, and other family members, play a crucial role in young children's development (Hartup, 1983; Rubin, Fein, & Vandenberg, 1983; Shantz, 1987). Although early social relations develop in the context of the family, as children move into toddlerhood and enter preschool, they spend increasingly more time in the company of other children. These experiences with relative equals complement those with adults who have greater authority, and hence ability to control children's behavior, than peers. Piaget (1932) argued that experiences with age-mates are necessary if children are to move beyond an egocentric orientation and begin to take the views of others into account. Because interactions with peers are reciprocal and not based on the constraints imposed by either socially sanctioned authority or necessary dependency, children are in a better position to engage in negotiation and compromise (Hartup, 1983; Rubin, 1982; Shantz, 1987). Children are often in situations in which power relations are not entirely equal. For example, one child may dominate in decision making or allocation of resources by virtue of age, size, knowledge of the situation, or personality style. However, social interactions with peers are more equal than those with adults. As such, they force the child to give greater consideration to the wishes, feelings, and viewpoints of others if mutually satisfying and cooperative relationships are to ensue. Thus, the social skills that are learned in the course of early peer relations are seen as complementary to those learned with adults and as necessary for future social relations (see also Sullivan, 1953).

⌐ Although recent work demonstrates that rudimentary perspective-taking skills develop within the family context and are evident even in the prosocial behaviors of toddlers (Zahn-Waxler et al., 1979), it is also clear that children learn much about the rules of social exchange in the peer group.⌐Turn taking, sharing, control of aggression, empathy, helping, sex role learning, role taking, strategies of conflict resolution, and moral reasoning all develop within the peer group as well as the family and appear to be central to the ability to establish friendships and maintain relationships with others. Thus, it is generally agreed that social competence has its roots in the quality of early family relationships (e.g., Hartup, 1983; Sroufe, 1983; Zahn-Waxler et al., 1982). At the same time, as children's social networks widen to encompass regular contacts with other children, the nature and complexity of their social reasoning and their social behavior show profound changes that signal a new phase of developmental organization.

At a general level, Brownell (1986) has discussed the convergence of social and cognitive development that occurs during the second year of life. She argues that as children's symbolic reasoning develops, as reflected in rapid strides in language ability, early causal reasoning, awareness of basic social routines, and the emergence of rudimentary perspective taking, parallel cognitive, social-cognitive, and social-developmental advances occur. Cognitive-developmental reorganizations appear to underlie these changes (e.g., Selman, 1981). In the social domain, for example, the object-mediated play of the 1-year-old is replaced by the more complex play of the toddler that includes more communication over a distance and longer sequences of turn taking, both of which require some awareness of the partner as a separate person (Brownell, 1986). In the preschool period, advances in self–other differentiation and role-taking skills are associated with the emergence of sustained bouts of cooperative play and pretending. The complexity of this play can likewise be related to changes in these and other underlying cognitive competencies. Conversely, children's social experiences with peers clearly influence their ability to make sense of and reason about the events going on around them (e.g., Corsaro, 1981), suggesting reciprocal relationships among cognitive development, social cognition, and social behavior. Thus, the emergence of prerequisite cognitive abilities and the experience of age-appropriate interactions with other children combine to lead to a fairly predictable sequence of development of children's social skills and social reasoning abilities.

Despite this relatively predictable developmental progression, children vary widely in their social behavior and in their appreciation of their social worlds. Individual differences in children's peer experiences and the quality of their relationships with peers are shaped in part by earlier experiences in the family. The quality of the early mother–child relationship appears to influence preschoolers' ability to play coopera- tively with peers, their tendency to be aggressive or withdrawn, their attractiveness as play partners, and their overall popularity in the peer group (e.g., Jacobsen & Wille, 1986; Lieberman, 1977; Sroufe, 1983). Several studies suggest that securely attached children are more likely to be socially competent in the peer group as preschoolers, whereas their anxious-insecure counterparts are more likely to experience difficulties with peers. For example, Sroufe (1983) found that children who had been more securely attached as infants showed more empathy, were more positive in their interactions with peers, and were less likely to respond negatively to peer initiations than their anxious and avoidant classmates. Lewis et al. (1984) reported that boys who were insecurely attached in infancy were rated by their mothers as more socially withdrawn in the peer group at age 6.

The quality of parent–child interaction in the preschool period also has concurrent influences on social behavior with peers, as well as on peer acceptance. A large body of research on child-rearing patterns and children's behavior in the peer group suggests that involved and nurturant parents who also set high standards for their children's behavior and use reasoning and explanations when enforcing limits have children who are more socially competent and prosocial with peers (see Maccoby & Martin, 1983, and Radke-Yarrow, Zahn-Waxler, & Chapman, 1983, for reviews). Conversely, parents who are rejecting, uninvolved, and often angry, and who frequently employ physical punishment to enforce limits are likely to produce children who are aggressive with peers (see Parke & Slaby, 1983, for a review). There is also evidence to suggest that certain types of parental deviance, such as psychopathology (particularly depression) and poor parental self- control (as reflected in child abuse), are each associated with toddlers' poorer control of aggression toward peers (George & Main, 1979; Zahn-Waxler, Cummings, et al., 1984).

Other studies have noted an association between parent–child relationships and peer popularity. For instance, MacDonald (1987) has reported that the positivity of parent–child affect exchange and the nature of their playful interactions are associated with peer-rated popularity. More popular boys and their parents displayed more positive affect during play and engaged in more physical rough-and-tumble play than comparison groups of rejected and neglected preschool boys and their parents.

The relationship between the quality of parent–child interaction and children's functioning in the peer group is undoubtedly complex. Findings may reflect, in part, cross-situational consistencies in behavior; that is, children who are positive and cooperative at home may also be that way with peers, whereas some children who are negative and noncompliant at home may likewise behave that way with peers. In addition, as Bell (1968) has suggested, children not only react to, but they also elicit, certain child-rearing practices by virtue of their temperament and their initial responsiveness to attempts at parental control. For example, children who are cooperative and compliant are likely to elicit reasoning, compromise, and negotiation from parents which may carry over to encounters with peers, whereas children who tend to be defiant and uncooperative will be more likely to elicit harsh and angry parental responses, which may influence the way they cope with conflicts in the peer group. In keeping with a transactional model of development, then, the relationships between child characteristics and parents' strategies of child rearing are reciprocal, and these in turn are thought to influence the quality of peer relationships.

A number of explanations have been proposed to account for the relationships between the quality of parent–child interactions and children's social competence with peers. Sroufe (1983; Sroufe & Fleeson, 1985) emphasizes the impact of early parent–child relations on the development of feelings of self-esteem and self-efficacy. Children who feel more competent and self-assured by virtue of their positive early experiences with nurturant and responsive caretakers will be better able to reach out to others. Their relationship history will thus carry over to their ability to form positive relationships in the peer group. According to this view, characteristic ways of relating to others and attitudes toward and expectations of others' availability in relationships develop from early experiences with caretakers and ultimately influence children's friendship choices and their general social behavior.

Maccoby and Martin (1983) have suggested that the nature of maternal control strategies and the affective tone of the relationship between mother and child will set the stage for more general attitudes toward cooperation and positive interactions with others versus more negative and aggressive encounters. Children's general willingness to comply with parents also may be apparent in the peer group where

more compliant and agreeable children are better able to play cooperatively with others. Parents' characteristic manner of handling social
encounters in the home teaches children prosocial strategies and
appropriate methods of conflict resolution that facilitate positive social
exchange in the peer group or exposes them to less mature strategies
that impede the development of social cooperative skills (Radke-Yarrow
et al. 1983; Zahn-Waxler et al., 1982). It has also been suggested (e.g.,
MacDonald, 1987) that family interactions influence children's ability to
regulate the expression of affect, which has an important impact on peer
relations; children who have difficulty either expressing positive affect
or inhibiting the inappropriate expression of negative affect will be more
likely to have difficulties getting along cooperatively with other children.

In general, then, current research and theory converge to suggest
that family experiences influence the nature of social development and
have a major influence on children's social experiences with peers.
There is also a growing emphasis on the quality of the emotional bond
between parents and children. A positive affective relationship with
parents is seen as one basic ingredient in children's social competence
with peers. Hartup (1983) emphasizes the importance of parental
behavior when he discusses the "synergy" between the family and peer
social systems. In keeping with a transactional model of development, it
would be logical to hypothesize that experiences with peers also feed
back in reciprocal fashion to influence the quality of parent–child
relationships, as well as relationships with siblings. Few parents of
adolescents would be likely to quarrel with this statement, but its
application to preschoolers may be less obvious. Certainly, there is little
research on this question with young children. However, it is likely that
parents' perceptions of their children will be influenced by their
observations of their children's social behavior with peers, which may in
turn have an effect on parental limit setting and the degree of
independence permitted. For example, parents' willingness to step back
and let children settle their own disputes might be expected to have an
impact on children's learning to negotiate, share, and compromise.
However, when parents perceive their children as excessively aggressive, they may be more likely to jump in prematurely to enforce the
nonviolent settlement of squabbles between peers, thereby depriving
their children of important learning opportunities. Parental perceptions
of their children's peer relationships probably also influence their
willingness to seek out peer experiences for their children, either by
enrolling them in preschool or inviting other children over to play.

Thus, parental attitudes and expectations might be expected to interact in a reciprocal fashion with children's social competence. In keeping with a theme that has been echoed throughout this book, there is coherence in children's behavior across development and consistency in their behavior in different social contexts, in this instance, in the family and peer systems (Hartup, 1983).

Peer Relationships in Preschoolers

> Jeremy and Jonathan, both 30 months old, are standing at the water table in the preschool classroom. Jonathan is filling a plastic container with water and spilling it out, watching the water splash down the drain. Jeremy watches and then goes to get another container. He, too, begins to fill his container with water and spill it out. The two boys stand side by side, both emptying and refilling their plastic pails, glancing at each other and exchanging a few words. They continue playing like this for several minutes until Jonathan drops his pail and runs off to ride the tricycle. Soon after, Jeremy, too, loses interest in this activity and finds something else to do.

This is a classic example of the parallel play typical of young preschoolers, who spend a good deal of their time watching, imitating, and learning from each others' play. Parallel play is marked by the similarity of the participants' actions and by their awareness of each other, despite relatively little direct verbal exchange or turn taking. It appears that by engaging in parallel play, children begin to learn about the synchrony of behavior that is necessary for more sustained bouts of cooperative interaction. Parallel play represents an early form of social interactive play that occupies a proportion of children's social activities across the preschool years, although the types of parallel activities that preschoolers select increase in complexity with age (Hartup, 1983). In the interaction just described, the children are engaged in an exploratory activity; with increasing age and cognitive sophistication, basic exploration gives way to more complex construction activities that children may engage in parallel fashion (Rubin et al., 1983). This vignette also illustrates the transient nature of young children's play encounters (Corsaro, 1981).

Four-year-olds Ian and Mike are building in the block corner, making a huge rambling structure. They are talking animatedly as they work, discussing the placement of the blocks and whether the building should be a garage or a castle. Mike adds some blocks to the foundation; then he steps back and watches while Ian adds some more blocks that jut out from the main structure. They continue to build, working together, taking turns, and talking as they play, engrossed in what they are doing. Zach comes along, picks up a block, and tries to add it to the building. Both Ian and Mike shout, "No!" and Ian says, "Don't! You can't build here!" Zach persists in trying to put the block on; Ian continues to protest and pushes Zach. The teacher intervenes.

This illustrates a number of typical features of preschool peer interactions. First, turn taking, social and task-oriented conversation, and cooperation toward a goal become increasingly important components of play in older preschoolers. This complex sequence of interactions indicates that the two boys are able to regulate their own behavior to take turns and work together. This vignette also suggests that Ian and Mike have some ability to share and to take the other person's point of view into account. Furthermore, the differentiation of self from other is needed before two individuals can coordinate their activities in such a fine-tuned and mutually regulated way. In addition, this type of cooperative activity requires some degree of means–end thinking and the ability to plan and work toward a goal. Finally, young children are capable of establishing strong bonds of friendship with others, and this may be reflected in prolonged bouts of joint play and cooperation. The cooperative play between Ian and Mike is an example of the marked strides that are made from roughly 30 months to 48 months in the development of preschoolers' social competencies.

At the same time, possessiveness, lack of sharing, and ultimate conflict also characterize social interactions among preschoolers (Shantz, 1987). Conflicts over space, toys, and activities are common occurrences in preschool classrooms, although similar to the episode described above, they are usually short-lived. In this instance, Ian and Mike did not want to share their ongoing activity with Zach; possibly they also did not want an outsider intruding into their relationship, either because their play had reached a level of mutually satisfying, although precarious, cooperation that could easily be destroyed by the addition of a third child, or because of a special bond between them that led to exclusivity in choice of play partners (Corsaro, 1981). Like possession struggles, the entry of a newcomer into an ongoing activity is often the source of conflict (see Corsaro, 1981; Shantz, 1987). In this instance, protecting one's turf, be it space, materials, or partner, becomes the overriding goal, and children do not take the feelings of the newcomer into account as they reject his bids outright. At this stage of development, too, there is a tendency to lash out physically and to protest verbally, rather than to negotiate a mutually agreeable compromise solution to the impasse.

> Jill and Julie are in the playhouse deciding whose turn it is to be the baby when Sam, a younger child, comes along. They grab him by the hand in a playful manner and Jill says, "Sam, you be the baby. I'll be the mommy." The discussion then ensues about what role Julie should take, the daddy or the big sister. Finally, they agree that she should be the daddy; so she goes off to the dress-up corner to get a hat.

Although it is often difficult for new children to enter an ongoing activity, at other times, children's groups form and reform spontaneously. Furthermore, research has shown that girls are more likely to incorporate boys into an ongoing activity than vice versa (Corsaro, 1981). In this instance, a younger child was brought into the play and given the role of the baby, suggesting a certain reality-based assignment of roles, despite the decision that Julie should be the daddy. This example also illustrates the opportunity for sex role learning and perspective taking afforded by young children's sociodramatic play. Finally, Jill and Julie avoided a conflict on role assignment by incorporating a younger child into the game, one who complied with their wishes that he be the baby. They also successfully negotiated what Julie's role in the play should be.

> Four-and-a-half-year-old Peter is running around the preschool classroom making believe he is a dragon. He is giggling and laughing and is excited, and he is unconcerned about where he is going. Thus, he runs right through the block corner, knocking down other children's buildings, pretending that he is the biggest dragon in the world. He runs up to other children in playful attack, making a ferocious face and growling at them, then bursting into laughter. The other children are not amused by this, however. One boy pushes Peter out of the way; another shouts, "Dumb-dumb, you're knocking down my house!" A third begins to cry and goes to tell the teacher.

In this example, a slightly older child is engaged in fairly complex fantasy play that involves adopting the role of an imaginary creature. This suggests a certain degree of flexible and creative thinking as well as some conception of hypothetical roles (Rubin et al., 1983). However, Peter is so engrossed in his own activity that he is unable to appreciate the impact of his rather boisterous play on others. Although his affect indicates that this is a game and that he is being playful, other children find him provocative and annoying and respond with varying types of protest: they respond physically, verbally, and seek adult intervention. This overexcited role playing of a quasi-aggressive sort may escalate to a full-blown aggressive incident between the child who is overly active and rambunctious and others who are engaged in more quiet problem-solving activities. Or, other children may join in, leading to an energetic chase or to playful wrestling. Such interchanges may help children learn to stop just short of real aggression or they may deteriorate into a fight, depending upon the degree of self-control exhibited by the participants.

These vignettes were meant to illustrate the enormous changes in children's social development that are apparent from the early to the late preschool period. The ability to engage in sequences of cooperative play in the context of complicated constructive and fantasy activities depends upon a number of gains in social abilities that are thought to derive from transitions in cognitive processes. Social exchanges that incorporate turn taking, mutual regulation and negotiation of goals, conversation, and role enactment suggest changes in self-control, representational and means–end thinking, perspective taking, rudimentary understanding of intentionality, memory, and language ability. When such exchanges also include joint planning toward a goal, they also imply some understanding of events beyond the here and now. They rely as well on the ability to attend to the partner's behavior and to respond appropriately, in terms of affective tone, verbal content, and ongoing motor activity. Thus, a good deal of synchronization must occur if the playful interaction is to be prolonged beyond the one or two turns characteristic of infants because inappropriate behavior from the partner is likely to lead either to conflict or to the termination of the interaction.

Study of the social interactions of preschoolers highlights the importance of conflict and its resolution and the development of prosocial behaviors as well as gains in cognitive skills. Shantz (1987) has suggested that conflict, defined as incompatible goals or behaviors between individuals, is central to change and developmental progression. She argues that conflict over toys, activity, role assignments, appropriate responses, and so on in the preschool setting sets the stage for numerous prosocial and antisocial interactions. Furthermore, through conflict and its resolution, children learn to regulate their behavior in the peer group as they practice and internalize appropriate rules of social exchange. Although a good deal of research on preschoolers' interactions has focused on aggressive encounters, Shantz concludes, from a review of the literature, that low level conflicts are more common and that they are usually solved before an outright aggressive interchange erupts. Furthermore, she notes that the content of children's conflicted interactions shows developmental change. Toddlers and young preschoolers are more likely to argue over possessions and space, whereas older preschoolers are more likely to have disputes about appropriate behaviors, classroom rules, ideas, or the way a fantasy role should be played. In this context, children learn to share, to take turns, to negotiate, and to compromise. They also learn about moral rules and conventions as well as about others' feelings and perceptions.

Despite the importance of conflict and its resolution and the focus on aggressive encounters, a much larger proportion of children's interactions tends to be prosocial. Cooperative and parallel play activities predominate among preschoolers (Rubin et al., 1983; Shantz, 1987). Young children also demonstrate the ability to show sympathy and concern for others; they help one another and comfort those who are distressed (Zahn-Waxler et al., 1982). Such prosocial behaviors are evident in the direct interactions among children, and they are rehearsed during sociodramatic play episodes. Although Piaget argued that the egocentrism of preschoolers precluded the development of such prosocial behaviors, much current research indicates that young children, although still concrete in their thinking, are capable of some degree of decentration, that their activities, thoughts, and feelings are not totally focused on the self, and that Piaget underestimated the cognitive and social capacities of preschool children (e.g., see Gottman & Parkhurst, 1980; Rubin et al., 1983; Shantz, 1987; Zahn-Waxler et al., 1979).

Preschoolers engage in a good deal of prosocial behavior that is reflected in the quality of their play and their concern for others. They are, however, also capable of showing a lack of concern for the rights and feelings of others, and this is evident in the relative frequency of possession struggles and in their responses to the social overtures of others. Corsaro (1981) conducted a detailed ethnographic study of the attempts made by preschoolers to enter ongoing social groups. He noted that roughly one half of the group entry attempts he observed met with initial resistance. Children were likely to claim ownership of the toys or space, to say that the area was overcrowded or that there were not enough toys for new members, to deny that the newcomer was a friend, to cite arbitrary rules about the groups' needs, or to issue a blanket refusal. Children who approached a group in an aggressive manner or who tried to take over were less likely to be accepted than those who used a more subtle approach that involved parallel play. Corsaro suggests that the high level of unsuccessful bids may reflect the fact that the newcomer disrupts the tenuous balance of an ongoing game or activity.

Friendship and familiarity also play a role in children's choices of playmates and in their willingness to let others join their ongoing activities. There is evidence that preschoolers have preferred playmates and even "best" friends who stick together and exclude others (Corsaro, 1981). Children also tend to prefer familiar to unfamiliar peers and are more likely to engage in prosocial behaviors, such as sharing, with children they know (Doyle, 1982). Prior peer experiences also appear to influence children's play. Children engage in more frequent and more elaborate fantasy play with familiar than unfamiliar peers (Gottman & Parkhurst, 1980). In another study (Harper & Huie, 1985), both prior experience with peers and familiarity with classmates were associated with children's participation in interactive play, whereas children without prior peer group experience were more likely to spend time in solitary activities. Time spent in solitary play seems to decrease over time as children become acclimated to the preschool classroom. In addition, there is evidence that the presence of familiar preschool peers in the same classroom facilitates the transition to kindergarten (Ladd & Price, 1987), possibly because familiar playmates serve a supportive function for each other in a new environment. Although it has been argued by some (e.g., Selman, 1981) that preschool children's egocentrism precludes the development of affective bonds of friendship that move beyond the momentary here and now, recent studies and anecdotal reports indicate that this characterization underestimates the ability of preschoolers to develop intense and mutually supportive bonds with age-mates (see Corsaro, 1981; Gottman & Parkhurst, 1980). For example, preschoolers establish specific emotional bonds with special friends who they favor as playmates, express affection toward, show concern for, and miss when they are absent.

Gender also influences the nature and quality of peer interactions. Same-sex friendships are more common across the preschool and elementary school years with children often actively avoiding opposite-sex playmates. The favored activities of boys' and girls' groups also differ markedly (Hartup, 1983). For example, boys tend to engage in more active and rough-and-tumble play than girls, who tend to spend more time in dramatic play and construction activities (e.g., DiPietro, 1981; Hartup, 1983). Boys also become involved in more frequent aggressive interactions, including property conflicts (Parke & Slaby, 1983; Smith & Green, 1975), whereas girls are likely to avoid the rough, aggressive, and active play of boys. Corsaro's observations in preschools indicate that boys have an easier time than girls gaining entry into mixed-gender play groups, and boys are also more likely to be accepted by an all-girls group than vice versa. Despite the predominance of separation by sex, there is evidence that opposite-sex peers sometimes develop strong attachments during the preschool years (Gottman & Parkhurst, 1980). However, it is not clear what happens to such friendships in the early elementary school years, when children's groups become even more strongly segregated by gender.

So far the discussion has focused on the nature of developmental changes in children's peer interactions and has described the typical patterns of behavior that are common among preschoolers. In addition, however it is necessary to explore the nature of individual differences. It was suggested in the discussion of family influences on competence in the peer group that children differ widely in their tendency to be sociable, shy, or aggressive; they also differ widely in the quality of their play. Moreover, these individual differences are thought to be important predictors of later development, partly as a result of their impact on other children. Even in preschool, children are very much aware of which children are the leaders and which are the troublemakers. Children who are more positive, cooperative, sociable, and concerned about the rights of others are more likely to be sought out as playmates, and this is likely to enhance their opportunities to interact with others, thereby developing their competence with peers even further. The ability to respond appropriately and reciprocally is also likely to be related to peer popularity; children who are more adept socially are more likely to be chosen as attractive partners.

Conversely, children who are disruptive, provocative, aggressive, and predominantly negative in affect are more likely to elicit negative responses from others and to be rejected by peers. Thus, children whose play is aggressive and disorganized or those who lack the skills to engage in mutual turn taking, sharing, listening, and responding appropriately in the context of the ongoing activity are likely to be avoided as playmates (Hartup, Glazer, & Charlesworth, 1967; Ladd & Price, 1987; Milich, Landau, Kilby, & Whitten, 1982; Rubin, 1982). Furthermore, Ladd and Price (1987) recently reported that time spent in cooperative play and extensiveness of positive social contacts in preschool were related not only to concurrent measures of peer popularity, but they also predicted peer status at the beginning and end of kindergarten. Similarly, aggressive and negative interactions in preschool were associated with a concurrent measure of peer rejection, and they predicted peer rejection in kindergarten. This relationship was especially strong for boys, who were more likely to be both aggressive and rejected. Moreover, there is evidence from this study and others (reviewed in Parke & Slaby, 1983) to suggest that aggression may persist in children who are intensely and inappropriately aggressive in preschool, possibly fueling a cycle of peer rejection that leads to continued inappropriate behavior with peers.

Sociable children, then, do well with peers, and aggressive children tend to be rejected, despite their interest in playing with others. There is also evidence to indicate that some children do not seek out play partners but tend to stay off by themselves on the sidelines. For example, Rubin (1982) observed the social interaction patterns of a group of preschoolers. Children classified as socially isolated spent more free play time unoccupied or watching the activities of others and less time in social conversation than their classmates, who had been classified as normally sociable or highly sociable. Socially withdrawn children not only initiated less interaction themselves but received fewer interaction bids from others. When isolated preschoolers were involved in play, it was more likely to be a relatively immature form of exploratory activity. Their decreased social involvement was also reflected in less socio-dramatic play with others, play that is seen as an important avenue of socialization and social-cognitive development. Even when paired with another child during free play, isolated children talked to themselves more and their partners less than comparison groups of more sociable peers. Children who seem "tuned out" and socially withdrawn are more likely to be ignored by classmates (Peery, 1979), providing them with fewer opportunities to engage in those social activities thought to enhance social competence.

Studies of children with behavior disorders indicate that difficulties with peers are a pervasive and continuing problem (Campbell & Paulauskas, 1979; Milich & Landau, 1982; Weiss & Hechtman, 1986). The few studies that have examined the social interactions of young children with externalizing behavior problems have found, not surprisingly, that they were more aggressive with peers than controls when observed in preschool (Campbell & Cluss, 1982; Schleifer et al., 1975), although they were not found to be less sociable with peers. Cohen et al. (1981) found that hyperactive kindergarteners were more likely to disrupt peers' play and to engage in solitary activities than their nonhyperactive classmates. Leach (1972) reported that 3-year-olds with marked separation problems in preschool were less competent with peers and that their tendency to avoid interaction and give in to peer conflict persisted over the first several months of school. Finally, Howes (1981) reported that dyads of "emotionally disturbed" children attending a hospital-based program were less likely to initiate social interaction successfully, engage in sustained bouts of reciprocal play, or show positive affect exchange than pairs of nonreferred controls. These few studies point to the poor social skills evidenced by preschoolers with varying types of behavioral disturbances and underline the need for additional research on these questions.

The evidence on nonreferred samples of preschool children suggests that both aggressive children and hyperactive-impulsive children are likely to be rejected by peers. Studies of school-age children confirm that clinically referred aggressive and overactive children are less popular with peers and are more likely to be overtly rejected by classmates than merely ignored (e.g., Dodge, 1983; Pelham & Bender, 1982). Furthermore, measures of peer rejection show relative stability over time (Dodge, 1983; Ladd & Price, 1987): rejected children who enter new peer groups are likely to display negative, annoying, and provocative behavior very early in the acquaintanceship process, and this behavior appears to lead to further rejection, even in a new group (e.g., Dodge, 1983; Pelham & Bender, 1982). In line with a transactional model, this suggests a cyclical pattern of influences between the rejected child's social status and his/her poor social skills. Inappropriate and annoying behavior initially leads to peer rejection, which in turn leads the rejected youngster to increase the intensity of his/her futile attempts to gain acceptance, leading to further rejection. Furthermore, persistent rejection by peers is likely to have a major impact on a child's self-esteem, something that may exacerbate social problems and contribute to other difficulties as well. Clinical evidence on children with behavior problems indicates that difficulties with peers tend to persist and to become more severe as children get older (Campbell & Paulauskas, 1979; Weiss & Hechtman, 1986).

Social Reasoning

In addition to studies of family influences on children's peer relations and those that examine the quality of children's play directly by watching them in preschools and other group settings, theorists and researchers have focused on children's understanding of social rules and social relations. Selman (1980) and other theorists (e.g., Damon, 1977) have suggested that children's reasoning about the social world develops in sequential fashion, with children going through stages of social-cognitive development that parallel Piaget's stages of reasoning about the physical world. According to this model, the first level, the egocentric or undifferentiated perspective, is apparent in young preschoolers and is reflected in a lack of distinction between the child's perspective (including perceptions, thoughts, and feelings) and that of others. Children at this level do not recognize that others can interpret experiences differently from the way they do; they also tend to confuse physical and psychological aspects of the social world. For example, young children may define a playmate as nice if the playmate gives them candy or a toy, rather than in terms of a psychological characteristic, such as concern for others. The second level, the subjective or differentiated perspective, is defined by the child's growing ability to understand that someone else's viewpoint may be different from his or her own. Children are beginning to be aware of psychological charac-teristics and the fact that different individuals may perceive events differently. However, they are unable at this stage to coordinate their own views with the views of others or to understand the reasons for differences in perspective. Children reach these stages at different ages, although, consistent with a Piagetian framework, all children go through all stages in the same sequence. Selman believes that most preschoolers are able to function only at the first level, although some older preschoolers reach the second level, which is more characteristic of elementary school children.

In the context of peer relationships, Selman and others (e.g., Damon, 1977) have tested this theory by examining children's develop-ing concepts of friendship. Selman's general theory of sequential stages of social development is confirmed by his work as well as by the work of others (reviewed in Selman, 1981). He calls the first level of children's friendship conceptions "momentary physical playmate," a term that denotes that the child's view of friendship is determined by proximity and frequency of contact. According to Selman, the child does not think in terms of an enduring relationship or seek playmates based on psychological characteristics. Rather, friends are playmates, and when children disagree, they are no longer friends. Furthermore, conflicts and fights occur over space and activities, rather than over other less tangible issues. Because the basis for friendship is physical, rather than psychological, the thoughts, feelings, and desires of others are not relevant. Although a child may be aware that another child wants the same toy, at this level of social reasoning, any sharing that occurs is most likely to be a function of dominance and submission, prior possession, or adult intervention and not due to the child's reasoning about how the other child feels when unable to have access to the coveted toy. Conflicts are resolved by physical fighting or by leaving the scene.

At the second level of friendship reasoning, children are beginning to take psychological characteristics into account. This stage is termed "one-way assistance" by Selman, who notes that these children define a friend as someone who does what one wants (e.g., lets you play with his toys). A friend is also someone "you like" and someone "you know" better than other children. Conflict is also seen as a one-way street; it is caused by the actions of one person toward another (e.g., not sharing toys). Thus, conflict can be resolved by one person's actions, such as giving up a toy. However, feelings are recognized. Children are friends with those they like and not friends with those they do not like. Furthermore, at this stage children recognize that one person's actions can influence how another person is feeling (you feel bad when someone won't let you play with him or his toys).

While research interviews confirm relatively concrete thinking among preschoolers and a limited ability to empathize with others or to conceptualize relationships as existing beyond the here and now, live behavioral observations indicate that children's social interactions with peers actually involve more complex social reasoning. Thus, as already noted, young children demonstrate some empathy, perspective taking, and concern for others when observed interacting with playmates, although they may not be able to articulate what they or others are feeling when asked directly or when required to imagine how they would feel in a hypothetical situation. Similarly, when asked about conflict resolution, young children may report that they would fight or tell the teacher, although observational studies of children's behavior suggest that they have a broader repertoire of situationally appropriate problem-solving strategies (e.g., Krasnor, 1982). For example, toy struggles, although they may lead to fights, may also result in some form of negotiation, sharing, or reasoning about why one child should play with the toy first.

Similarly, Selman's model of friendship concepts suggests that preschoolers rarely form meaningful friendships with other children that involve concern, caring, sharing, or awareness of the other child's absence or that involve a more long-term bond. However, observations in preschools and of children interacting at home indicate that this is not the case (e.g., Corsaro, 1981; Gottman & Parkhurst, 1980). Young children clearly establish close relationships with other children that involve spontaneous sharing of toys as well as of thoughts and feelings, albeit at a different level than one would expect from school-age children. Young children are capable of expressing worry and concern for the welfare of friends and of missing them in their absence, clearly an indication of some appreciation of a relationship that goes beyond the here and now. Children's ability to negotiate to solve disputes also suggests somewhat greater social reasoning ability than is implied by Selman's model (Krasnor, 1982). Furthermore, analyses of young children's conversations indicate awareness of the listener's needs and characteristics, as well as more conversational reciprocity than is implied by theories that emphasize the egocentrism of preschoolers (e.g., see Gottman & Parkhurst, 1980; Shantz, 1987; and Shatz, 1983, for discussions of this and related issues). Finally, the data on preschool children's perceptions of classmates indicate that they are relatively accurate in identifying children who are inappropriate and aggressive, as well as those who are socially adept. This finding suggests that young children possess at least some rudimentary awareness of the behavioral characteristics of peers. They are also aware of which behaviors contribute to liking and which lead children to be avoided by peers.

In summary, the rapid changes that occur in young children's social abilities with peers have been well documented. From toddlerhood to the preschool period, children master the basic rules of reciprocity that are necessary for successful social interaction and social conversation as they establish relationships with children outside the family circle. These experiences with peers parallel and complement experiences in the family; experiences with others also influence and are influenced by changes in children's reasoning about their social world. However, children also show wide variations in sociability and the ability to deal with conflict, which appear to affect their acceptability as play partners. The long-term impact of children's early experiences with peers remains a topic of current interest and debate. It is to this issue that I now turn.

The Clinical Implications of Peer Problems

There is wide agreement that difficulties in the peer group are frequently a concomitant of both internalizing and externalizing behavioral disturbances in young children (Campbell & Paulauskas, 1979; Rutter & Garmezy, 1983). However, it is less clear whether peer problems should be viewed as a correlate, cause, or consequence of other difficulties (Rutter & Garmezy, 1983). The prognostic significance of peer problems also has been the subject of some discussion and speculation.

A number of short-term longitudinal studies of nonclinical samples suggest that both aggressive behavior toward peers and social withdrawal show some stability across the preschool years and into early elementary school (e.g., Buss, Block, & Block, 1980; Fagot, 1984; Halverson & Waldrop, 1976; Kohn, 1977; Ladd & Price, 1987). Indeed, longitudinal studies of aggression in both referred and nonreferred samples also indicate marked long-term stability, a finding that has led Olweus (1979) to suggest that aggression may be as stable as IQ. Furthermore, there is evidence that aggressiveness shows continuity across generations (see Parke & Slaby, 1983, for a review). In general, these longer term studies have been conducted with children who were identified as aggressive at school-age. Thus, it is unclear how generalizable these results are to preschoolers. Fewer studies have been conducted on the long-term stability of social withdrawal.

Similarly, studies have indicated that children's reputations in the peer group are stable and that children who are rejected in one peer group also tend to behave in ways that lead to rejection in a new group (e.g., Dodge, 1983; Pelham & Bender, 1982). There is also some recent evidence to suggest that peer status is relatively stable from preschool to kindergarten (Ladd & Price, 1987). The potential importance of findings such as these is dramatized by a classic study conducted by Cowen and his colleagues (Cowen, Pederson, Babigian, Izzo, & Trost, 1973). These investigators found that peer rejection in third grade was predictive of psychiatric problems in adulthood and that peers were better able to identify abnormality in classmates than were teachers. This widely cited study has served as a major impetus for research on the nature and long-term sequelae of peer difficulties in childhood.

Contrary to the popular belief that negative and inappropriate behaviors in young children are rarely significant, severe problems in preschool may not be transient; peer difficulties, along with other symptoms, especially of externalizing problems, may persist (e.g., Campbell, Ewing, et al., 1986; Fischer et al., 1984; Hughes, Pinkerton, & Plewis, 1979; Kohn, 1977; Westman, Rice, & Bermann, 1967). The studies that have examined this question will be discussed in more detail in Chapter Eight. In this context findings may be interpreted as evidence for the persistence of peer difficulties in some disturbed preschoolers. What little evidence exists suggests that peer difficulties by themselves are not likely to be clinically significant. Thus, the young child who goes through a period of frequent toy struggles or who has some difficulties playing cooperatively with others, in the absence of other problems in social or cognitive development, is probably going through a difficult developmental transition that will be outgrown. However, the highly aggressive youngster who also has a range of other difficulties with self-control and compliance appears to be at risk for continuing problems that are likely to include conflicts with peers.

The data on the persistence of externalizing problems are much clearer than the findings on social withdrawal, which tend to be more equivocal. It is generally agreed that children who are shy and withdrawn in one group may be accepted in another (Asher, 1983) and that internalizing problems in general are not likely to persist in preschoolers (Fischer et al., 1984). However, some studies have found that shy, withdrawn children continue to function more poorly, both academically and socially, than their more sociable peers (Kohn, 1977).

The mechanisms that mediate the relationships between peer competence and outcome remain to be explicated. As noted earlier, peer difficulties may be one important indicator of problem severity. The abilities to establish friendships and to function adequately in the peer group are among the major developmental tasks of early childhood. Children who are having difficulties negotiating a range of developmental transitions that include separation from mother, the development of autonomy and a sense of self, the establishment of reasonable internal controls over impulses, and the ability to cooperate with age-mates are clearly at higher risk for continued problems in adaptation than children who cope with these developmental tasks more easily. Thus, peer difficulties may be a correlate of problem severity and hence associated with poor outcome. However, in keeping with a transactional model of development, persistent peer problems are probably also both a cause and a consequence of poor outcome at each developmental transition point. Poor peer relations might be expected to have an impact on a young child's self-esteem and feelings of self-efficacy, which in turn may exacerbate symptoms. At the same time, difficulties with impulse control, immature social reasoning, or frequent expressions of anger and defiance will influence the quality of a child's relationships with peers. Furthermore, as already noted throughout this book, the expression of symptomatic behavior, including getting along with other children, is often related to ongoing stresses within the family. In an attempt to illustrate some of these complex issues further, I will return to the case studies.

Case Illustrations

The children from our longitudinal study who were described in Chapter Three varied greatly in the quality of their relationships with peers, both at the initial interview and over the course of their early development. However, severe initial peer problems and peer relationships that worsened with development tended to be associated with poorer outcomes at age 9. Other children, despite problems in the family, appeared to function well with peers and to derive a good deal of support from the peer group.

Jamie L's parents contacted the project initially partly because of their concern with his peer relationships. Even as a 3-year-old, Jamie was exceedingly aggressive with peers. His parents and preschool teacher agreed that he tended to become overexcited around other children. Jamie's parents described him as aggressive and wild; he tended to disrupt the play of other children in nursery school and to provoke fights by running up to others and grabbing toys or interfering in their activities. As a result of this behavior, other children did not want to play with him and Jamie spent much of his time in solitary activities. Despite this, he very much wanted to play with others. However, when he did approach other children, he tended to be rough and forceful, attempting to dominate their play, and the interaction almost invariably ended in a fight. This only served to increase Jamie's isolation even further because children actively avoided him. Not only was Jamie rejected by his preschool classmates but he was also avoided by other children in his neighborhood; furthermore, their parents were reluctant to invite Jamie over to play or to have their children visit him. These problems were still in evidence at age 4.

Jamie's difficulties with peers have remained a continuing theme throughout his development. At the age 6 follow-up, both his mother and his first grade teacher commented on his poor ability to get along with other children. Jamie's mother noted that the frequency of aggression had decreased, although he got into the occasional fight that was pretty serious. Whereas school-age children rarely engage in physical fights with peers but instead rely on verbal aggression (Hartup, 1974; Shantz, 1987), Jamie continued to get into physical fights with other boys in his class. In addition to these relatively dramatic encounters, Jamie evidenced more subtle but annoying behaviors, such as those found to lead to rejection by classmates (Dodge, 1983; Pelham & Bender, 1982). Thus, he was described by his teacher as disturbing others, interrupting ongoing classroom activities, and clowning. These behaviors may have represented inappropriate attempts to gain peer attention and acceptance.

Peer problems continued to be serious at the age 9 follow-up. Jamie's mother described him as having no close friends, although she also noted that he wanted friends very badly and worried a good deal about not having friends. Despite his desire for friends, however, Jamie was still getting into fights with others, acting provocative and disruptive in school, and behaving in ways guaranteed to lead to rejection. His mother saw him as unable to compromise or follow games with rules, as socially immature, and as a bully. The few children with whom he did play tended to be younger than he, children he could boss around and control. Jamie's difficulties in the peer group appear both chronic and severe. Even though he had reached the age at which boys' peer contacts tend to be extensive, he still could not interact cooperatively with others. Thus, Jamie appears to be a continuing risk for poor interpersonal relations. In addition, it should be emphasized that Jamie has been afforded numerous opportunities to spend time with other children. He attends structured after-school activities with other children, such as Scouts, but these experiences are uniformly negative for him.

Thus, throughout development, Jamie's relationships with peers have been poor, characterized by excessive aggression, an inability to compromise or share, and difficulties in reflecting on the impact of his behavior on others or in anticipating the consequences of his aggressive outbursts. These inappropriate behaviors appear to be one manifestation of Jamie's persistent and severe difficulties with self-control and frustration tolerance, and they appear to have contributed to his history of rejection by peers, something that has persisted from preschool to the present, both in school and outside. The peer rejection that Jamie has experienced may in turn not only interfere with the acquisition of more appropriate social behaviors by depriving him of the typical experiences with peers that facilitate socialization but may also exacerbate peer problems, as Jamie's fruitless attempts to make friends become increasingly desperate, further undermining his self-esteem. In this instance, then, early peer problems may be interpreted as contributing, in a sort of snowball effect, to the persistence of general difficulties at school and home.

In contrast, Annie J has consistently gotten along well with peers, and it may be that her good peer relationships have in part compensated for her chronically troubled relationship with her mother. When Annie was first seen in the project, she had had only very limited experiences with other children. At the age 4 follow-up, despite her mother's reports of continuing problems at home, Annie was doing well in preschool, as reflected in her cooperative play with classmates. Similarly, at age 6, although her mother continued to see Annie as overactive, inattentive, and uncooperative at home, Mrs. J reported that Annie did well with other children. Indeed, Annie's teacher saw this as a particular strength because she commented spontaneously on Annie's sociability and good relationships with her classmates. This same pattern was in evidence at the age 9 follow-up. Although Mrs. J still reported that Annie was overactive, distractible, argumentative, and a worrier, she also reported that Annie had a number of stable friendships with girls in the neighborhood and that she played well with other children, was concerned about the welfare of her friends, and got a good deal of satisfaction from playing with others. In addition, Annie was involved in several extracurricular activities with other children and she excelled at these. Again, consistent with reports since preschool, her third grade teacher reported that she was doing well socially and academically.

Despite the evidence discussed earlier, linking the quality of parent–child relationships to success in the peer group, Annie is doing well in this domain. This may reflect her relatively more positive relationships with her father and sister which have served to compensate somewhat for her relatively impaired relationship with her mother.

Annie's success with peers paired with her good academic performance and her excellence at ballet may all contribute to her feelings of competence and self-worth, which have permitted her to focus some of her energies on more adaptive pursuits outside the mother–child relationship. Furthermore, her early successes in the peer group might have contributed to feelings of self-esteem that helped her to achieve success outside the home. In addition, there is a good deal of evidence indicating that some resilient children are able to overcome problems in the home environment that place other children at risk (Garmezy, 1987) and that girls are more resilient than boys (Rutter, 1981; Rutter & Garmezy, 1983). Another less optimistic possibility is that Annie is functioning well outside the home currently, but that as she reaches adolescence or young adulthood, problems in interpersonal relationships beyond the mother–child dyad will surface.

Robbie S has shown a less consistent pattern of relationships with peers. No peer problems were noted when his mother was first interviewed, although Robbie had been in day-care from a very early age and, therefore, had had extensive contact with other children. When he was observed in preschool at 3 years, 4 months of age, the school observer specifically commented on his cooperative play with other children, despite the fact that he was the youngest child in the class. His preschool teacher likewise reported that Robbie was doing well; she saw him as highly sociable and not at all aggressive or provocative with others. Similarly, Robbie was continuing to do well with peers at the age 4 follow-up.

However, as family problems worsened and as Robbie became embroiled in his parents' divorce proceedings, his peer relationships deteriorated as well. In kindergarten, he was described as very aggressive with peers. His teacher was especially concerned because he seemed to lash out at others without provocation, for example, throwing things at them, apparently out of frustration. Similarly, at the age 6 follow-up, Robbie continued to evidence problems with peers in school. His first grade teacher described him as aggressive and disruptive; he tended to bully other children and often got into physical fights at recess. Even during 30-minute classroom observations conducted during structured, teacher-directed activities, Robbie was observed to get into three separate altercations with children sitting near him. Because of his aggression with peers and his poor behavioral control in general, Robbie was ultimately placed in a special class for children with behavior problems. Yet, Mrs. S also noted that Robbie had friends in the neighborhood, including a best friend who lived up the street; she reported that they could play together for hours without incident.

By the age 9 follow-up, his family situation had settled down somewhat, and Robbie was seen as somewhat improved, although he was still getting into the occasional fight, particularly at recess. Both his mother and teacher were more concerned with Robbie's inattention and need for adult direction than with his peer relationships. He continued to have the same friends in his neighborhood with whom he was described as playing well. Robbie's peer problems, then, seem to occur against a background of stable friendships that have lasted from early childhood to the present. He has a history of good peer relationships from early childhood, as well as a positive and warm relationship with his mother. Thus, it appears that Robbie has a number of strengths that bode well for future interpersonal relationships and that his aggressive outbursts are related rather directly to ongoing stresses within the family rather than to an inability to relate to other children.

Finally, Teddy M was first seen at just younger than $2^1/2$ years. At that time peer problems were not a particular concern, although Mrs. M described Teddy as prone to get excited around other children. She also appropriately attributed this to his age and his relative lack of experiences with age-mates. Teddy started preschool when he was $3^1/2$ years old and did well socially. By the age 6 follow-up, however, Mrs. M was somewhat concerned about Teddy's shyness with other children. He preferred to stay at home to play with his brother rather than go to visit friends. Although Mrs. M noted that Teddy had friends with whom he played in school, he tended not to initiate play with them; rather, he waited for them to invite him over. Even then, however, he was often reluctant to go without his brother. However, Teddy's first grade teacher commented on his good social skills and noted that he was well liked by other children. Because of Teddy's shyness and what his parents saw as his social immaturity, he was retained in first grade. When seen at age 9, his teacher reported that he was doing well in second grade. His mother remained concerned about his shyness and failure to initiate play with others. Although Mrs. M reported that Teddy did not have any close friends, she did note that he had several friends with whom he had played for several years. Overall, then, it appears that Teddy may be less outgoing than many children his age, relying a good deal on his older brother for companionship, but he does not seem to have impaired relationships with other children. Rather, he seems to be functioning reasonably well in the peer group, as elsewhere, despite some unevenness in his development.

Summary

In this chapter peer relationships have been discussed with a focus on the developmental importance of experiences with age-mates. The interplay among family influences, peer experiences, and social-cognitive functioning have been emphasized. In particular, the quality of parent–child relationships is seen as having a major impact on the quality of children's relationships with peers via the impact of child-rearing strategies on children's early social skills, feelings of self-efficacy, and concern for others. Children appear to learn prosocial behavior patterns, conflict resolution strategies, and awareness of the feelings of others in the family setting, and these have an effect on their acceptance in the peer group. Experiences in the peer group in turn facilitate social development by giving children a range of experiences with sharing, role taking, affect regulation, and the control of aggression, among others, experiences that are unique when they involve age-mates rather than adults.

Typical patterns of peer interaction in the preschool setting were also described to illustrate some of the major developmental changes observed in the preschool years. Early peer interactions consist of interest in and curiosity about the peer and what he/she is doing, and this develops into imitation as reflected in the parallel play of young preschoolers. Children then begin to engage in more reciprocal exchanges that involve turn taking and sharing. With further development, the peer encounters of preschoolers can include rather elaborate games and sociodramatic play bouts that include role assignments, the negotiation of joint goals, shifts in roles, and successful attempts at conflict resolution, which appear to influence and be influenced by changes in underlying cognitive structures. Observations of peer interactions may provide a window on the development of some social cognitive processes. However, observational studies of social behavior and interview studies of children's reasoning lead to somewhat different conclusions about the relative sophistication of young children's social skills. Social reasoning studies suggest that children are more limited in their social skills than do observations of their actual behavior. Thus, it appears that children may "know" how to behave in socially appropriate and sensitive ways but be unable to describe the process or their underlying motivations.

Individual differences in patterns of behavior in the peer group may also be important. Patterns of aggression and social withdrawal may be a signal of developing problems. Furthermore, aggressive and shy children are more likely than their more skilled counterparts to be avoided or ignored by playmates. This may give them fewer opportunities to learn to behave appropriately with other children and further exacerbate peer problems. There is also some evidence to suggest that peer problems may be of prognostic significance, particularly when they occur in the context of a number of other problems in social development that seem to have an impact on the quality of interpersonal relationships in the family and beyond.

CHAPTER SEVEN

Treatment Approaches

So far I have discussed the nature of relatively common behavior problems manifest in the preschool period and have examined the complex relationships between family interaction patterns and child behavior. I also have discussed typical patterns of social development and contrasted them with atypical or problematic social behavior in the peer group and the family. The onset and early course of children's problems were also traced in illustrative cases. Although allusions were made to a variety of interventions, none was discussed in detail. In this chapter the major approaches to problem behavior in preschool children will be discussed and evaluated.

First, however, it is important to point out the surprising paucity of literature available on intervention with children of preschool age. Most descriptions of treatment focus on school-age children. Furthermore, studies that have evaluated the efficacy of traditional psychological treatments have concentrated almost exclusively on children of school age or older. Thus, recent controlled studies of psychotherapy outcome with children, with all their limitations (see Casey & Berman, 1985; Kovacs & Paulauskas, 1986; and Tuma & Sobotka, 1983, for reviews), have not considered the impact of traditional relationship building or psychodynamic approaches (including play therapy) with young children. Similarly, family therapy outcome studies have tended to focus on learning, behavioral, and psychosomatic difficulties experienced by children of elementary school age and adolescence (Alexander & Malouf, 1983; Masten, 1979). There are, however, three exceptions to this trend. Behavior modification programs, including parent training programs, are often geared to parents and their preschoolers as targets of behavior change. Primary prevention programs that emphasize social and emotional development and compensatory education programs that attempt to enhance cognitive and preacademic skills frequently focus on preschoolers and their parents because they aim to prevent the onset of problems or to ameliorate problems that are apparent in early childhood. Finally, a handful of studies have examined the impact of various therapeutic preschool programs for emotionally disturbed and/or developmentally delayed children.

These distinct strands in the therapy literature reflect a number of trends including referral patterns, the types of problems recognized and considered significant at different ages, and the tendency of traditionally oriented therapists to eschew research in general and the prescriptive approaches to treatment that are amenable to empirical scrutiny. As noted in Chapter Three, behavior problems in young children are less likely than those in older children to come to the attention of mental health professionals unless they are accompanied by severe developmental delay or profound social withdrawal, problems that do not lend themselves easily to traditional treatment approaches. When the more typical behavior problems, such as aggression, noncompliance, peer problems, or tantrums, do come to the attention of professionals, they are often dismissed as age-appropriate or as likely to be outgrown. When they are treated, problems such as these are most often dealt with using behavioral interventions because they are observable and often can be controlled, at least in the short term, with appropriately timed rewards and punishments. Prevention and early intervention programs that developed out of the Great Society perspective of the 1960s have, on the whole, produced some improvements in social and cognitive functioning (Clarke-Stewart & Fein, 1983). However, they have targeted groups of high risk children living in poverty in multiproblem families. Therapeutic preschool programs have been developed from a range of theoretical perspectives that run the gamut from structured behavioral programs, through more academically oriented programs, to those that derive from a traditional psychodynamic approach. The relative efficacy of these various types of preschool programs has not been evaluated systematically.

Regardless, children similar to Jamie and Annie, who were described in previous chapters, have tended to fall through the cracks. They are from intact and relatively well functioning families with adequate financial resources and the wherewithall to seek appropriate treatment, making them ineligible for many programs geared to young children. Furthermore, surprisingly little is published about what to do for such children or families, nor are there many resources available. Treatment programs that focus on the behavior problems of preschoolers from a broad perspective that includes family relationships are not readily available, especially if the preschooler is developing well intellectually. Thus, much of what I have suggested to parents and much of what is discussed in this chapter is based on common sense, knowledge of developmental processes and the developmental needs of young children, and on prior experience with school-age children and their families.

As pointed out by Kovacs and Paulauskas (1986), psychological treatment with children usually involves some combination of traditional psychotherapy, behavioral or cognitive-behavioral interventions, family therapy, and drug therapy. The choice of modality, or modalities, is determined primarily by the discipline and theoretical orientation of the clinician conducting the assessment, the nature of the setting (e.g., private practitioner, mental health clinic, pediatric setting), and the financial resources and motivation of the parents. A related issue is which family member, or members, is the focus of treatment. In traditional approaches the child receives therapy on a weekly or twice weekly basis, with parent guidance seen as an adjunct to the main treatment with the child; the problem is conceptualized as residing primarily within the child or in the child's ability to cope with environmental stress. Behavioral parent training, however, emphasizes work with the parents who are taught to change their ways of interacting with their child to change the child's behavior in the natural environment. In this framework the parents' ways of handling the child are identified as the target of change, and in many cases, the child may not even be seen. When children are included, it is usually to observe patterns of parent–child interaction to provide feedback to parents, and to assess outcome, rather than to include children as direct targets of intervention. In contrast, family approaches usually focus on the family system as a whole as the unit requiring change, although in some instances the marital dyad might be the target of intervention, even though the presenting complaints might emphasize problems in a child.

In this chapter the most commonly used treatment approaches are discussed briefly, with an emphasis on work with preschoolers and their families. The focus is on parent training, compensatory education, and therapeutic nursery schools. Parent training programs are discussed in detail because there is a good deal of information available on the efficacy of such programs with parents of young children. Primary prevention and compensatory education programs are examined because they have been carefully evaluated and because mental health workers who deal with families that do not fit into the category of "high risk" in the traditional sense have much to learn from the approaches used in some of these programs. The few studies that have examined therapeutic nursery schools are also discussed. Finally, I return to the case illustrations to highlight the various combinations of treatment approaches that may appear warranted in a particular instance and to evaluate efficacy from a clinical perspective.

Issues in Therapy with Preschool Children

From both a clinical and a research perspective, it is important to consider a number of issues when making recommendations for treatment and when evaluating the relative merits of various treatment approaches. Heinecke and Strassman (1975) point out that it is not meaningful to ask merely whether treatment with children is effective. Rather, one must start with the basic assumption that treatment can enhance development for some children under some circumstances. Thus, it is necessary to evaluate the relative effectiveness of specific treatments for particular problems in children of a given age, with a number of contextual factors considered simultaneously. Among the more obvious factors to consider are the developmental status of the child, the nature of the problem, the time of onset and severity of the problem, and existing family resources (Alexander & Malouf, 1983; Heinecke & Strassman, 1975; Kovacs & Paulauskas, 1986). A number of variables identified in previous chapters, such as family intactness, parental mental health, the quality of the marital relationship, parental motivation, and material resources, are important in determining whether therapy will be tried, what approach is most appropriate, and whether it will lead to change. Furthermore, as pointed out in Chapter Three, the diagnostician must make a clinical decision about whether the difficulties that led to referral are age-appropriate, normal variation, problems that are likely to reflect no more than a difficult developmental transition or transitory reaction to stress, or problems that appear more serious and are likely either to persist or to lead to other problems as development proceeds. In addition, even if the problems are deemed to be age-appropriate or transitory manifestations of a stressful developmental transition, assessment may suggest that work with the family is in order. For example, in some cases, it may seem necessary to educate parents about development to help them understand the likely reasons for their child's age-appropriate but upsetting behavior; in others, it may seem important to modify parents' expectations and strategies of child rearing; in some instances, it may be necessary to deal with hidden issues, such as marital distress, that may have led to dysfunctional family relationships and consequent discomfort, with the focus inappropriately on the child's problems.

Treatment recommendations for parents and preschoolers must make the child's developmental level and more immediate psychological needs a central consideration. Thus, psychodynamic treatment approaches that tend to be long-term and to focus on intrapsychic change, personality reorganization, or the resolution of unconscious conflict may be less relevant to the problems of preschoolers than treatment modalities that deal with the child in the here and now, are relatively structured and goal-oriented, and emphasize the child's problems within a family and social context. Because preschoolers are so dependent upon family members and other caregivers, treatments focused only on the child seem misdirected; changes in the caretaking environment will usually be necessary to bring about changes in the child.

Harter (1983b) has conducted a theoretical analysis of the cognitive-developmental limitations of preschoolers, suggesting a number of reasons why traditional psychodynamic approaches to treatment seem inappropriate. Taking a Piagetian perspective, she concurs with Selman (1980) and argues that the cognitive-developmental functioning of preschoolers is characterized by relatively concrete, egocentric, and nonreflective thought. Furthermore, because preschoolers have only a limited recognition of the range of human emotions, more abstract, insight-oriented, and cognitive techniques would not be expected to be effective with this age group. For example, if preschoolers have not yet developed the self-consciousness or self-reflective capacities to be able to recognize their own problem behavior, to identify and label complex emotions in themselves or others, or to understand and reason about their own motivations, it would not be reasonable to assume that therapeutic techniques that rely on self-reflection and the understanding of the meaning of one's own behavior would be successful. Harter also suggests that traditional free association is hindered by the tendency of preschoolers to confuse fantasy and reality, thus causing some youngsters to stifle frightening thoughts. She proposes that egocentric thinking and prelogical thought interfere with the ability of preschoolers to comprehend interpretations because they have difficulty accepting the therapist's view of events and are unable to make the complex links necessary to integrate the therapist's interpretation of events with happenings in their daily lives.

Harter's work also suggests that young children have difficulty recognizing the simultaneous presence of two emotions, particularly contradictory ones, thus making it difficult for them to deal with ambivalent feelings toward others. She proposes that emotion recognition in self and others develops through a sequence of levels from concrete and egocentric to more complex, abstract, and other-oriented, similar to levels proposed by Selman (1980, 1981) in his discussion of the development of friendship concepts and interpersonal understanding. Similarly, according to this view, young children have difficulty conceptualizing latent or hidden feelings, nor do they clearly differentiate between their own feelings and those of parents during the preschool years. In addition, preschoolers do not yet have a clearly developed sense of self or of self-esteem because they tend to think in terms of concrete attributes of persons, such as gender or size, rather than in terms of abstract psychological attributes. Finally, preschoolers cannot grasp the notion of a therapeutic relationship because they do not conceptualize helping and trust in the same way as adults or older children do (Kovacs & Paulauskas, 1986).

Much of this analysis makes sense, but it also may underestimate the capabilities of young children, at least insofar as their ability to identify some salient emotions and to have some rudimentary notions of their causes. Furthermore, it is important to distinguish between the capacities that young children exhibit in social interaction and their abilities to step back and reflect upon their behavior and its meaning. Although it is not likely that preschoolers can engage in metacognition (thinking about mental processes) or recursive thinking (thinking about other people's thoughts about themselves), it is not known which, if any, of these cognitive capacities is a necessary ingredient of therapeutic change. Indeed, many adults probably never develop to Selman's higher levels of social reasoning. The relationship between these levels of reasoning and the ability of individuals of any age to profit from a therapeutic relationship requires study in its own right. Support and respect from a caring adult may have an impact on a child's sense of self-esteem (e.g., Bretherton, 1985), independent of more sophisticated analyses of relationships. Thus, a cognitive-developmental analysis of the limitations of dynamic therapies raises many of the same issues that confront the developmentalist trying to integrate children's overt behavior with their verbal understanding of internal cognitive and affective processes, as well as interpersonal relationships. This is clearly an area worthy of further research.

Cognitive-behavioral techniques that have as their goal cognitive restructuring or training in problem-solving strategies also are probably beyond the grasp of most preschoolers (Cohen et al., 1981), given their limited tendency to reflect spontaneously upon their thought processes, their decision-making style, or the impact of their behavior on themselves or others. However, independent of these potential cognitive-developmental limitations, the importance of interventions that include other members of the family and/or the wider social environment appears obvious. The extant literature suggests that structured techniques that modify parenting strategies and provide parents with improved management skills and information about children's developmental needs appear to have particular promise. Before discussing these approaches, several common approaches to intervention are described briefly.

Therapeutic Models and Levels of Analysis

Therapeutic approaches have been classified by Alexander and Malouf (1983) in terms of etiological formulations, the goals of intervention, and the level at which intervention occurs. Thus, they distinguish among biological models, intrapsychic and cognitive processing models that emphasize individual internal (conscious and/or unconscious) processes, learning theory models that focus on overt behaviors, interactional or family systems models that stress relationships, and sociocultural models that focus on broader social forces. This seems a useful scheme for conceptualizing major approaches, although those that appear to have the most promise for work with preschoolers and their families tend to cut across these levels of analysis or to target several levels simultaneously.

Until recently, only the traditional psychodynamic approaches had anything resembling a developmental perspective (Alexander & Malouf, 1983). Whereas the orthodox Freudian focus on unconscious conflicts, psychosexual development, and fixation and regression (e.g., Klein,

1932) is relatively out of synchrony with recent advances in developmental theory, ego-analytic and object relations theories have had a major impact on developmental formulations of attachment and peer relations (e.g., Bowlby, 1969; Mahler, 1968; Sullivan, 1953). Although these theories have not spawned systematic interventions for preschoolers that have been evaluated empirically, some of these ideas have been incorporated into relatively eclectic dynamic interventions (e.g., Fraiberg, 1980). Biological approaches to treatment recognize maturational influences on development, but psychosocial developmental factors and their interaction with biological processes tend to be ignored. Family systems theories include notions of family development, but individual needs and developmental trajectories do not figure prominently, at least explicitly, although therapeutic interventions are generally tailored to be consistent with children's developmental levels and competencies. Behavioral parent training programs have recently been broadened to incorporate a more developmentally informed view (Eyberg, 1987) and to consider bidirectional influences (Patterson, 1980). Factors in the wider social environment (Dumas & Wahler, 1985; Wahler, 1980) must also be taken into account when designing programs and evaluating outcome.

Biological Approaches

At the most basic level, biological models of psychopathology rest on the assumption that physiological or neurological dysfunctions underlie aberrant behavior and that, to be useful, treatments must alter faulty biological mechanisms. Despite this assumption, however, the actual "disease process" underlying most behavior disorders is not known. The pharmacotherapy revolution reflects the current biological trend in psychiatry. In the child mental health field virtually thousands of studies have examined the use of various psychotropic medications with school-age and adolescent children diagnosed as showing attention deficit disorder, depression, anxiety, and a range of other problems in psychosocial adjustment (Alexander & Malouf, 1983; Gittelman & Kanner, 1986). Although the effectiveness of particular medications, most notably the impact of the stimulants on hyperactive children, has been well documented, little is understood about the nature of drug effects, their modes of action, or their long-term impact on biological functioning or psychological development. Thus, although some practitioners believe that stimulant medication is the treatment of choice for hyperactive children, the use of behavior modifying drugs with very young children would appear to be especially ill-advised given our limited knowledge of their effects on growth and development. Furthermore, the few studies that have examined the use of methylphenidate (Ritalin) with preschool hyperactive children have suggested that negative side effects outweigh positive changes in behavior (see Campbell, 1985). Finally, even in older children, medication is only effective, in the long term, when combined with other treatments that focus on child-rearing practices and family interaction patterns.

Modifications of diet have also received a good deal of attention, primarily in the lay press and from parents. Feingold (1975), whose diet has received the most attention, has argued that allergies to particular foods and food additives are a main cause of hyperactivity and related behavior problems in children and that dietary changes can lead to dramatic improvements in the behavior of many hyperactive children. However, controlled studies of the impact of food additives on behavior (Conners, 1980) have not substantiated these claims. In a review of controlled diet studies, Kavale and Forness (1983) concluded that the therapeutic effects of dietary treatments for hyperactivity and related disorders are negligible. Conners (1980) notes that although some small proportion of children, especially young children, may be especially sensitive to particular foods and that these sensitivities may be reflected in behavior problems, the positive effect publicized widely by Feingold is the exception, not the rule.

Increased sugar consumption has also been proposed as a cause of attentional problems and self-control deficits (e.g., Conners, 1984), and similar to food allergies, the role of sugar consumption in the development of behavior problems is accepted relatively uncritically, based on clinical anecdotes, by many parents and pediatricians (Bennett & Sherman, 1983). Milich, Woolraich and Lindgren (1986) critically reviewed the empirical studies assessing this question and concluded that the evidence, on the whole, did not support the contention that sugar intake was associated with hyperactivity or other behavior problems. They did acknowledge, however, in line with the food additive data, that a small subgroup of younger children may be especially sensitive to the effects of increased sugar consumption; they also stressed the need for more research documenting a causal link between sugar and behavior before alternative explanations can be ruled out. In general, then, dietary approaches to treatment of young children's behavior problems have not gained much credence in the mental health community. Rather, reliance on dietary changes as the primary treatment for behavior problems may be one convenient way to avoid coming to grips with relationship problems or ineffective child-rearing practices that are more difficult to change.

Intrapsychic and Cognitive Processing Approaches

Intrapsychic or traditional psychodynamic approaches to treatment focus on changing personality organization, resolving unconscious conflicts, or otherwise changing intraindividual mental processes that are not observable or easily operationalized. Although most practicing child clinical psychologists identify themselves as psychodynamic in orientation (Tuma & Sobotka, 1983), as already noted, there is very little in the way of systematic research that evaluates the efficacy of the many approaches that fall under this rubric. The few studies that do exist are poorly designed and do not meet basic standards for empirical research on therapy outcome (see Hartmann, Roper, & Gelfand, 1977, and Kovacs & Paulauskas, 1986, for discussions of these issues, which are beyond the scope of this chapter). In addition, studies have not considered the impact of therapy on children younger than 6 years. Furthermore, the relevance of these approaches to the problems of young children can be questioned, as noted earlier. Thus, not much space will be devoted to them.

Because, as discussed earlier, it is unclear to what degree pre-schoolers can conceptualize problem behavior, verbalize directly about problems or concerns, or understand the meaning of a therapeutic relationship, traditional therapeutic approaches tend to rely on play as the medium of expression that is most natural and comfortable for young children. Although the therapeutic relationship is seen as central, as is the establishment of an accepting environment in which conflicts, concerns, and worries can be expressed, the therapist facilitates the child's expression through play, either as playmate or participant observer, and intervenes little in the child's life beyond the protected environment of the playroom. This is in contrast to most other approaches in which the therapist intervenes directly in the child's family environment, either with specific suggestions about changes in parental behavior or with more subtle attempts to change parental attitudes. Play therapy approaches run the gamut from nondirective play therapy as exemplified in the work of Axline (1969), in which the supportive environment is seen as facilitating development and helping the child to reach his/her potential through the expression of feelings and the resolution of conflicts, to more psychoanalytic approaches in which interpretation of the play is seen as central to change (e.g., Klein, 1932). Despite the intuitive appeal and wide use of play techniques, controlled studies on the effectiveness of play therapy with clinically identified preschoolers are lacking. The reader interested in more detailed discussion of the various schools of play therapy is referred to Schaefer and O'Conner (1983).

More recently, a rapprochement between operant behavior approaches and those that focus on internal processes has evolved and a range of techniques called cognitive behavioral have been developed. The aim of these approaches is to utilize the rational, thinking side of the personality and to influence the way people interpret events and react to them, giving them some cognitive control over thoughts and feelings. Whereas various cognitive approaches have been moderately effective with school-age children (Urbain & Kendall, 1980), young children appear to be less amenable to these techniques, given their level of cognitive development. In particular, the cognitive approaches used with children involve reflecting on their own cognitive processes (e.g., attention, impulse control, decision making) as well as on the impact of their behavior on others (consequential thinking). Preschoolers appear to have difficulty stepping back to think about these internal processes. Also, although as their perspective-taking abilities develop, preschoolers are beginning to become more aware of the effects of their behavior on others, it is unlikely that specific training in cognitive restructuring or in the reinterpretation of ongoing events will generalize to influence their behavior in the natural environment.

Modifying Overt Behavior

Behavioral approaches that target and modify overt behaviors have been utilized with children of all ages for the past 20 years. Scores of studies have demonstrated that learning principles can be employed to change children's behavior (see Devany & Nelson, 1986, and Hobbs & Lahey, 1983, for recent reviews). Thus, it has been demonstrated that troublesome behaviors such as tantrums, aggression toward peers, noncompliance with requests, and social withdrawal can be modified when rewards (either social or tangible) are given for appropriate behavior and withheld for inappropriate behavior (e.g., time out, withdrawal of privileges) or when appropriate behavior is modeled and reinforced. Methods such as time out, the use of contingent praise, and the use of tangible rewards such as toys or treats for good behavior are used almost routinely in many preschool and day-care centers, and many parents, across a range of educational levels, employ behavioral approaches when setting limits on their children.

Much of the empirical work in this area has focused on training parents to be more effective in setting consistent and predictable limits on their children's behavior. Earlier outcome studies, based on strict operant conditioning procedures, indicated that formal treatments showed short-term effectiveness with behavior disordered preschoolers but that gains did not automatically generalize to other behaviors or were not maintained consistently after treatment ended (Alexander & Malouf, 1983; Eyberg, 1987). This early work derived from a strict learning theory view in which behavior change was conceptualized in mechanistic terms and was seen as deriving solely from the child's learning history defined in terms of environmental contingencies. Such a unidirectional view is inconsistent with most current thinking in the field of child development or child psychopathology. Furthermore, the developmental level of the child was not considered routinely; consequently, the meaning of the parent-identified behavior was not placed in a developmental context. Thus, exploratory behavior ("getting into everything"), age-appropriate defiance and testing, or bed-wetting might have been targeted for change if it was annoying to the parent who sought treatment, although the behavior in question might well have been developmentally appropriate or even an important expression of a developmental issue.

In line with recent theoretical advances, the focus of many parent training programs has been narrowed to emphasize a particular age range and broadened to consider the behavior from a developmental point of view (Eyberg, 1987). Programs also have been expanded to incorporate a systems view of the family and, therefore, to address more general family interaction processes that may influence the ability of parents to appropriately implement and follow through on behavior management programs for noncompliant and aggressive children (Brody & Forehand, 1985; Dadds, Schwartz, & Sanders, 1987; Webster-Stratton, 1985). Some therapists have attempted to build in experiences to promote generalization across settings (Sanders & Christensen,

1985); still others have added educational components aimed at improving parents' understanding of normal developmental processes, in an attempt to change parents' cognitions about the meaning of a particular behavior at a specific development period. Programs may focus on the parent–child relationship by teaching parents more appropriate and responsive ways of interacting with their preschooler (Eyberg, 1987). Thus, behavioral parent training programs now are likely to include both didactic information about the use of rewards and punishments and components that are more characteristic of relational and/or cognitive restructuring approaches to treatment. Several of these are discussed in detail later on in this chapter.

Interactional or Family Systems Models

Whereas family systems models run the gamut from those that emphasize symbolic processes to those that stress overt behavior patterns, family interactional or systems models all focus on interpersonal rather than intrapsychic processes. Although one family member, most often a child, may be identified as the problem, from this perspective, the problem lies within the family and the child's symptoms have functional significance for the family as a whole. Thus, family therapists examine, among other issues, intergenerational boundaries, family alliances, the structure and nature of relationships within the family, whether particular family members are isolates, how power is distributed, and how decisions are made. From a systems perspective, symptoms are seen as maintaining some form of equilibrium within the family, even though it may be dysfunctional. For instance, an oppositional and defiant preschooler may be seen as removing the focus from marital problems and thereby allowing the parents to avoid dealing with a more threatening problem, or anger toward the spouse may be expressed primarily through disagreements over child rearing, which are then reflected in child misbehavior. Children's problems also may serve to keep extended family members such as grandparents involved in child care or other aspects of family functioning, leading to blurred boundaries across generations and often placing decision making in the hands of nonnuclear family members (see Alexander & Malouf, 1983; Haley, 1976; Minuchin, 1974). Parents may successfully avoid interaction and intimacy by focusing all their attention and energy on a difficult preschooler, or a mother who is overinvolved with her child may use problem behaviors as a rationale to avoid the separation experiences associated with preschool entry. In each of these examples, the child's behavior serves other needs within the family system. Indeed, although a particular child in the family may be identified as the problem member, there is evidence that parent-referred children do not always differ from nonreferred siblings (Patterson, 1980) or from unrelated controls (Lobitz & Johnson, 1975). Furthermore, from a family systems view, it may be argued that behavioral approaches that merely attempt to modify the symptomatic behavior in the problem child are likely to fail if other aspects of the family system are not also considered during treatment. Some family systems theorists (e.g., Framo, 1975) argue that child behavior problems are inevitably associated with marital dysfunction, although studies indicate that this is not the case (Dadds et al., 1987).

Family systems approaches appear promising and there is accumulating evidence of their efficacy with school-age and adolescent children and their families (Alexander & Malouf, 1983), although the effectiveness of only the more behaviorally oriented family treatment techniques has been evaluated systematically. As noted earlier, no controlled studies have examined the efficacy of family therapy when the referral problem focuses on preschool children's behavior difficulties. It seems clear from some of the cases described earlier that family problems are indeed an important component of the child's ongoing difficulties. More work in this area is clearly warranted.

Sociocultural or Community Interventions

The approaches discussed thus far focus on children and/or families. However, efforts also have been directed at larger units including communities or particular groups within the population. In general, these programs fall under the rubric either of primary prevention or early intervention, rather than treatment in the traditional sense. These programs tend to be tied more closely to political viewpoints and social policy initiatives than to the mental health community, although mental health institutions such as community mental health centers derived from the prevention focus (Winett, Stefanek, & Riley, 1983) that grew out of the Great Society programs of the 1960s and 1970s. Prevention efforts emphasize enhancing development in young children (Alexander & Malouf, 1983; Peterson & Roberts, 1986). Thus, community intervention or prevention programs are based on the premise that the well-being of children and families can be improved through a range of programs that target health, nutrition, work and living conditions, and family life, as well as cognitive and social development (Winett et al., 1983). As noted by Peterson and Roberts (1986), community programs tend to focus on enhancing competencies and adaptive functioning, while deemphasizing psychopathology. Rather, it is assumed that appropriate interventions, timed at crucial periods of development or provided to particular groups who may be at risk, will serve to prevent problems and, thus, the need for more costly treatments that are focused on psychological maladaptation.

Interventions as diverse as nutritional supplements for infants and mothers, "Sesame Street," and vaccinations are all based on notions of prevention, although they target different levels of functioning and different subgroups of the population. In general, community prevention programs occur at the level of a social system, such as the preschool or day-care center, the community clinic, or the neighborhood, and they are focused on large numbers of children, rather than on a few who are specifically referred once a problem has been identified. Early intervention programs, such as Head Start identify high risk groups who are then eligible for the program. Thus, although all or most 3- and 4 year olds may benefit from preschool attendance, the specialized curricula designed for children living in poverty are not necessary for middle class children living with educated parents in stable families. Although Head Start and other compensatory education programs for low income children have been criticized as hastily conceived, inadequate, and costly (Winett et al., 1983), there is convincing evidence that many of these programs have a positive impact on cognitive and social development, whereas some long-term follow-up studies suggest that a range of gains in social and academic functioning are maintained (e.g., Lazar & Darlington, 1982). Several early intervention and primary prevention programs for preschoolers are discussed next in more detail.

Therapeutic Approaches for Preschool Children

Although it appears useful to examine treatments from the perspective of models and levels of analysis, as already noted, the lines between these various treatment approaches are becoming increasingly blurred. As models of development become more complex and as more and more data underline the importance of family and social context variables in understanding children's development, both normal and abnormal, therapeutic approaches have become less doctrinaire and more eclectic. Thus, the therapeutic preschool programs, parent training approaches, and primary prevention programs to be discussed next focus on the child and family from more than one perspective. Thus, they may combine behavior management with educational intervention or family treatment. Furthermore, some systematic attempt is made to evaluate outcome using objective measures of behavior change.

Therapeutic Preschool Programs

Although therapeutic preschool programs are often prescribed for young children with behavioral and/or developmental problems, there is a lack of systematic research on their effectiveness. Therapeutic preschools, similar to several of the other approaches to treatment that have been discussed, tend to vary widely in philosophy, theoretical orientation, focus, and degree of parental involvement. They may have little in common except that the children tend to be seen for more than the one hour per week, which is typical of many treatment programs, and they are seen in groups of same-age peers. Programs that derive from a psychodynamic framework are often relatively unstructured play therapy groups in which the goal is helping the child to express feelings and conflicts. As in individual therapy, the therapist may interpret the child's play, and the symbolic meaning of the play is seen as central to understanding the child's problems. The children's interactions with peers may also be a focus of the therapy. Parent groups or individual meetings with the parent usually supplement preschool attendance and the attempt is made to provide general support and guidance for the parents in understanding and dealing with their child's difficulties, although concrete advice is not often given. Other programs may be more structured and didactic, with a focus on children's cognitive and language development, and the ability to get along with other children. More structured programs may or may not incorporate behavioral procedures, such as time out and rewards for good behavior. The nature and amount of parental involvement will also vary. Furthermore, some programs combine problem children and normal children in the same program, whereas others only include children with difficulties.

In general, therapeutic preschool programs have not been evaluated empirically; when they have, investigators have relied primarily on case studies and clinical impressions to assess improvement. Cohen, Bradley, and Kolers (1987) suggested recently that this lack of systematic evaluation partly reflects the psychodynamic orientation of many preschool treatment programs, which, as noted earlier, tends not to be associated with rigorous, controlled assessments of outcome. Cohen et al. also suggested that the heterogeneity of both children and treatments does not lend itself to the design of outcome studies. Because programs are often developed to meet the individual needs of particular children, it is difficult to conduct research that evaluates the efficacy of specific aspects of treatment. Furthermore, children with a range of cognitive and socioemotional problems are often treated together and outcome measures are rarely comprehensive, making interpretation of negative findings difficult. Thus, it is not surprising that little is known about which preschool-based treatments are most effective for which children.

Only three studies have systematically examined the effectiveness of a multifocused therapeutic preschool program with clinically referred, nonautistic, behavior-disordered children. Anderson, Long, Leathers, Denny, and Hilliard (1981) assessed the impact of a comprehensive day treatment program on the behavior of a small group ($n - 23$) of low socioeconomic status (SES) children, ages 3 to 6, with behavior problems. Five girls and eight boys were described as anxious and withdrawn; nine boys and one girl were described as aggressive. Treatment consisted of a half-day therapeutic program and a half-day of preschool in which children were integrated into a regular nursery school setting. Children were seen five times a week for an average of 17 months. The program was structured, focusing on preacademic skills and social development. In addition, parents were seen weekly for work on parenting skills and the provision of emotional support. Outcome was assessed by the teachers themselves who completed behavioral rating scales describing children's behavior at the start and completion of treatment. Although, not surprisingly, most children were rated as improved, anxious and withdrawn children were more likely than aggressive children to be rated as improved by teachers. Although this study suffers from serious methodological flaws including nonblind and biased assessments of change, the lack of a comparison group, and the use of a very limited assessment instrument, it is noteworthy that teacher ratings suggest a differential response to treatment, especially in view of the length and intensity of the program.

Woollacott, Graham, and Stevenson (1978) assessed the impact of a relatively unstructured mother–child treatment program provided for 25 2$\frac{1}{2}$- to 3$\frac{1}{2}$-year-olds. Treated children were compared with demographically matched untreated children from an epidemiological study of young children's behavior problems. Although parent reports of behavior problems pretreatment indicated that the groups showed comparable difficulties (discipline problems, separation anxiety, developmental delay), the treated group had more serious problems as well as more frequent separation experiences associated with hospitalization. Mothers and children attended the year-long treatment program for 5 hours per day once or twice per week. The goals of the mother–child treatment included improving mother–child communication and helping mothers become more aware of their children's emotional needs and developmental levels. In addition to these combined sessions, mothers attended parent support groups and also had the opportunity to meet individually with the social worker. Despite the intensity of treatment and the combined focus on maternal needs and child problems, maternal reports of improvement were comparable for the treated and untreated groups 1 year later, at the conclusion of treatment. However, the lack of more comprehensive and objective assessments of change are a major drawback of this study because it is known that women who seek treatment for their young children are often more depressed and anxious and perceive their children more negatively than comparable groups of mothers who do not seek help (Gath, 1968; Shepherd, Oppenheim, & Mitchell, 1971). In addition, although this treatment regimen was intense, it was also unstructured, and the lack of focused educational or skill-building components for either children or mothers may account for the poor results. Furthermore, lack of paternal involvement in treatment as well as failure to consider family issues may have undermined treatment efficacy.

The work of Cohen and her colleagues (Cohen et al., 1987) improves immeasurably upon these earlier studies. These investigators examined the efficacy of a comprehensive day treatment program for emotionally disturbed and developmentally delayed 3- to 6-year-olds. Assessment data were obtained from both parents and teachers; the children were administered tests of cognitive and language functioning prior to the start of treatment, after 8 months of treatment, and at discharge. Treated children were compared with a demographically matched group of children attending local day-care centers. Children in the clinical group attended the program for half a day five times per week for 1 to 2 years. Individualized cognitive, language, and social activities were designed by a multidisciplinary team of mental health workers and educators. In addition to building cognitive, language, and social competence, goals included limiting disruptive and aggressive behavior, helping the children to become active participants in the peer group, and encouraging the verbal expression of feelings. Parents were expected to work with their children in the playroom setting. They also had regular contact with a social worker.

Results were examined for subgroups of children with different presenting complaints: developmentally delayed children, language-delayed children, and behavior-disordered children. All the delayed children were also socially withdrawn, and approximately 25% also showed problems of undercontrol. The behavior-disordered children were of average intelligence and were more likely than those in the other two groups to come from single-parent families. One half of the day-care attenders (comparison group) likewise were from single-parent households. Children in the developmentally delayed groups made the greatest gains in both cognitive and language functioning and in teacher-rated behavior, although they did not reach the level of the comparison group on cognitive measures. Improvement was most noticeable after 8 or 9 months in the program. Although teacher ratings did not indicate that the behavior problem group showed significant gains in social competence or behavioral control, parents rated their behavior problem children as showing fewer problems, both internalizing and externalizing, at both posttest assessments. Cohen et al. (1987) conclude that day treatment programs are most effective for children with developmental delays who are especially helped by a structured cognitive and language intervention, provided it is sufficiently intense and prolonged. The effectiveness of the program for behaviorally disordered children who were not also delayed is less apparent from the data obtained. They also note that family motivation contributed significantly to outcome and that the families of the behavior-disordered children were most difficult to engage. However, the program did not appear to provide parents with focused ways of dealing with disruptive and noncompliant behavior, nor is it clear what teachers did to facilitate change in behavior. It is likely that a structured program focused on behavioral control and prosocial interaction with peers and also paired with comprehensive parent training would be more effective with behavior-disordered preschoolers.

Parent Training Programs

As noted earlier, parent training programs are among the most promising and widely used interventions for behavior problems in preschoolers. Most recent reviews of child-focused treatment are relatively enthusiastic about the impact of parent training on a variety of child problems including aggression and noncompliance in children across a wide age range (Alexander & Malouf, 1983; Hobbs & Lahey, 1983; Kazdin, 1987), although these authors also note the inconsistencies in the literature. Weisz, Weiss, Alicke, and Klotz (1987) conclude that behavioral parent training programs tend to be more effective and long-lasting with younger than older children. However, Eyberg (1987) is the only author to address the impact of parent training programs on behavior problems in preschoolers specifically, and she concludes that all programs are not equally effective. Eyberg (1987), Kazdin (1987), and others (e.g., Dadds et al., 1987) emphasize both program characteristics and family factors that are associated with treatment follow through, treatment efficacy, and maintenance of treatment effects. Programs with the most general effects on parent–child interaction and the most long-term efficacy, assessed specifically in samples of preschoolers, go beyond strict operant training in reinforcement contingencies and the use of time out and deal, as well, with other aspects of family functioning. These successful programs all teach parents to use contingent and descriptive praise, to ignore annoying behaviors, to decrease criticism and vague commands, and to use time out for destructive, aggressive, and noncompliant behavior (e.g., Dadds et al., 1987; Eyberg & Robinson, 1982; Webster-Stratton, 1985). However, they vary on several dimensions, including group versus individual administration, the presence or absence of the child during treatment sessions, the length of treatment, paternal involvement, and the use of other treatments, in addition to the behavior management training.

In our own work, we utilized a program that combined a standard behavioral parent training program (Becker, 1971) with didactic information about normal development in late toddlerhood and the preschool period. Parents met for eight 2-hour sessions in small groups of four to eight parents. Both the behavioral training only group and the behavioral-developmental group targeted specific behaviors for change and did weekly homework assignments. The developmental portion of the curriculum focused on issues, such as developing autonomy and independence, development of self-help skills, learning to express and control emotions, enhancing peer relations, and balancing parental needs with children's needs. The rationale for this approach was that parents needed to understand and be aware of developmental issues and transition points to change their children's behavior effectively and appropriately. It was also reasoned that parents would become more tolerant of age-appropriate behavior if they could see it from a developmental perspective. Only one half of the parents in the problem group were interested in group participation, suggesting differences in motivation. Eight were assigned to each treatment and seven served as waiting list controls. At posttest there was no consistent group differences as a function of treatment, in either parent report or observational measures, although consumer satisfaction was high. Furthermore, at the 1-year follow-up, treated and untreated groups did not differ. These disappointing results may reflect the small sample size and the insensitivity of some of the measures to change in parental behavior. In addition, the information on development, although it elicited a good deal of parental discussion, may have been too general and abstract to lead to changes in parental behaviors or expectations. A review of the literature indicates that treatments that provide more direct supervision and feedback to parents as they interact with their children appear more promising.

An interesting and effective approach to parent training was developed recently by Sanders and Christensen (1985). They compared the effectiveness of a regular parent training program conducted in the home with parent training combined with planned activities training. Children (mean age = 4 years) had been referred for oppositional behavior. Ten families were assigned randomly to each treatment. The parent training given to all parents included teaching them to prompt and praise appropriate behavior, to give clear instructions and commands, to ignore irritating behavior, and to use time out for aggression and noncompliance. Parents were observed with their children at home and given feedback on their own behavior. Parents in the planned activities condition were also given a generalized set of problem-solving strategies to use in situations such as shopping trips, birthday parties, visits, and car rides, situations that are often stressful for families with preschool children. Parents learned how to prepare children for upcoming events, to plan activities meant to avoid conflict, and to state expectations for good behavior explicitly beforehand. These skills were modeled by the therapist, role played by parents, and coached. Both the parent training and the planned activities treatments were effective as indexed by observations obtained at home during breakfast, structured parent–child play, bathtime, and bedtime. Moreover, at a 3-month follow-up, therapy gains were maintained. Indeed, children and their parents did not differ from a nonreferred comparison group. The observations, modeling, and feedback appear to be attractive features of this program, as is the selection of situations about which parents complain frequently.

Webster-Stratton (1984) and Eyberg and Robinson (1982) have used an approach that combines training in operant child management methods as outlined above with training in more general ways of interacting sensitively and positively. Such a combined approach makes sense from several vantage points. Research on children's socialization indicates that qualitative features of the mother–child interaction, particularly positivity and warmth, are associated with general compliance and a willingness to comply (see Chapter Four). Mutual expectations and the relationship history appear central. Thus, it may not be that helpful to modify specific disciplinary practices if more general qualitative aspects of the mother–child relationship are not changed as well. Second, work by Dumas and Wahler (1985) indicates that in troubled mother–preschool child dyads, mothers often respond indiscriminately to children's behavior, with positive, negative, or neutral behavior occurring independent of the child's antecedent behavior. Moreover, these mothers exhibit high rates of negative and unsupportive behavior, which tends to fuel child noncompliance and attention seeking. It appears that a poor relationship has developed in these dyads and that the children have learned that interaction with their mothers is basically unrewarding. Third, this formulation of parent training that targets both specific parenting behaviors and more qualitative aspects of the relationship is congruent with clinical experience and the formulation of the problems of many young children, as illustrated by Annie and her mother who were described earlier.

Webster-Stratton (1984) compared parent training groups that involved videotaped modeling and discussion of the principles of child management and relationship building with an individual treatment regimen in which the mother, child, and therapist met weekly. Both groups were seen for approximately 16 hours of treatment. Both treatment methods were compared with a no treatment, waiting list control group. Children were referred because of oppositional behavior and ranged in age from 3 to 8 years (mean = 4 years, 8 months). Both treatment groups made considerable gains, relative to controls, as reflected in maternal ratings of child behavior and observations of mother–child interaction. Mothers used more praise and less criticism after treatment, and children were less noncompliant and negative. Treatment gains were maintained at a 1-year follow-up. Webster-Stratton suggests that the group experience may have been effective because it served as a support for mothers and because the modeling and discussion of a range of problems may have facilitated generalization.

Eyberg and Robinson (1982) emphasize the impact of treatment on interaction patterns within the family, and they suggest that strengthening the parent–child relationship leads to broader and more long-term effects on family functioning. Parents (three couples, four single mothers) and seven children (mean age = 4 years 11 months) who were referred because of a range of externalizing problems including disobedience, aggression, destructiveness, hyperactivity, and tantrums were seen in individual treatment sessions of approximately 1 hour per week for 9 weeks. Treatment included observations of parent–child interaction, followed by explanations, modeling, coaching of more appropriate behavior, and feedback. The relationship enhancing portion of treatment included teaching the parents active listening, as well as appropriate responsiveness to their children's initiations and verbalizations, the ability to follow their children's lead in a nondirective play situation, and the provision of emotional support. This was followed by training in more typical child management skills, including contingent and consistent praise, ignoring and not criticizing, and the use of time out. Parent report and observational measures indicated changes in the behavior of both parents and children at the completion of treatment. Moreover, parenting skills had generalized to untreated siblings who were also observed to be more compliant at the end of treatment.

The role of father involvement in treatment was examined by Webster-Stratton (1985) using this approach. Parents and their oppositional children (mean age = 60 months) participated in treatment. One group consisted of 18 two-parent families (several included boyfriends or stepfathers, but all fathers or father surrogates were involved in child care and attended most treatment sessions) and the other of 12 father-absent families. Although both groups of mothers made significant changes and gains were maintained at a 1-year follow-up, women whose spouses or boyfriends participated in treatment were more positive with their children who in turn were more compliant. Moreover, significantly more two-parent families were classified as responders based on their overall response to treatment, whereas single mothers were more likely to be nonresponders. These findings underline the importance of support from a close family member in facilitating changes in parenting practices. However, it is unclear from this study whether father involvement directly influenced child behavior because fathers changed their child-rearing strategies and/or increased their involvement in child rearing, whether fathers' presence in treatment served to encourage mothers to modify their behavior toward their children, whether fathers' presence had a more general and indirect but supportive effect on mothers that facilitated change, or whether some combination of these factors accounts for the findings.

The role of father involvement in treatment may also be related to the quality of the marital relationship because it has been suggested that marital discord may interfere with successful parent training. Persistent conflict between parents would be expected to undermine the ability of parents to work together and provide consistent limits on and rewards for child behavior. This is in line with clinical impression and with the literature on the relationship between child conduct disorders and marital problems (see Chapter Four and Emery, 1982). Dadds et al. (1987) assessed the combined effects of parent management training and partner support training in couples with a preschool child showing oppositional behavior. One half of the couples had reported that they were satisfied with their marriages and one half reported significant levels of marital distress. One half of the maritally distressed couples and one half of the maritally satisfied couples were randomly assigned to parent management training alone, while the remaining couples received parent management training paired with partner support. Parent training included instruction in the home using contingent praise and time out, as well as generalization training to stressful situations, such as bedtime and shopping, which was described earlier. Couples in the partner support treatment also learned to work together to solve problems and to provide each other with mutual support. Although parents in all groups were more effective with their children posttreatment, the maritally distressed group who did not receive partner support training did not maintain these gains at a 6-month follow-up. Dadds et al. (1987) note that aversive interaction between parents is associated with concurrent child misbehavior. Furthermore, fathers in the parent support training were more likely to participate in child care. This suggests mutual and bidirectional influences among improved parent communication, decreased stress and resentment, and improved parenting skills. However, more research will be required before the active ingredients of these programs and their mutual interactions can be delineated. It is worth emphasizing that these authors point out that their marital intervention is designed only as an adjunct to parent training and that in more severely distressed couples, more intense systems therapy may be indicated.

Taken together, these studies indicate that broad-based parent training approaches that take into account other aspects of family relationships and also involve direct observations of parent–child interaction or at least include role playing, coaching, and feedback have the most obvious impact on the child and family and are most likely to lead to changes that are maintained at follow-up. In addition, it appears that families living under more stressful conditions or parents who feel less supported socially and emotionally may be either less able to follow through with treatment initially or less able to maintain gains once treatment is over. This was true for the single-parent mothers in the Webster-Stratton (1985) study and the maritally discordant families followed by Dadds et al. (1987). Other studies likewise indicate that factors outside the parent–child dyad influence willingness to seek treatment and treatment response. These include family composition (Webster-Stratton, 1985), father involvement and support for treatment, social support (Dumas & Wahler, 1983, Wahler, 1980), and maternal depression (Greist & Wells, 1983). For example, in our own work single mothers were less likely to participate in treatment, as were families with more overall stress and disruption. Parents who participated in treatment were also more likely to remain in the study. These data highlight the fact that those families most in need of treatment are often the ones without the emotional resources or instrumental supports (such as transportation or child care) to allow them to make use of available services, even when there is no charge, as was the case in our study.

Primary Prevention and Early Intervention

A large number of programs have been instituted in the elementary schools to improve the social and emotional functioning of children identified as at risk on the basis of their low SES, family disruption, poor social interaction with peers, or teacher ratings of mild to moderate behavior problems (e.g., Cowen et al., 1975). Two widely cited primary prevention programs focused on preschoolers. Shure and Spivack

(1979) designed and implemented a curriculum to train improved interpersonal problem solving on the assumption that poor peer relations might mediate poor outcomes in young children. Inner city children attending day-care and preschool programs in Philadelphia were given a graded series of group discussions daily for about 20 minutes for 3 months. The curriculum focused on helping children to identify problems or conflicts (e.g., two children want to play with the same toy), generate solutions to the problem, and think about the impact of the various solutions on others and themselves. Despite numerous criticisms of this work (e.g., Peterson & Roberts, 1986), data suggest that the treatment had some impact on children's social functioning and self-esteem. However, in the absence of parental involvement and a more general focus, long-lasting effects would not be anticipated.

Rickel and her coworkers (Rickel & Dyhdalo, 1981; Rickel, Smith, & Sharp, 1979) instituted an early intervention program for high risk preschoolers and their parents. Children were identified as shy and withdrawn, aggressive, and/or as showing learning problems by pre-school teachers. All participants were inner city, black children. Parent training was combined with an individually designed program focusing on cognitive skills, self-esteem, and self-expression that was administered in the school by therapy aides. Children were randomly assigned to active treatment and to an attention control. Both at the end of treatment and at a 2-year follow-up, when children were in first grade, treated children performed better, both on a measure of cognitive development and according to teacher ratings of behavior. Shy, withdrawn children maintained their gains better than their aggressive peers.

Most early intervention programs for preschoolers have focused more directly on academic skills, although they have differed widely in the degree of structure, the nature and amount of parent involvement, the age of entry, the length of the program, the nature of the curriculum (e.g., drill vs. discovery learning, language vs. concept development), and the relative emphasis on cognitive and language development as opposed to building social competence. These issues have been reviewed in detail recently by Clarke-Stewart and Fein (1983). Most of these intervention programs, similar to the ones just described, have focused almost exclusively on poor children living in highly stressed families. The goal of these programs was the remediation of skill deficits to facilitate adjustment to elementary school and to enhance academic functioning. Some programs appeared to merely prevent deterioration in treated children relative to controls, whereas others appear to have led to more long-term gains in academic functioning and behavioral adjustment (Clarke-Stewart & Fein, 1983; Lazar & Darlington, 1982). In general, parent involvement, length and intensity of program, and structured content appear to be some of the parameters associated with more obvious gains.

Lazar and Darlington (1982) recently examined the long-term efficacy of 12 independently designed infant and preschool early intervention programs. Although programs differed on a range of factors, all emphasized cognitive development using structured curricula and intense treatment with low adult–child ratios. Overall, findings after follow-up intervals ranging from 5 to 10 years indicated that low-income children who had participated in comprehensive early intervention programs were less likely to repeat a grade and to be in special classes than untreated controls, even when initial background factors were controlled statistically. Although gains in IQ scores were not maintained beyond a 2-year follow-up across programs, children's view of their own competence and parents' aspirations for their children were positively influenced by early program attendance. Lazar and Darlington (1982) conclude that "high quality programs with careful design and supervision, using a variety of strategies can be effective for different types of low-income children" (p. 65). Other outcome assessments of early intervention programs for low-income infants and preschoolers likewise document changes in cognitive and social functioning as well as mother–child interaction (e.g., Andrews et al., 1982; Lee, Brooks-Gunn, & Schnur, 1988; Slaughter, 1983).

The programs reviewed by Andrews et al. (1982) are among the more comprehensive and ambitious because they incorporated simultaneous programs for mothers and infants followed into preschool. Thus, a detailed curriculum on child rearing and child development, home management, child health, and community resources was paired with learning experiences for the children and support for mothers. The program was based on the rationale that changes in mothers' attitudes and knowledge, parenting strategies, ability to utilize existing resources, and self-esteem would be more likely to have a lasting impact on the child's environment than preschool experience alone. Posttest data revealed changes in children's cognitive functioning and in a variety of mother–child interaction measures. For example, program mothers were more positive, more sensitive, less restrictive, and more effective in their use of language and teaching strategies; children were more positive and verbal in interaction with their mothers. Some gains were maintained at a 1-year follow-up.

The findings from the programs reviewed by Lazar and Darlington (1982) and Andrews et al. (1982) indicate that intensive interventions with a multidimensional focus on children and their parents, which employ structured curricula and provide a range of services over time, are most likely to be effective. Yet, the early criticisms of Head Start and other early intervention programs (e.g., Jensen, 1969) were based on the misguided assumption that preschool experience per se should lead to long-term gains and ameliorate a range of deficits in cognitive and social functioning. As noted by Lazar and Darlington (1982) and others (e.g., Lee et al., 1988; Zigler & Valentine, 1979), the initial expectations for these programs were unrealistic. A year of preschool experience was expected to bridge the gap in cognitive, language, and social development between children reared in poverty and middle class children, despite massive differences in early experience and ongoing environmental input and support for academic and social competence. These more recent evaluations, however, highlight the need to modify the family environment and to provide additional resources to help parents support their children's development.

These findings have obvious implications for programming in the mental health arena as well. Intensive programs that focus on providing parent training and family intervention, as well as structured, therapeutic preschool experiences for young children with behavioral and emotional problems are sorely needed. As Kazdin (1987) recently argued, only intensive treatments that provide a range of services over time can be expected to have a long-lasting impact on disturbed children and their families. The theoretical framework espoused at the start of this book emphasized the importance of understanding children's development from a dynamic, transactional, family systems perspective in which aspects of the family's social context are seen as having both direct and indirect effects on the child. Thus, it is not surprising that treatment approaches that are compatible with this view and that focus on preschoolers and their families in a wider social context were the ones most likely to lead to positive change.

Illustrations from the Longitudinal Study

By the time they were 6 years old, the children in our longitudinal study had received a range of different treatments; 38% of the children whose parents had considered them hard-to-handle in late toddlerhood and the early preschool years had been referred for some form of psychological or educational help by the time they were in kindergarten or first grade (Campbell, Ewing, et al., 1986). These treatments were given in addition to the parent training groups that were offered to study parents when they entered the project. These additional treatments ranged from speech therapy or remedial reading programs at school through special class placement to more intensive family interventions that often included a combination of family therapy or parent counseling and a behavior management program. In some cases help with marital communication and support was combined with behavior management, similar to the treatment described by Dadds et al. (1987). Several children were also in play therapy and two had been given a trial of medication to control aggression and/or attentional deficits. Other parents (13%) sought advice from pediatricians, school principals, or classroom teachers but did not enter into formal treatment programs. Thus, parents of 51% of the initial problem group sought some form of advice or formal help by school entry. In contrast, only one child (4%) in the control group was in any formal program (speech therapy). Another 15% of comparison parents sought advice from their pediatricians about problems such as bed-wetting, nail biting, and finicky eating habits, but not about major problems in undercontrolled or overcontrolled behavior.

Two of the children described in detail in Chapter Three were in some form of treatment program when followed up at age 6, and parents of two of the children did not seek help beyond that provided in the parent groups described earlier. Teddy, who was seen initially as showing only age-appropriate activity and exploration and who was progressing well, had not received any form of additional help when followed up at age 6. This seemed appropriate, given his stable family situation and his satisfactory development. Teddy's parents had attended a parent group, where they received information about appropriate developmental expectations and the developmental needs of toddlers and preschoolers. They also listened to the concerns of other parents, some of whom had children who were far more difficult to control than Teddy. This helped the Ms to place Teddy's age-appropriate exuberance into a more realistic developmental perspective. It also helped Mr. and Mrs. M to set priorities, deciding which behaviors clearly required firm limits and which behaviors could be overlooked or tolerated as typical for that developmental period.

Annie and her family clearly could have benefitted from treatment beyond that provided in the parent group. Both Mr. and Mrs. J attended the group regularly and they improved their child management skills somewhat. The Js were encouraged to provide Annie more contingent praise and positive attention, and to be less critical. They were also helped to establish more reasonable and age-appropriate expectations for Annie and not to let conflicts over toilet training and eating escalate. However, we were less successful in helping the Js to understand Annie's emotional needs or to modify Mrs. J's very negative perceptions of Annie. This was beyond the scope of the group, except in a superficial way. Work on these issues with the Js would have required a more intensive individual and/or family approach, possibly one aimed at helping the Js to understand the underlying dynamics of their family interactions, as well as to improve the mother–daughter relationship. The Js, however, saw the problem as Annie's difficult behavior and were resistant to our suggestion that they might require additional help. As Annie entered school and was home less often, and as Mrs. J became involved with her younger daughter, her concerns about Annie abated. Mrs. J did not seem motivated to change her conflict-ridden relationship with her older daughter. Throughout, she continued to see the problems she identified as inherent in Annie, rather than as a reflection of dysfunctional relationships within the family system.

Jamie's parents likewise attended a parent training group and they worked hard at implementing our suggestions for limit setting, use of time out, etc. However, as noted in Chapter Three, we had little new to teach them because they were already doing most things we suggested. Mr. and Mrs. L focused their efforts on trying to improve Jamie's self-control and his relationships with other children, and they did benefit from the support they received from the therapists and the other parents. Although the Ls viewed Jamie's behavior as slightly improved at the completion of the group sessions and they felt more in control of the situation, problems did continue. At the end of kindergarten, Jamie was assessed by the school psychologist because of problems with self-control in the classroom and on the playground. Thus, he tended to get wound up and overexcited: in the classroom, Jamie often called out inappropriately or disrupted the activities of other children; on the playground, he frequently provoked fights with peers. As a result, he was on a behavioral program at school that included time outs, special rewards for good behavior, and all-too-frequent visits to the principal's office when time outs were inadequate. Jamie's parents worked closely with the school to monitor his progress and to make sure that there was consistency between the expectations voiced at home and at school. In addition, Jamie had regular meetings with the school guidance counselor who worked with him on self-control and peer relations, trying to help Jamie to prevent his peer conflicts from getting out of hand. These seem to be appropriate interventions because Jamie's difficulties did not appear to reflect other problems in the family and because his parents appeared to be handling his problems with considerable skill, patience, and sensitivity. Jamie made some strides and his behavior problems were under somewhat better control as he entered first grade.

Robbie's mother, Mrs. S, also attended a parent group. Mr. S did not accompany her because he attributed Robbie's difficulties to his wife's inadequate parenting skills. As noted in previous chapters, lack of paternal involvement and interparental blame and hostility are often correlates of behavior problems in children. Although Mrs. S was extremely responsive to our suggestions and followed through, setting appropriate limits and providing Robbie with a good deal of positive feedback and emotional support, his problems persisted, as would be expected, given the tense and conflict-ridden home environment. In the group, Mrs. S focused specifically on Robbie's difficulties with self control and compliance. At the completion of the group sessions, Mrs. S stated that she was in better control of Robbie's behavior and more consistent in her limit setting. However, it was obvious that family conflicts were contributing to Robbie's difficulties. Therefore, we also suggested that Mr. and Mrs. S might benefit from treatment elsewhere, focused on broader marital and family issues. Unfortunately, Mr. S was not interested in pursuing this suggestion. As noted in Chapter Three, Robbie's parents separated when he was 4 years old. Robbie experienced considerable upset as a result of the separation. His mother sought counseling to be better able to help Robbie cope with the separation, and he was eventually referred for play therapy. In addition, his mother received parent counseling and supportive therapy in an effort to help her deal with Robbie's difficult adjustment, as well as with her own anger and depression. In regard to Robbie's adjustment to the separation, Mrs. S needed help ensuring a stable, predictable, and supportive environment for Robbie, preparing him for the changes in his living situation, and helping him to cope with the turmoil associated with visitation arrangements. She also needed support and advice about limit setting because in view of her own distress, it was sometimes difficult for her to continue to set sufficiently firm, consistent, and appropriate limits on Robbie's behavior. In play therapy Robbie had an opportunity to express his confusion, anxiety about abandonment, anger at his parents, and concerns about the future, and he appeared to establish an excellent relationship with his male therapist. Although Robbie coped well in preschool and weathered the initial separation, continued interparental conflict and unstable visiting arrangements seemed to undermine his ability to cope. In kindergarten he became seriously aggressive with other children and noncompliant with the teacher, and a behavior management program was instituted. Robbie and his mother have continued in various forms of treatment over the years. These have included special class placement and individual psychotherapy for Robbie; Mrs. S has also sought advice from time to time about managing Robbie's behavior effectively or about helping him to weather a stressful life change.

Summary

In this chapter, the various treatment modalities used most frequently with young children were reviewed. Developmental considerations in treatment selection were touched on briefly, and it was concluded that more structured and didactic treatments that focus on parenting skills and family relationships appear most appropriate for preschoolers and their families. Furthermore, these more structured treatments have been subjected to at least some degree of empirical scrutiny. The impact of traditional forms of psychotherapy (play therapy) or of more contemporary family therapy approaches on preschoolers and their families have not been evaluated systematically. Certainly, family approaches have much promise, especially when combined with interventions that focus on parenting behavior. In addition, intensive preschool programs that help young children learn to control aggression with peers and to function more cooperatively and prosocially in the peer group may also hold promise, although systematic interventions of this sort are only beginning to be developed for children with behavior problems who are not also developmentally delayed or at risk for other reasons (e.g., Cohen et al., 1987).

There is evidence from early intervention and primary prevention programs suggesting that intensive, long-term, structured programs that also include parents can help young children overcome some early deficits in cognitive and social functioning. There is reason to believe that this model of comprehensive early intervention is also applicable to children and their families who are at risk because of parental psychopathology, family disruption, or poor parenting skills, or for children and families in which the childhood behavior problems are not clearly associated with one of these family risk factors. It is surprising that so little empirical work has been conducted on treatments for preschoolers with more typical behavioral difficulties, such as over-activity, noncompliance, and aggression (see also Eyberg, 1987).

Finally, the range of treatments used by children in our longitudinal study was discussed. Children and their families were seen in many different treatments that focused on the children's academic and social skills, parenting skills, and family relationships. Furthermore, it was common for children and their families to be seen in several forms of treatment, either simultaneously or successively. This may suggest that our ability to help troubled families with the techniques currently available is limited, or it may underline the resourcefulness of some families who were willing to try different approaches. What seems clear from this review is the need for more integrated treatment programs that can help families with difficult preschoolers early on, before problems escalate.

CHAPTER EIGHT

Follow-Up and Outcome

Few studies have actually followed preschoolers longitudinally, from early childhood to elementary school and beyond. However, the few that have are reviewed, as are several other studies that have followed children from school age to adolescence and young adulthood. In general, studies suggest that some proportion of children with early and severe problems continue to have difficulties later on, although outcome is mediated by a range of factors. In this chapter these studies are reviewed. Next, data from our own ongoing longitudinal study, tracking children's development from kindergarten entry through third grade, are presented. Finally, I return to our case studies to illustrate the course of problems in early childhood.

Longitudinal Studies of Toddlers and Preschoolers

Studies that have followed small samples of young children in the general population from infancy through school-age indicate that problem behaviors are relatively common and that they often are associated with a particular developmental period. For example, difficulties with sleeping, eating, and crying are most common during infancy and early toddlerhood; concerns with bowel and bladder functions and with struggles for independence and autonomy become more salient at about age 2; by age 3, management and discipline problems predominate; fears and worries, as well as aggression with peers, may concern parents during the late preschool period or at kindergarten entry; and school difficulties emerge as more serious parental concerns by age 6 or 7 (see Chapter Three and Campbell, 1989, for a review). Early longitudinal data indicated that in nonclinically referred children, such difficulties are usually transient (MacFarlane et al., 1954). More recent, large-scale studies with much larger samples indicate that this is the case for most, but not all, young children with early difficulties. Findings are consistent in that family factors and child characteristics appear to predict outcome.

In a large-scale epidemiological study, Werner and her colleagues (Werner, Bierman, & French, 1971; Werner & Smith, 1977) followed a cohort of children born in Hawaii in 1955. Birth records were obtained; maternal ratings of infant behavior were gathered at 1 year; children and families were assessed at 2, 10, and 18 years of age. While severe perinatal complications were associated with mental retardation, mild perinatal stress predicted learning and behavior problems at age 10, particularly in the context of high activity level at age 1, and a poor mother–child relationship, family instability, and low maternal educational level, assessed during infancy or toddlerhood. Werner and Smith (1977) conclude that the interaction among biological impairment, difficult infant behavior, and environmental factors, including a low standard of living, was predictive of moderate mental health problems at age 10. However, of children with serious learning and behavior problems at age 10, only 20% had clear-cut neurological signs. Furthermore, learning and behavior problems at age 10 tended to persist and to develop into antisocial behavior in adolescence, again particularly in boys from poor homes; of the children that became delinquent in adolescence, most had been identified as having significant problems by age 10. Werner and Smith (1977) interpret their data within a transactional model and emphasize the interacting contributions of biological vulnerability, environmental instability, and the quality of parent–child relationships in determining outcome.

The epidemiological study conducted by Richman et al. (1982) in London leads to similar conclusions in that problems were seen to persist in a relatively high proportion of children who were identified as showing clinically significant problems at age 3. Children identified as showing problems from maternal report were especially overactive, inattentive, attention seeking, difficult to control, irritable and negative in mood, and likely to have problems getting along with siblings and peers, relative to matched comparison children who were not rated as having significant problems. At initial assessment childhood problems were associated with a range of adverse family factors, including maternal depression, a poor marital relationship, punitive child-rearing practices including frequent spankings, parental disagreement over child rearing, high parental criticism of the child, and lack of maternal warmth. Poorer housing and more financial difficulties also characterized the problem group.

A significant proportion of children in the problem group continued to have difficulties with restlessness and overactivity, attention-seeking behavior, temper tantrums, discipline, and sibling relationships when followed up 1 year later. Problems persisted in 63% of the problem group at age 4 and in 62% at age 8. Furthermore, teacher ratings also confirmed more problems at age 8 in the group rated by mothers as more difficult to handle at ages 3 and 4. Overactivity, concentration difficulties, discipline problems, unhappiness, and poor sibling relationships were still the primary concerns at follow-up. Serious peer problems were also in evidence. Although early family adversity did not predict outcome, persistent difficulties were associated with ongoing problems within the family, including continued marital dysfunction, maternal illness and depression, and more external psychosocial stress. Finally, persistent problems were related to the children's poorer cognitive and academic functioning, especially for boys. Also, some children who had not shown problems initially did develop them over the course of the follow-up period, and problems in family relationships and maternal depression were associated with the onset of problems as well.

A cluster analysis of symptom ratings at age 3 indicated that approximately 33% of the sample fell into one of two clusters defined in part by restlessness and discipline problems; the remaining clusters were described primarily by bowel and bladder control problems and may be considered transient developmental difficulties related to maturation and self-regulation. Of the two clinically significant clusters, one describing 23% of the sample was defined by feeding difficulties and a high activity level. This cluster of symptoms by itself did not appear to predict poor outcome. Of most relevance is the cluster made up of 10% of the sample; children high on restlessness and overactivity, tantrums, discipline problems, poor concentration, negative mood, and difficulties with siblings at age 3 had the most family problems and the worst outcomes. This cluster of symptoms was associated with low maternal warmth, high criticism of the child, and a poor marriage. At age 4, 89% of this group was still having difficulties; at age 8, 67% were still considered to have clinically significant problems. Taken together, these findings indicate that moderate to severe levels of overactivity, attention problems, and management difficulties at age 3, especially in the context of family problems, are associated with poor outcome at school age. These findings were particularly strong for boys.

McGee and his colleagues conducted a large epidemiological study of children in New Zealand (McGee & Silva, 1982; McGee, Silva, & Williams, 1984). Children were first recruited into the study at age 3 and followed up at ages 5 and 7. Children with stable behavior problems, that is, problems that persisted from age 5 to age 7, came from more discordant families characterized by higher rates of separation and single parenting, poorer family relationships, and more frequent school changes. In addition, their mothers were younger, of lower mental ability, and more likely to report symptoms of anxiety, depression, and minor physical complaints than mothers of children without problems. Thus, it is likely that these children received poorer parenting than comparison children. Consistent with our own data and those of Richman et al. (1982), children with persistent problems were described by both parents and teachers as primarily hyperactive and aggressive, rather than sad, anxious, or withdrawn. In addition, stable behavior problems were associated with reading difficulties and poor school achievement. Yet, most indices of pregnancy and delivery complications, neonatal difficulties, neurological impairment, and developmental milestones did not differentiate children with stable behavior problems from those without. McGee, Williams, and Silva (1984) conclude that children with stable behavior problems have experienced a range of stresses in their lives, which interact in complex fashion to produce and/or maintain disordered functioning.

Data from several other longitudinal studies of preschoolers confirm these findings. Bates and colleagues (Bates & Bayles, 1988; Bates et al., 1985) found that maternal reports of difficult temperament in infancy, primarily irritability and fussiness, predicted later ratings of behavior problems at preschool and kindergarten age. Furthermore, behavior problems were associated with low levels of positive affective engagement and play in toddlerhood, conflicts over independence, discipline problems, and negative maternal control. Similarly, Fischer et al. (1984) found that early reports of externalizing problems in day-care, characterized by discipline problems and aggression, predicted persistent problems as reported by parents 5 to 7 years later. Shy and withdrawn behavior in early childhood was not associated with continuing difficulties according to Fischer et al. However, Bates and Bayles (1988) found that internalizing problems showed a high degree of continuity from ages 3 to 5. Persistent internalizing problems were associated with maternal depression and low levels of maternal affectionate involvement and age-appropriate play. In another longitudinal study of preschool attenders (Lerner, Inui, Trupin, & Douglas, 1985), more severe behavior problems in preschool, as determined from teacher records, were associated with a range of difficulties by adolescence. In our earlier work, we followed up a sample of clinically referred hyperactive preschoolers at ages 6 and 7. Both maternal (Campbell, Schleifer, Weiss, & Perlman, 1977) and teacher (Campbell, Endman, & Bernfeld, 1977) reports indicated that problem preschoolers continued to be rated as more hyperactive and aggressive at follow-up. Observations of mother–child interaction and the child's classroom behavior partially confirmed these adult ratings.

Taken together, then, an accumulating body of evidence suggests some degree of continuity, contrary to the earlier view that behavior difficulties in toddlers and preschoolers were relatively insignificant. Although it is clear that isolated symptoms or constellations of mild symptoms are most usually indicative only of transient problems that are likely to disappear with development, constellations of more serious problems appearing in early childhood may signify difficulties that are likely to persist, at least to middle childhood. It is important to emphasize that not all children with early and severe problems continue to have difficulties; furthermore, the nature of their problems may change or become less severe with development, depending upon the environmental supports available to the child. It is less clear whether more internalizing problems persist in young children. Finally, it appears from the small amount of existing literature that ongoing family stress and disruption and a poor mother–child relationship are often associated with continued difficulties, especially for boys (Lewis et al., 1984; Richman et al., 1982).

Longitudinal Studies of School-Age Children to Adolescence and Early Adulthood

In numerous studies samples of clinically identified children have been followed from elementary school to adolescence, and in a few more recent studies children have been followed to early adulthood. Because referrals for childhood problems, especially learning difficulties, poor school achievement, and externalizing behavior problems, tend to peak from about age 8 to 12, studies have focused on following children in this age group to adolescence. These studies have been reviewed in detail elsewhere (Weiss & Hechtman, 1986); because findings are relatively consistent, they are discussed only briefly, although Weiss and Hechtman's classic study is discussed more fully.

In general, follow-up studies suggest that problems persist in roughly one half of the youngsters identified as showing externalizing problems during the elementary school years. Many of these studies have followed samples identified as hyperactive. Data suggest that problems are most likely to persist in children from troubled families and/or where symptoms of hyperactivity and attentional problems are associated with high rates of aggression (e.g., Milich & Loney, 1979; Gittelman, Mannuzza, Shenker, & Bonagura, 1985; Paternite & Loney, 1980; Wallander, 1988). Thus, it appears that hyperactivity and attention problems by themselves do not predict poor outcome. Rather, the combination of these symptoms with aggression and other indicators of antisocial behavior appear to predict later delinquent and antisocial behavior. Children with lower IQs are also more likely to have continuing difficulties, partly because low IQ is a proxy for other aspects of psychosocial adversity and partly because youngsters who perform poorly in school are more likely to have difficulties coping in our complex society. However, child factors alone are rarely adequate to determine whether an aggressive child will grow into an antisocial or delinquent adolescent or young adult. Negative outcomes are strongly predicted by parental psychopathology (particularly antisocial behavior or alcoholism in the father), punitive child-rearing practices, and marital dysfunction (Loney, Kramer, & Milich, 1981; Milich & Loney, 1979; Wallander, 1988; Weiss & Hechtman, 1986). As noted throughout, it is the complex interactions among these factors that predict continued difficulties in establishing and maintaining relationships, following the rules of society, and developing adequate cognitive and/or social skills to remain in school or to hold a job. Although many studies have followed up aggressive and hyperactive children to determine rates of delinquency, drug and alcohol abuse, and other forms of antisocial behavior, they have tended not to examine more subtle problems in interpersonal functioning, self-esteem, or achievement.

In the first major long-term follow-up study of hyperactive children into young adulthood, Weiss and Hechtman (1986) examined both more subtle indices of adjustment and more obvious indicators of antisocial behavior. Children were first followed from elementary school age to adolescence. When hyperactive adolescents were compared with normal controls, they were found to be functioning more poorly at school and with peers. Thus, they had repeated more grades at school and were receiving lower marks on their report cards. They were also less likely to have friends and they reported lower self-esteem. Discipline problems and antisocial behavior were more salient than the initial problems of inattention and overactivity, although they still differed from controls on measures of these symptoms.

Subjects were followed up again approximately 15 years after initial diagnosis (mean age = 25 years). About one half of the sample of hyperactives was doing well at follow-up, whereas the remaining half had mild to severe difficulties. Overall, those with persistent problems tended to complain of inattention, restlessness, and impulsivity, as well as a range of other symptoms including interpersonal problems and anxiety. Relative to controls, hyperactive adults received more psychiatric diagnoses, with 23% meeting diagnostic criteria for antisocial personality disorder. In addition, there were trends suggesting somewhat elevated rates of drug and alcohol abuse and aggressive behavior in hyperactives compared with controls. However, contrary to findings from some studies, Weiss and Hechtman note that most of these individuals were not involved in major offenses. Only a small subgroup of hyperactive subjects accounted for elevated rates of contact with the law and had engaged in more serious antisocial activities, such as theft and selling drugs.

In addition to psychiatric status, Weiss and Hechtman examined more general indicators of functioning, academic achievement, and work history. Hyperactive subjects had completed fewer years of formal schooling and worked in somewhat lower status occupations than controls, although groups were matched on the social class of family of origin. They had also experienced more job changes, both self-initiated and because of layoffs. Finally, their employers were less satisfied with their job performance than was the case for controls. However, the rate of unemployment was not higher in the hyperactive group. Observational and self-report measures also indicated that hyperactive subjects had poorer social skills and lower self-esteem than controls. In general, consistent with findings from other studies, family stability, social class, intelligence, and the constellation of initial symptoms predicted outcome. Those who had been described as hyperactive, aggressive, emotionally unstable, and unable to tolerate frustration were more likely to be doing poorly at follow-up than those with more circumscribed initial symptoms. Interviews with hyperactive subjects indicated that those who were doing well in early adulthood often attributed their improved self-control and sense of responsibility to the support of a caring adult, most often a parent, but also a grandparent, teacher, or guidance counselor who showed a special interest in the child.

Findings from the Longitudinal Study

As already noted, we have been involved in a longitudinal study of parent-identified hard-to-manage preschoolers, who, along with a sample of nonreferred comparison children, have been followed from age 3 to age 9, with periodic assessments of the child's functioning in a range of situations. Parent and teacher reports have been obtained, children have been observed in structured and unstructured laboratory situations, their classroom behavior has been observed, and family functioning has been assessed. As pointed out in Chapter Three, parent-identified children differed from the comparison group on a range of measures obtained at the time of entry into the study. These included parent and teacher reports of hyperactive–distractible behavior and aggressive–noncompliant behavior; groups did not differ on scales assessing anxiety. Independent laboratory observations revealed that problem youngsters differed from controls on measures of activity level, inattention, and impulsivity obtained during free play and experimenter-administered structured tasks (Campbell et al., 1982). Mothers of problem children were more likely to provide direction and negative control during an unstructured play period, but problem children showed only a nonsignificant tendency to be more aggressive and noncompliant than controls in this setting (Campbell, Breaux, Ewing, Szumowski, & Pierce, 1986). Observations in the preschool classrooms of study participants indicated that they also were more aggressive with peers, and problem boys were less compliant with teacher requests than were other children in the sample. Problem children did not differ from controls in their tendency to approach peers or to engage in cooperative play (Campbell & Cluss, 1982). Finally, although the families of the problem children were, on average, from a lower social class and experiencing higher levels of psychosocial stress, there were wide individual differences on background measures.

Parent report and laboratory measures were repeated 1 year later when the children were 4 years old (Campbell et al., 1984). Despite the fact that many of the more difficult children in the sample who would be expected to have the worst outcomes were lost to follow-up, the groups continued to differ at the age 4 follow-up assessment. Thus, children in the problem group were still rated as more hyperactive-distractible and aggressive-noncompliant by their mothers, and they differed on laboratory observations of activity, inattention, and impulsivity.

At age 6, children were again observed in the laboratory and at school. Mothers were interviewed; mothers and teachers completed questionnaires. As before, teachers were informed only that the target child was a participant in a longitudinal study of development. These findings have been reported in detail elsewhere (Campbell, Ewing, et al., 1986). Briefly, when the entire group of hard-to-manage 3-year-olds was compared with controls at the age 6 follow-up, the two groups continued to differ on maternal and teacher ratings of externalizing, but not internalizing, symptoms. Both mothers and teachers rated the problem youngsters as significantly more hyperactive, inattentive, and aggressive than controls. In addition, mothers rated them as less competent with peers, and teachers rated them as showing less adaptive functioning in school. Classroom observations confirmed that children in the initial problem group tended to be more active and distractible, as well as more disruptive and aggressive, than comparison children. Laboratory observations of free play, of activity level during structures tasks, and of mother–child interaction during problem solving did not reveal group differences at age 6.

In addition to group comparisons, early predictors of later symptom ratings were examined (Campbell, Breaux, Ewing, & Szumowski, 1986). Similar to the age 4 data, maternal behavior in the laboratory at age 3 continued to predict maternal ratings of hyperactivity and aggression at age 6. In addition, concurrent, but not earlier, stress ratings were associated with hyperactivity ratings, such that mothers living in more stressful family circumstances rated their children as more hyperactive at age 6. Initial (age 3) child characteristics and observed behaviors also predicted symptom ratings at age 6. Thus, boys who were more active during free play in the laboratory and more negative and noncompliant when observed playing with their mothers at age 3 received higher hyperactivity ratings at age 6. Negative behavior during play also predicted aggression ratings 3 years later. Finally, initial symptom ratings were highly correlated with symptom ratings later on.

The findings presented so far indicate a relatively high degree of continuity between initial assessments of problem behavior at age 3 and similar assessments obtained 3 years later when children entered school. However, it is also clear that there were wide individual differences in children's functioning at school entry. Some problem youngsters were doing fine at follow-up; some had mild problems; still others continued to have relatively severe problems. This was examined in several ways. First, we asked how many children in the initial problem group met objective criteria for disorder at age 6; these youngsters (persistent problems) were then compared with those who did not meet criteria (improved group) and to controls on both follow-up and initial measures. Children were considered to show persistent problems if they met DSM-III criteria for attention deficit disorder at age 6, if they scored above a cut-off score of 70 on the Aggression dimension of the Achenbach Child Behavior Checklist (CBCL; Achenbach & Edelbrock, 1983), or if they were rated by their mothers as showing either moderate or severe problems on the follow-up interview. (The CBCL is a widely used and well-standardized checklist for assessing childhood symptoms; scores are derived from a computer program that provides age and gender appropriate norms. A standard, T, score of 70, which is 2 SD's above the mean of 50, is considered clinically significant.) Exactly 50% of the original problem group met one or more of these clinical criteria at age 6 and were considered to be showing persistent problems; the remainder were considered improved because they did not meet any of these criteria.

A reanalysis of the data was conducted in which persistent problem children, improved children, and controls were compared. Results indicated that most group differences at age 6 were accounted for by the children with persistent problems. Improved youngsters did not differ from controls on most measures and they were rated as significantly less symptomatic than the persistent problem group by teachers as well as parents. Comparisons between the persistent problem group and improved children on initial (age 3) measures yielded few differences. However, consistent with those reported earlier, more negative and controlling maternal behavior and more severe initial ratings on both hyperactivity and aggression characterized the persistent problem group. In addition, when the pattern of initial symptoms and symptom changes over time were examined, children with persistent problems were found to have both more numerous early signs of oppositional/conduct disorder, to have higher overall symptom ratings, and to show less developmental change in symptoms from ages 3 to 4 and 4 to 6 than children who improved (Campbell, 1987).

At the age 9 follow-up assessment, mothers were administered a structured diagnostic interview, the Diagnostic Interview Schedule for Children—Parent Version (Edelbrock et al., 1985), which incorporates DSM-III criteria for major childhood disorders. Symptoms are scored on a 3-point scale from 0 = absent to 2 = definitely present. The interviewers were both blind and independent; they knew nothing of the children's earlier behavior or group status. In addition, mothers and classroom teachers completed questionnaires. Data were examined in terms of group status at age 6 (i.e., persistent problem, improved, control). Children in the persistent problem group were more likely than children in the other two groups to meet diagnostic criteria for at least one externalizing disorder (attention deficit disorder, oppositional disorder, or conduct disorder) at follow-up; 67% of the persistent group continued to meet diagnostic criteria at age 9 compared with only 29% of the improved group and 16% of controls, a statistically significant difference. However, groups did not differ in the proportion meeting criteria for an internalizing disorder (separation anxiety, overanxious disorder, dysthymia). However, several children in the persistent group who were reported at age 9 to show symptoms of an externalizing disorder were also described as depressed and/or anxious.

Even when children did not meet specific diagnostic criteria, they still showed elevated symptom levels, as assessed by questionnaires and interviews. Thus, children in the persistent problem group were reported to show significantly more symptoms of attention deficit disorder, as assessed by the diagnostic interview than either comparison group at the age 9 follow-up; mothers of children in the persistent problem group also reported significantly more symptoms of oppositional and conduct disorder than mothers of controls. Consistent with the diagnostic data, symptom counts on internalizing problems did not differentiate across groups. It is worth noting that mothers across the groups reported relatively high rates of anxiety and fearfulness, particularly in regard to school performance and peer acceptance, concerns that are clearly age-related.

Maternal ratings on the CBCL were consistent with the diagnostic data. When ratings on behavior disorders were scored according to appropriate age and gender norms, children in the persistent problem group received significantly higher ratings than their improved peers and than the comparison group on the dimensions Hyperactive, Aggressive, and Delinquent and significantly lower ratings on Social Competence (including behavior with peers, participation in organized activities, and behavior at home). They were also rated as more socially withdrawn than comparison children. However, by age 9, children seemed to be better controlled in school. Relatively few received elevated ratings from teachers on the Achenbach Teacher Report Form, and group differences were significant only on the Nervous–Overactive and Externalizing scales, with persistent problem youngsters differing from controls. It should be kept in mind that three children from the persistent problem group were in special classes either full- or part-time by the age 9 follow-up; another four were receiving some form of school-based remedial help; two had repeated a grade. Five children were on stimulant medication for their hyperactivity. All of these factors may have influenced teacher ratings because study children may not have stood out relative to classmates. Furthermore, despite these teacher ratings, most children in the persistent problem group had received some form of educational and/or psychological service by age 9, as detailed in Chapter Seven.

We also examined several earlier predictors of maternal ratings of behavior problems at age 9. Negative maternal control during play and the free play composite score, derived from observations of the child's attention to toys during free play, both observed in the laboratory at age 3, continued to predict maternal ratings of hyperactivity at age 9, even when gender, IQ, and social class were controlled. Thus, mothers who were more negative and whose children were more unfocused in their play continued to see their youngsters as more overactive and difficult to control 6 years later. Finally, both maternal and teacher ratings of externalizing problems at age 6 predicted maternal ratings of similar problems at age 9. These data indicate predictability over time and across informants, confirming that ratings of persistent problems reflect more than negative and biased assessments of children's behavior by their mothers.

Another approach we took to examining individual differences in initial measures and their implications for predicting later functioning involved the use of cluster analysis. A discussion of the intricacies of this statistical technique are beyond the scope of this book. The interested reader is referred to Aldenderfer and Blashfield (1984). Briefly, this technique allows the researcher to find relatively homogeneous groupings of children who are similar in their pattern of measures and different from other groupings. Because both theory and clinical intuition convinced us that background variables and the quality of the mother–child relationship, as well as child characteristics, should be important in defining subgroups, the following measures obtained at age 3 were utilized: maternal ratings of hyperactivity, maternal ratings of aggression, maternal reports of infant temperament (obtained at age 3 from the structured interview, including reports of irritability, feeding difficulties, sleep problems, and consolability), Binet IQ, a family stress rating (1 = no stress other than target child, 3 = severe and ongoing stresses in the family independent of or over and above the child's behavior problems), and the mother's behavior during the interactive play observation in the laboratory. Scores were standardized so that they were on a similar metric (i.e., mean of 0 and *SD* of 1). A cluster solution with six clusters was selected at most interpretable and consistent with theoretical expectation. Two clusters, containing just three children (one, the most disturbed child in the sample, and two from extremely dysfunctional families who were later lost to follow-up), are not discussed further. The remaining four clusters are described in more detail (see Figure 8.1).

Cluster 1 is composed of six children, all of whom have remained in the study. At age 3, they were described as difficult infants who were

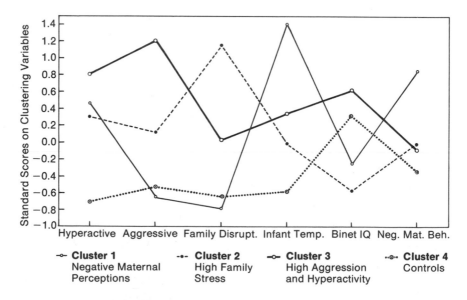

FIGURE 8.1. Cluster analysis of age 3 data.

high in activity level but low on aggression or noncompliance. Their mothers were particularly negative and controlling during the laboratory observation of play. As a group the children were average in ability, and in all cases the family situation was highly stable. This group is noteworthy because of the relatively negative maternal descriptions of the child's behavior and the high levels of negative and controlling maternal behavior during the play observation. Cluster 2 was originally composed of 13 children who were not considered particularly difficult infants but who were rated as active and aggressive at intake. While mothers were moderately negative and controlling, this group was characterized by extremely high levels of psychosocial stress, with most families coping with major difficulties at intake. These included severe marital discord or disruption, unemployment, and physical and/or psychological disorder. Six of these families were lost to follow-up. This group was considered the high-stress group. Cluster 3, consisting of 10 children, was characterized by the highest levels of hyperactivity and aggression, despite low levels of family disruption, low levels of negative maternal control, moderate infant difficultness, and high IQ. This group, the high-symptom group, is one in which a biological vulnerability to disorder must be considered. All of these families remained in the study through the 6-year follow-up, although two were lost by age 9. Finally, the fourth cluster of 30 children includes the entire control group and eight problem youngsters. Overall, this cluster is low on hyperactivity and aggression, low on family disruption, low on negative maternal control, and high in IQ. As might be expected, at both ages 6 and 9, cluster 3 (which overlaps 70% with the persistent problem group) is doing worst. Indeed, 75% met DSM III diagnostic criteria for an externalizing disorder at age 9.

Taken together, the data from this ongoing longitudinal study are consistent with those reported by other investigators, most notably Richman et al. (1982), in indicating that problems persist from preschool to school in a substantial proportion of children identified by parents as difficult to manage at age 3. Family stress, high maternal ratings of hyperactivity and aggression, and high levels of negative maternal control appear to be associated with the identification of a child as problematic early on and with high symptom ratings at age 6. High initial symptoms of both hyperactivity and aggression, a negative mother–child relationship, and observed overactivity and inattention at age 3 predicted maternal ratings of externalizing problems at age 9. While additional analyses remain to be conducted on this data set, particularly those dealing with family factors, a clinical examination of the findings may provide some additional leads to factors associated with different outcomes.

For example, it is interesting to note that one half of the children in the group characterized by negative maternal perceptions (cluster 1) at intake were doing very well at follow-up and their mothers no longer perceived them as difficult. This probably reflects some combination of changes in the mother–child relationship, changes in the family as a whole, and the children's developing independence and competence. It appears that these mothers were able to allow their children more autonomy as they got older, and the children, for their part, were less confrontative and more sure of themselves. In addition, these mothers may be better suited to parenting a school-age child and less able to tolerate the testing and defiance characteristic of toddlerhood. Other children in this group were continuing to have difficulties with classroom behavior and academic achievement, although the quality of the mother–child relationship had changed dramatically, and mothers, having a better understanding of their children's difficulties, were supportive. One of these children was in a special class for children with learning problems. In one instance, the mother–child relationship remained tense and the child appeared to be relatively defiant and anxious.

Many children in the high-stress group (cluster 2) were lost to follow-up. Of those that remained, one half were doing well at follow-up. These families appeared to have stabilized over the period from age 6 to age 9. One of the children who was continuing to have difficulties at age 9 was getting along somewhat better at home but was in a special class at school. Two children were living in continuously and seriously stressed family environments, and both met diagnostic criteria for oppositional disorder at age 9.

Problem youngsters who were clustered with the controls at intake were doing well overall. The few who were not functioning adequately were living in stressful family circumstances, either by virtue of on-going mother–child conflict that was not picked up on our observational measures (but was reported by mothers during interviews) or family disruption. Finally, children in cluster 3, the high-symptom group, were overall doing poorly, as noted earlier. Three of these children (of the eight seen at age 9) were also learning-disabled. These children were characterized by high initial symptom levels that tended to persist across measurement periods, although in some cases, problem severity may have been influenced by other factors in the family environment.

Given the length of the follow-up period, it is not surprising to note that a number of families that were intact at the start of the study separated over the ensuing 6 years. By the age 9 follow-up, five separations/divorces or deaths had occurred among parents of the children in the problem group and there were two remarriages; this means that seven of 29 families experienced a significant change in status (24%); in contrast, only one family in the comparison group changed status over the period of the study (4%). Overall, children in the initial problem group who experienced marked family change tended to be doing poorly at follow-up. Several of these youngsters, both boys and girls, were sad and anxious at follow-up, and it appeared that these problems were related to coping with the loss attendant upon parental separation.

The range of outcomes in the sample was diverse. Some children were doing fine at follow-up; others had learning problems that emerged in the early school years. In some cases these were evident earlier in delayed language development or articulation and expression difficulties; in others they were a surprise. Other children clearly met criteria for attention deficit disorder and some were on medication or had been at some time between ages 6 and 9. As might be expected, learning problems and hyperactivity tended to co-exist in some children. Others appeared more oppositional than hyperactive at follow-up, although again, the two also coexisted in other youngsters. Finally, despite early aggression and hyperactivity, some children seemed to be more anxious and/or depressed at follow-up. Again, anxiety or high levels of dysphoric mood either coexisted with other difficulties (hyperactivity, noncompliance, or learning problems) or occurred alone in the context of family change. Overall, based on maternal interviews, the range of outcomes across the entire group of problem 3-year-olds seen at age 9 is depicted in Figure 8.2. It is also worth noting that although comparison children also showed signs of anxiety, these tended to be more isolated fears and worries rather than part of a symptom picture that included a range of difficulties with psychosocial functioning and academic achievement. These issues are illustrated more specifically with a discussion of the four children described in previous chapters.

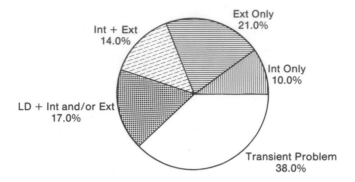

FIGURE 8.2. Diverse outcomes of problem 3-year-olds based on Diagnostic Interview Schedule for Children diagnoses/symptom ratings. Diagnoses were based on independent interviews with children's mothers at age 9. LD = learning disorders; Int = internalizing; Ext = externalizing.

Case Illustrations

The four children discussed throughout this book are considered in terms of their continuing development and their outcome at age 9. In each instance parents complained of problems from infancy onward and these youngsters all showed some difficulties with self-regulation when seen at age 3. However, these four youngsters differed widely in terms of the pattern and severity of initial problems, the quality of the mother–child relationship, the nature of the family environment, and their development at age 4.

Jamie L

Jamie was among the more aggressive and difficult children in the sample, despite a stable and supportive family. Although he had made some gains by age 4, difficulties were still apparent, and he continued to have many more problems with compliance, restlessness, activity, and peer relations than the average 4-year-old in the sample. Jamie was followed up again just after his sixth birthday. He was reportedly much better able to focus his attention and control his activity. However, Mrs. L stated that her current concerns about Jamie included his "testing limits," his difficulty confronting new situations, and his attention-seeking behavior in school. She noted, when questioned about specific behaviors, that he tended not to listen in school, still had difficulty controlling his temper, that he needed constant structure and discipline and that he continued to get into fights at school, especially at recess. Mrs. L continued to use time out, reasoning, and the withdrawal of privileges as preferred disciplinary strategies, although Jamie's father was inclined to get angrier and to be less patient with Jamie as Jamie got older. According to both interview and questionnaire measures, Jamie was no longer seen as particularly hyperactive or distractible; he did not meet DSM-III criteria for attention deficit disorder at age 6. However, on the Achenbach CBCL his mother rated him in the clinical range on scales assessing aggression and disobedience.

During the laboratory observation of free play at age 6, Jamie did not appear disorganized or unfocused. However, he was restless and fidgety on structured tasks and he left his seat frequently. He also made a surprisingly large number of errors on a visual matching task; his performance was impulsive and careless.

Jamie was on a behavioral program at school and was seeing the school guidance counselor in an attempt to deal with his anger and poor self-control in the school setting. In particular, there had been several incidents in which Jamie had initiated fairly serious fights with other children. In addition, he often talked out in class and interrupted the ongoing activities of the teacher and other children. Jamie had also been assessed by the school psychologist. His school teacher reported that things were under control and surprisingly did not rate him in the clinical range on any scales on the teacher report version of the Achenbach CBCL. Furthermore, despite his social and discipline problems, Jamie continued to function at a superior level intellectually and he was doing excellent school work; he also participated in extracurricular activities.

At age 9, Jamie was still having significant problems at home and at school. He met DSM-III criteria for conduct disorder, socialized, because he continued to get into regular and fairly serious fights with other children and had begun to steal from his parents. He was still a discipline problem as well. Although he also was described as impulsive and fairly active, he did not meet criteria for attention deficit disorder because he was not having difficulty paying attention. However, his mother described him as a youngster who was chronically unhappy, had low self-esteem and was socially immature. On the Achenbach CBCL, completed by his mother when he was 9, Jamie was rated in the clinical range on the scales Social Withdrawal, Aggressive, and Delinquent, consistent with the clinical picture at age 6. Although his mother reported that Jamie wanted to play with other children, his immature social behavior and aggressiveness tended to alienate them. At age 9, he was reported to have no close friend. His fourth grade teacher noted his excellent intellectual ability, high achievement test scores, and presence in a program for gifted youngsters. However, she also saw him as having significant problems with peers, with classroom discipline, and with self-control; on the teacher version of the CBCL, he was rated as just below the clinical range on the Aggression scale. Jamie and his family were being seen by a psychologist.

It is instructive to examine the developmental course of Jamie's difficulties. Problems with attention have abated since the preschool years, and he no longer appears particularly distractible. He is able to sit still and attend to things that interest him, and he is performing well academically in school and succeeding in some extracurricular activities that require concentration and practice. Thus, his superior intelligence, curiosity, and the considerable environmental support provided by his family and school have obviously paid off in some areas. However, he continues to demonstrate poor impulse control and early signs of antisocial behavior, to have relatively serious peer problems, and to suffer from chronic unhappiness, all of which are likely to presage persistent social and interpersonal difficulties as Jamie reaches pre-adolescence. This is a rather pessimistic example of relatively poor outcome, despite a superior family environment and extensive psychological intervention from early childhood. In terms of predictive factors, Jamie's initially high levels of both hyperactivity and aggression, as well as the intensity of his aggressive encounters with peers, may be significant. The early onset of his problems with self-regulation and undercontrol may also be important clues to his persistent problems. As noted in Chapter Three, factors such as family instability and harsh child-rearing practices are clearly not contributing to the maintenance of difficulties in this instance; constitutional/temperamental factors appear most salient.

Annie J

Annie was a youngster whose difficulties seemed to result from insensitive and inept parenting, as well as inconsistent and inappropriate parental expectations. She was involved in an intense struggle with her mother over who was in control; her parents seemed unable to provide her with the needed environmental supports for developmental change; consequently, each developmental hurdle became a major battleground. Nevertheless Annie made a smooth transition to pre-school where she got along well with both teachers and peers. When followed up at age 6, the marked discrepancy between Annie's behavior with her mother and with others was still apparent and her mother's perceptions of Annie's behavior appeared to be grossly distorted. In the intervening 2 years, Mrs. J had given birth to a daughter who was developing normally, although she was also being overwhelmed by an intrusive and insensitive mother. However, Mrs. J reported that she was having an easier time with her second child whom she perceived as easier to care for—more cuddly and less irritable and defiant than Annie had been.

Annie eagerly greeted the home visitors and there were certainly no longer any signs of separation anxiety. She was friendly and cooperative, eager to begin each new task, and almost never fidgety, bored, or off-task. She performed at the superior level on the Wechsler Preschool and Primary Scale of Intelligence and was disappointed when testing was over. She took the examiner to her room to show her her favorite toys. Overall she was a cooperative, sociable, but sadly needy youngster who appeared to be starved for attention, affection, and positive feedback. During the laboratory assessment, Annie likewise became engaged with the tasks easily; her play was focused and directed to a few salient toys; she was not at all impulsive or inattentive. In school she was also performing well and her first grade teacher saw her as showing no problems, except a tendency "to talk too much to her neighbors." On the teacher version of the CBCL, she was rated as a socially competent youngster with no behavior problems. Observations in the classroom confirmed the teacher's report that she was behaving appropriately in school.

Unfortunately, Mrs. J painted a different picture. She reported that Annie had had a difficult time adjusting to kindergarten and that there had been several instances of school refusal. She complained of continued difficulties with discipline, inattention, overactivity, and poor impulse control. Indeed, Annie met DSM-III criteria for attention deficit disorder with hyperactivity according to maternal interview. On the CBCL, her mother rated her above the clinical range on the scales Depression, Social Withdrawal, Somatic Complaints, and Aggression. Furthermore, she reported problems with bed-wetting, nightmares, anxiety, fearfulness, and loneliness, providing a picture of an anxious, unhappy, and possibly angry youngster, rather than a child with primarily externalizing problems. In contrast, her teacher did not endorse one symptom item!

This marked discrepancy between maternal and teacher reports was still apparent at the age 9 follow-up. Annie's third grade teacher reported that she was functioning at grade level and above in all academic areas and that she was getting along well socially. The third grade teacher, similar to the first grade teacher, did not endorse any symptom items on the CBCL. Mrs. J did acknowledge that Annie was doing well in school, and she did report that Annie had friends and was involved in a number of outside activities. In particular, Mrs. J noted that Annie was taking ballet lessons and that she excelled at dancing. Although Mrs. J was able, then, to recognize some of Annie's strengths, she also continued to report numerous problems at home. She complained of a number of externalizing and internalizing symptoms that she saw as relatively specific to her own relationship with Annie. Thus, Annie was still described by her mother as impulsive, overactive, inattentive, defiant, angry, immature, and aggressive. In addition, Mrs. J was concerned about Annie's anxiety, sadness, moodiness, and tendency to worry about things. She described Annie as an overly sensitive youngster who tended to become easily upset by events around her, such as the death of a neighbor's dog and the move of a close friend. Mrs. J rated Annie above the clinical range on five scales of the CBCL: Depression, Social Withdrawal, Somatic Complaints, Hyperactivity, and Aggression. According to the structured diagnostic interview with Mrs. J, administered by an interviewer who knew nothing of Annie's earlier history, she met DSM-III criteria for attention deficit disorder with hyperactivity, for overanxious disorder, and for chronic dysphoric mood. This picture of relatively severe and pervasive psychopathology is certainly inconsistent with Annie's behavior at school and with peers. Mrs. J also noted that her younger daughter had recently started preschool and had experienced very severe separation anxiety, suggesting that a pattern of mother–daughter problems around separation–individuation was about to be repeated.

Annie's problems would appear to stem primarily from insensitive parenting reflected in her parents' inability to respond to and meet her emotional needs and their failure to recognize and appreciate her many strengths. Her mother also appeared intrusive and overconcerned, primarily about what she saw as Annie's problems, and she seemed to lack genuine warmth, acceptance, and affection. At age 6, Annie appeared to be a highly anxious youngster with low self-esteem and an overwhelming need to please. At age 9, despite her many accomplishments, Annie was still apparently highly anxious and possibly depressed. As noted earlier, it is possible that Annie was indeed a more difficult than average infant and that her early behavior contributed to an escalating pattern of mother–daughter conflict, although this is impossible to assess. In any case, it seems clear that lack of positive maternal behavior paired with overintrusiveness and a poor understanding of the developmental and psychologic needs of young children played a significant role in the persistence of Annie's problems at home.

Annie's continued difficulties with her mother at age 9 may also reflect desperate efforts for acceptance and recognition in the face of persistent rejection, which only has served to exacerbate her anxiety, sadness, and anger even further. In addition, Mrs. J appears unable to empathize with Annie or to help her cope with major developmental transitions (such as entry into kindergarten) or other stresses that are understandably upsetting to young children (such as her friend's move). At age 6, Annie's dependent behavior with other adults and her neediness were seen as possibly the result of an earlier insecure and anxious attachment relationship (see Sroufe, 1983). However, her ability to relate to other adults and to function relatively adequately in the peer group since early childhood suggest that Annie has adapted reasonably well to her family situation and that she has learned alternative ways of having some of her emotional needs met, at least superficially. Although it is obvious that Annie is not really a child showing attention deficit disorder, she may well be at risk for continued problems with anxiety, dysphoria, and low self-esteem, which all appear to be realistic reactions to her history of maternal rejection. Furthermore, if one accepts Bowlby's (1969) hypothesis that the relationship with the primary caregiver is the prototype for all later attachments, it is logical to predict that Annie may well have difficulty establishing trusting relationships with significant others in early adulthood. Or, she may be resilient enough to develop into an intellectually and socially competent young woman, despite these early setbacks. Only continued follow-up will permit answers to these questions.

Robbie S

Robbie initially presented as a fairly active and impulsive youngster with poor self-control. Although he was relatively noncompliant at home, he got along well with peers in preschool and was not described as aggressive. However, as his family situation deteriorated and his parents ultimately separated, his behavior problems worsened. He was showing a variety of symptoms at age 5, some consistent with his initial difficulties with attentional control and compliance, others characteristic of young children coping with separation. At the age 6 follow-up, things had not improved. The conflict between Robbie's parents had resulted in numerous court appearances and a lack of stability for Robbie. He continued to be sad and anxious and to have sleep problems. He was also active, inattentive, noncompliant, and angry much of the time, both at home and at school. He met DSM-III criteria for attention deficit disorder and received high ratings on both the internalizing and externalizing portions of the Achenbach CBCL. Laboratory observations were consistent with maternal reports of problem behavior. Robbie was aggressive in his play and somewhat out of control. He was also restless and inattentive on structured tasks, and he tended to test the limits with the examiner. He also made many careless and impulsive errors on a visual matching task.

Teacher reports also indicated problems with attention, compliance with classroom rules and regulations, and task completion. In addition, Robbie was getting into some relatively severe fights with other children. Finally, he was making limited academic progress despite better than average intellectual abilities. Classroom observations indicated that he was disruptive and irritating with other children, uncooperative with the teacher, frequently out of his seat, and that he often did not listen to the ongoing lesson. By the end of first grade, Robbie had not learned to read at all. Ultimately, he was enrolled in a special class for children with learning and behavior problems where he began to make some progress.

At age 9, problems were still in evidence, although Robbie also had made some progress academically. Although his family situation had stabilized over the intervening years, there was still conflict between his parents over visitation, and his father did not always follow through on planned visits and outings, leaving Robbie upset and angry. At school Robbie remained in a special class for children with behavior problems, although he was mainstreamed for most academic subjects. He was functioning at grade level in reading and arithmetic despite his earlier problems. Robbie's special class teacher was particularly concerned about his inattention, poor self-control and consequent need for constant direction and structure, although she felt that he had made considerable gains, both socially and academically, and that he was well motivated. She saw Robbie as very responsive to feedback and praise. However, Robbie also had been getting into fistfights during recess and at lunch with two boys who tended to tease and harass him, and he had been spending a portion of each day sitting in the principal's office. Mrs. S painted a similar picture. She was primarily concerned about Robbie's attentional problems, which was reflected in her interview responses. According to the structured diagnostic interview administered to Mrs. S, Robbie met DSM-III criteria for attention deficit disorder with hyperactivity. On the CBCL, his mother endorsed items leading to elevated scores on the dimensions of Social Withdrawal and Aggression, reflecting his recent fights with peers and some discipline problems at home.

It appears that Robbie is a youngster whose initial difficulties reflected a combination of temperamental difficultness (constitutional), a possible genetic vulnerability to psychopathology, and family tensions (environmental). His problems appear to have been exacerbated by the continuing instability in his life. Indeed, although we may characterize him as consistently active, inattentive, and noncompliant since early childhood, his aggression, anxiety, and cognitive problems appear to wax and wane in tandem with environmental stressors. In addition, Robbie's somewhat delayed language development may have contributed to his early reading problems. It is possible to speculate that he was a youngster at risk for problems and that given the severity and chronicity of family problems, his difficulties have both worsened and become more stable. In terms of predictive factors, the combined contribution of high initial symptoms and ongoing family disruption appear to account for Robbie's relatively poor outcome, consistent with research findings from other follow-up studies.

Teddy M

Teddy was the least problematic of the four children described when seen initially. It was our impression that his parents' interpretations of his early behavior and their expectations for quiet and compliance were somewhat unrealistic and that Teddy's behavior was pretty much age-appropriate. Although his play was somewhat unfocused when observed in the laboratory at age 4, he seemed to be doing well in general, and there were few signs of any real problems.

At the time of the age 6 follow-up, the M family was still living in the same house and the family situation remained unchanged. Mrs. M no longer saw Teddy as overactive or distractible. She described him as "happy" and "pretty easy going," although he was somewhat fearful of the dark and of thunderstorms. Mrs. M also reported that Teddy was somewhat shy with other children, waiting for them to initiate contacts and that he was reluctant to visit them, preferring to remain at home with her. Despite his apparent shyness, he had several friends he played with regularly and he was also involved in structured activities that brought him into contact with other children. His mother no longer saw him as showing significant problems, as indicated by her responses both to the interview and structured questionnaires. She also reported that Teddy was doing well in school, something that was confirmed by his teacher who described him as a "delightful child" who was "well liked by his classmates" and "enjoys learning." Teddy's teacher rated him well below the clinical range on all scales of the Achenbach Teacher Report Form. Observational measures confirmed parent and teacher reports of no significant problems. Teddy was cooperative and engaged during the laboratory assessment of free play; he performed willingly and well on structured tasks, with no signs of impulsivity, inattention, or fidgetiness. When observed in the classroom, he was also involved in appropriate classroom activities, attentive to teacher directives, and cooperative with peers.

At the age 9 follow-up, it was surprising to discover that Teddy had repeated second grade because his parents had been concerned about his shyness and social immaturity. Although the school had not seen the need for him to remain behind, because he was one of the younger children in his class, they acceded to his parents' wishes. Mrs. M still expressed some concerns about Teddy's shyness and failure to initiate peer contacts. She also noted that his school work was often disorganized and messy. However, he was apparently functioning at grade level and above in all academic areas. Both maternal and teacher reports indicated no significant behavior problems.

Teddy is a good example of a child whose development was well within the normal range. During the preschool years, Teddy's parents tended to misinterpret his age-appropriate activity level, relatively short bouts of sustained play, and limited ability to share toys as problems. Mr. and Mrs. M's high expectations for good behavior and their earlier pressures for maturity may well have placed Teddy under considerable stress, and this may have been apparent in his anxiety and fearfulness at age 6; these may have been age-related fears and timidities that resulted from starting school. Thus, Teddy's difficulties appear to be minimal, well within the normal range for children his age; his shyness and mild fearfulness do not appear to be having a major impact on his social and academic functioning. Certainly, relative to most of the children in the study who had been seen by their parents as having significant difficulties in late toddlerhood and the early preschool period. Teddy is doing very well and there is little reason to be seriously concerned about persistent problems as he enters third grade. Teddy's outcome is consistent with findings from the few other longitudinal studies reported in this chapter. Low levels of initial symptoms, a stable family environment, and a positive parent–child relationship would be expected to predict a good outcome in elementary school.

Summary

In this chapter the few longitudinal studies of hard-to-manage toddlers and preschoolers who were followed up to elementary school were examined, as were follow-up studies of hyperactive and aggressive elementary school children followed to adolescence and early adulthood. In general, there is a surprising convergence of findings. Approximately, one half of the children with moderate to severe externalizing problems in early childhood continued to show some degree of disturbance at school age, with boys doing more poorly than girls at follow-up. Similarly, clinically referred school-age children, especially boys, who present with symptoms of both hyperactivity and oppositional or conduct disorders, have a 50–50 chance of showing some form of continuing difficulty in adolescence or young adulthood. However, the links between preschool behavior problems and later disturbances are unclear. Furthermore, it should be pointed out that some children do not reach clinical attention until they enter school; this may reflect parental tolerance or reluctance to seek help in some cases in which problems had their onset in the preschool period but for one reason or another went unrecognized. However, problems in some children clearly have their onset with the stress of school entry or as a function of newly emerging difficulties in the family.

In addition, studies have examined predictors of good and poor outcome at various ages. Most studies suggest that family discord or disruption, negative and conflict-ridden parent–child relations, and maternal depression or anxiety are associated both with the onset and persistence of problems. Some studies identify predictive relationships, whereas others suggest that ongoing family difficulties are associated with ongoing problems in the child. In addition, all follow-up studies are consistent in showing that high levels of initial symptoms in the child, especially in boys, are associated with continuing difficulties. In particular, high levels of aggression and disobedience in the context of a high activity level and poor peer relations are associated with persistent problems both from preschool to elementary school and from elementary school to adolescence. Furthermore, children with lower IQs are more likely to have persistent difficulties that may also be reflected in specific learning disabilities or more general deficits in cognitive functioning and school achievement.

Although it is now fairly evident that earlier disorder predicts later difficulties in adjustment, it also appears that children with early symptoms can show a range of outcomes. Furthermore, it is likely that a variety of factors contribute to outcome and that the relevant factors and their complex interactions may be different for different children living in different family and social environments. Children with the same symptom picture at one point in time may have different outcomes and these are likely to be mediated by different factors. This complexity was illustrated both by general findings from our own longitudinal study of parent-identified hard-to-manage preschoolers followed up at ages 6 and 9 and by case illustrations from this study. Thus, in one instance a child with high levels of initial hyperactivity and aggression had a relatively poor outcome despite low levels of ongoing stressors or other risk factors for disorder. He continued to be aggressive, difficult to discipline, and disruptive at follow-up, although attention and school achievement were not problems. Also noteworthy were his continuing peer problems and his sad mood, which may well be reactions to his other difficulties. In a second example, a boy with relatively severe initial symptoms of hyperactivity and noncompliance (but not aggression), complicated by a family history of psychopathology and ongoing family turmoil, continued to show serious behavior problems at follow-up. He was not only aggressive with peers and noncompliant, but he met criteria for attention deficit disorder and he had learning and behavioral difficulties at school requiring special class placement. Furthermore, at age 9, his peer relations had also worsened, and over the years a number of signs of anxiety and sadness emerged as well. These problems were apparent against a backdrop of a positive mother–child relationship. In a third instance, a negative mother–child relationship was associated with sadness and anxiety in a girl who was functioning well outside the home. This youngster had made a reasonably good adjustment to family conflict, which may also reflect ongoing marital distress and maternal depression. However, her long-term prognosis remains unclear. Finally, one boy with relatively mild initial symptoms and no clearly identifiable risk factors or family problems was doing well at follow-up despite initial parental concerns about high activity and inattention and later worries about immaturity and shyness. Taken together, these data and case illustrations underline the complexities inherent in identifying causal mechanisms in the development of disorders in children, in predicting future adjustment, and in delineating the specific factors contributing to or mediating outcome, both generally and in the individual case.

CHAPTER NINE

Conclusions and
Social Policy Implications

In this book the major developmental transitions facing preschoolers have been discussed. Early indicators of behavior problems have been described, albeit with many caveats about the clinical implications of difficult behavior in early childhood. It was argued that child characteristics interact with family factors and factors in the wider social environment to determine whether children will function well or poorly in early childhood and that complex transactions among these factors also will determine how well adjusted children are at school age. A warm and supportive parent–child relationship, augmented with firm, reasonable, consistent, and flexible child-rearing practices, and a generally positive emotional climate in the home were seen as particularly important factors facilitating optimal child development. Conversely, a conflicted parent–child relationship, arbitrary, punitive, and/or uninvolved parenting, and high levels of family discord were associated with the development of problems, and these were likely to persist if the family climate, including child-rearing practices, did not become more positive over time.

Relationships with siblings and peers were also seen as having an important influence on young children's social development. Experiences with age-mates and siblings help young children to negotiate the tasks required to become cooperative members of a social group, as they learn to compromise, inhibit aggression, share, and understand the other's point of view. Furthermore, parent–child relationships, sibling relationships, and peer relationships appear to influence one another in systemic fashion. Thus, problems at home can have ramifications in the peer group and vice versa; for example, children living in stressful family circumstances may become aggressive at school or children who are rejected by other children may become noncompliant and moody at home. Other factors in the preschool or day-care environment, such as inadequate supervision or insensitive care, may precipitate problems at home. Similarly, external stresses on the parents, such as problems at work or with extended family, may have an impact on parental availability or patience and thereby precipitate or exacerbate problems between parents and children. Children's problems may appear as transient situational disturbances or reactions to stress that disappear as external stressors lessen or, in the context of particular child characteristics, such as negative mood and poor self-regulatory abilities, when there are multiple and ongoing family stresses, problems may become more severe and persistent.

A transactional model is based on the assumption that development is neither linear nor necessarily predictable, especially when single factors and individual cases are considered. According to this view, young children are often able to overcome early difficulties, given a supportive and responsive environment. It is also clear that some proportion of children with early and relatively serious behavior problems will continue to have difficulties throughout the early childhood years. The limited data suggest that problems may persist despite access to currently available treatments. Furthermore, the combination of provocative and aggressive child behavior, inadequate parenting strategies, and continuing family difficulties is most clearly associated with chronic problems. However, individual children appear to develop problems for different reasons, and there are likely to be a variety of routes to disorder, as well as different factors influencing problem persistence and severity. Thus, different combinations of factors may lead to problem onset in the individual case; even when similar etiological factors appear to be present, their relative importance may vary from one individual to another. Finally, one factor may be causal in one case and a consequence of problems in another. For example, rejection by peers may lead to aggressive behavior in one child, whereas in another, aggressive behavior may lead to peer rejection. As has been evident throughout, it is almost impossible to know where and how to draw causal inferences. Some of these issues were illustrated by case vignettes throughout this book.

Despite the complexity inherent in this field of study and the difficulty in establishing clear-cut causal links between particular environmental factors and the child's behavior, there are a number of conclusions that have been drawn in preceding chapters linking environmental factors to the onset and/or persistence, as well as the amelioration, of children's problems. At a practical level, research findings regarding child and family development and later outcome have social policy implications, and many current social policy debates have important ramifications on young children and their families (e.g., Maccoby, Kahn, & Everett, 1983; Stipek & McCroskey, 1989). Among the more heated debates are those revolving around policies concerning child care and parental leave (e.g., Hopper & Zigler, 1988; Phillips, 1986; Stipek & McCroskey, 1989). Educational programs for parents and for health professionals also need to be addressed. The lack of availability of comprehensive treatment programs for preschoolers with behavior problems needs to be given serious attention by the mental health and pediatric communities. Children and families similar to those described in this book have been widely neglected by the mental health community, which has targeted children of school-age and adolescence for intervention efforts, as well as preschoolers with more serious cognitive and emotional disorders. Young children with less obvious problems tend to fall through the cracks because they are frequently ineligible and/or inappropriate for those programs that are available. This lack of policy initiatives in a variety of areas affecting preschoolers reflects a combination of economic factors, political priorities, and misinterpretations and oversimplifications of research findings (Maccoby et al., 1983; Woodhead, 1988).

Recently, several authors, addressing social policy issues that affect infants and preschoolers, have pointed to the need for transactional, ecological, and systems models when translating developmental data into policy initiatives (McCartney & Galanopoulus, 1988; Woodhead, 1988). Woodhead in particular cautions against the overly simplistic interpretation of research findings that can lead cost-conscious legislators to favor one-shot and quick solutions to complex problems (see also Zigler, 1987). Indeed, one could argue that the current trend away from government spending on social programs is, in part, a direct result of the failure (or lack of well-documented success) of various prevention and treatment programs to effect sweeping social changes or to have long-lasting effects on outcome. Woodhead discusses the case of Head Start and other early intervention programs for impoverished preschoolers, which have waxed and waned in popularity and consequently in funding levels. Funding of such programs at any point in time appears to depend upon the findings from specific studies, the nature of public expectations, and the types of outcome measures employed. Although recent studies indicate that early intervention programs for dis- advantaged children are effective, even in the long-term, when they are structured, have a reasonable staff:child ratio, and involve parents, the nature of the change process is poorly understood (Haskins, 1989; Woodhead, 1988).

The initial rationale for early intervention was the expectation that cognitive enrichment would lead to permanent gains in cognitive functioning (Hunt, 1961). Not only did naive optimism about the impact of early intervention lead to expectations of significant and permanent gains in IQ, some suggested that enrichment programs for dis- advantaged preschoolers would break the cycle of poverty. Woodhead (1988) and Zigler (1987), among others, point out the negative social policy implications of overblown expectations. When these expectations were unrealized and deemed unrealistic, funding suffered and funding cuts rarely took into account the relative merits of different programs. A more realistic appraisal of early intervention programs, one that is more consistent with the accumulated evidence, suggests that all programs, whether prevention programs for disadvantaged children or treatment programs for children with difficulties, must be evaluated within a family and social context. Thus, Woodhead (1988) argues that compensatory preschool education programs influence the child's self-esteem and social competence as well as the attitudes and expecta- tions of significant others in the child's environment (parents and teachers). Complex transactions among these child and environmental factors are likely to mediate outcome. This model can be applied to a number of other social policy issues that have an impact on a large number of young children and families.

Education for Parenting

Although childbirth education classes of various sorts are widely available to pregnant women and their husbands, such programs tend to help couples prepare for and deal with the delivery. They do not prepare parents for the profound psychological impact of becoming a parent or for the multiple changes that occur in the marital relationship and the family system (e.g., Belsky, 1981). Little guidance is given to new parents about what to expect from a newborn or about how to best manage routine caretaking tasks, which may seem overwhelming to new parents. Few programs are available to teach parents more generally about children's early development or developmental needs. It is assumed that most parents just "know" what to do or that they discover the best methods of coping with a particular problem or developmental phase by learning from their social network or, at worst, by trial and error. Although parenting groups are often available for parents who are "at risk," many parents, educated, sensitive, and child-centered ones, as well as those with fewer resources, could benefit from educational programs that provide support (especially to first time parents) and information on the development of infants and toddlers.

For instance, it may be helpful to new parents to understand something about their infant's developing perceptual and sensory systems, as well as the fact that face-to-face social interaction and close bodily contact are important for early socioemotional development. Understanding that infants vary widely in temperament and personality and that they may have different needs depending upon, for example, their self-soothing ability, activity level, and alertness, may also be helpful. As infants begin to explore the world of objects and show fear of strangers, understanding the developmental underpinnings of these major advances may help parents to cope with them more effectively, for example, by more appropriately childproofing the house to permit exploration and by being sensitive to the approach of strangers or to separations. Parental responsiveness to distress is also an important consideration for parents. All too frequently, parents worry about "spoiling" a 2-month-old if he/she is picked up when he/she cries. Understanding that a 2-month-old and a 12-month-old differ greatly in their levels of cognitive and social development, their ability to meet their own needs and communicate about them, and their understanding of cause-effect relationships would appear to make parenting an easier task. Certainly, when children reach toddlerhood, many parents sorely need help setting appropriate limits. In some instances parents may require support to help them ride out the tantrums that may accompany this sometimes stormy and difficult developmental period. Often parents have a hard time providing a supportive environment that will facilitate exploration and the development of autonomy but not elicit conflict-ridden defiance.

Unfortunately, programs that teach parents about the rudiments of development are rarely available. All too often parents enter parenting programs when things have gotten out of hand, and it is clear that a

6-week or a 12-week parent training program by itself will do little as a therapeutic intervention (see Chapter Seven). Furthermore, such programs tend to be based on naive behaviorism with little concern for the differing needs of children at different developmental levels. In addition, annoying behaviors are usually identified as the problem requiring modification, and parents are not encouraged to think about underlying causes or other ways of conceptualizing what the real problem might be. Rather, simple solutions, such a star charts and time out, are prescribed for most, if not all, presenting complaints. Normal perturbations in development are rarely addressed, nor is a link made between stressful events in the family and a child's aggressive, defiant, or clinging behavior. It is indeed surprising how educated and sensitive parents sometimes think that their preschooler is buffered from ongoing stressful family events. Thus, it would seem that many minor problems which can escalate and become more serious, even though they may remain transient, could be prevented or ameliorated by some relatively straightforward pointers for parents. Such programs could be made available through a range of pediatric, developmental, and educational facilities for a small fee. Parents of children similar to Annie and Teddy might have benefited from such information when their children were infants and toddlers; their increased knowledge might have influenced their sensitivity and understanding, making things easier on parents and children alike. A parent education (i.e., developmental) component should also be incorporated into more comprehensive programs for families considered at risk.

Education for Health Professionals

When Robbie's mother contacted her pediatrician about her difficulties handling his behavior in infancy, she was told that he would outgrow the problem and not to worry about it. This was a common experience of parents in our project, one that we continue to hear about with disturbing frequency. Although it is appropriate not to overpathologize common developmental problems, such a response shows a lack of sensitivity to parental concerns and needs. Thus, whereas such advice may be reassuring to some parents, it may confuse and upset other parents whose children are extremely difficult or who are uncertain about how to cope with a particular developmental issue and are seeking advice. Even when the problem is something that is likely to be outgrown, as many problems are, parents may need support and specific suggestions about management strategies that are more effective than those they are using. Unfortunately, general training programs for pediatricians, nurses, or other primary care providers do not routinely include courses on normal social and cognitive development. Developmental issues are more likely to be covered in specialty programs, such as behavioral pediatrics or pediatric nursing, although individuals with such specialized training are more often found in teaching hospitals or specialty clinics, not as primary care providers. Yet, parents bring their questions about common developmental problems and their concerns about behavior management to their pediatrician or family physician first. This has prompted Routh, Schroeder, and Koocher (1983) to propose that clinical psychologists (presumably ones with a developmental background) join forces with pediatricians working in group practices, health maintenance organizations, and other frontline facilities. Although I heartily agree with this recommendation, it should also be pointed out that many psychiatrists, psychologists, and social workers receive little basic grounding in developmental issues; mental health training programs tend to focus on pathology and its ramifications. However, in-depth knowledge of normal child and family development would seem to be a crucial prerequisite to work with young children and their families, whether one is providing primary services or services to children on a referral basis. Work with young children and their families requires special training, training that helps the pediatric or mental health worker to understand parental concerns within a developmental framework while not minimizing them as insignificant.

Child Care

The child care controversy has become extremely heated recently, and the issue of day-care has resurfaced in the political arena. Indeed, this is clearly the most serious public policy issue concerning young children and families that currently faces the country because it is obvious that many young children spend their most important hours in less than adequate facilities. Unfortunately, the child care debate has focused rather simplistically on whether day-care is good or bad for infants (e.g., Belsky, 1988; Clarke-Stewart, 1989), and emotions on this topic have run high. Critics of child care have played on the guilt that many women feel when they return to work; proponents of child care have sometimes emphasized the potential benefits of quality care and minimized the drawbacks of child care in general. More recently, behavioral scientists embroiled in the child care debate have become more active in the political arena, where it is clear that issues of the quality of care have not received adequate attention (Gamble & Zigler, 1986; Phillips, 1986). Obviously, child care is not a monolithic construct; young children with working parents may be cared for at home by a relative or paid baby-sitter, at a neighbor's house, in a family day-care facility, in a day-care center, or in some combination of in home and out of home care. In each instance, the quality of care and the nature of the child–caregiver relationship will vary widely. In both family and center day-care, adult:child ratios will vary considerably and caregivers will differ in their training and knowledge of child development. Although the extant research can be interpreted to support either the pros or cons of nonparental care (Belsky, 1988; Clarke-Stewart, 1989; Clarke-Stewart & Fein, 1983; Phillips, McCartney, Scarr, & Howes, 1987), there is accumulating evidence indicating that quality of care interacts with family factors to determine the impact of day-care on children's development (e.g., Howes & Olenick, 1986). Thus, the question becomes, not whether child care is good or bad, but under what conditions young children in nonparental care fare well and what conditions need to be modified to facilitate development in those children who are not doing well.

From a transactional and ecological perspective, one must consider the convergent factors in the child, family, and child care facility that are associated with good versus poor adaptation to nonparental care. The anecdotes presented in Chapter Four suggest that when children spend too much time away from home, when the quality of care is poor, providing children with inadequate attention, affection, and emotional support, and when there are major tensions in the home that interfere with adequate parenting, children are apt to develop major problems. Several of the children described earlier were reacting to a subtle, but insidious, form of emotional neglect. Dealing with only one facet of this complex interplay of factors will probably not be adequate to ameliorate children's problems. However, standards for child care facilities would make a small dent in one aspect of the problem by pressing for adequate numbers of properly trained and/or experienced caregivers who might be more sensitive to the needs of young children.

In this regard, the quality of care, defined grossly in terms of the ratio of children to caregivers and staff training in child development and child care, becomes crucial. For example, staff:child ratios of 3:1 for infants and 4:1 for toddlers have been proposed, based on an analysis of the needs of young children for individual care, attention, and social interaction with adults (see Phillips, 1986). Although the data on day-care quality are far from complete, it is evident from extant findings that staff:child ratios, staff training and experience, the stability of caregivers, and programming rather than custodial care are associated with developmentally appropriate gains in children's cognitive functioning and social competence (Clarke-Stewart, 1989; Phillips, 1986). These general issues need no longer be open to debate; support is needed for continued research on specific issues of child care quality.

Although it is now documented that quality can make a difference, it is also well known that children with the most needs are often those who are left in the least adequate facilities. At a minimum, providers of care to young children should be trained to understand children and their development. The fact that caregivers are often untrained and unskilled, working for low wages and in facilities with high turnover should be a cause for concern among parents, child development specialists, and politicians alike. Staff:child ratios in such facilities are often inadequate to meet either necessary safety standards or the psychological needs of young children. One adult cannot possibly meet the needs of five or six infants or toddlers for basic caregiving, as well as social and cognitive stimulation, although 30 states permit such ratios for infants and 46 for toddlers (see Young & Zigler, 1986)! Poor pay and low status lead to rapid staff turnover when there is substantial evidence that stable caretakers are important to young children's sense of security and well-being.

The history of federal standards for day-care centers and family day-care homes provides a sobering picture of the interplay between political concerns and children's welfare (see Phillips, 1986; Young & Zigler, 1986). Although standards were drawn up and published as the HEW Federal Interagency Day Care Requirements (1980), they were withdrawn because of cost constraints; furthermore, these are *minimum* standards, "a standard below which the child's development could be impaired" (Young & Zigler, 1986). Although these standards appear adequate in some areas (e.g., staff:child ratio and group size), specifications for staff training and programming are more ambiguous. More recently, Congress passed the 1985 Model Child Care Standards Act in response to allegations of sexual abuse in day-care and preschool facilities (see Phillips, 1986, for a detailed discussion of this legislation and its weaknesses). This legislation, consistent with government policies on deregulation and limited federal involvement in state-run programs, is seen as advisory rather than mandatory. Its main thrust is the requirement that states institute background checks of new staff, supposedly as a way of decreasing incidents of child abuse by caregivers. The effectiveness of this approach remains to be determined. Although every effort should be made to monitor and minimize such crimes against children, this legislation fails to deal, except in vague and nonspecific terms, with general issues of quality of care. Thus, it does not delineate specific requirements for staff training or supervision, staff:child ratios, or programming, although as Phillips (1986) notes, staff:child ratios and staff training and qualifications have been related most clearly to outcomes. Despite these findings, it is these dimensions that are left to the discretion of the states. Clearly, this bill, which was reactive to a specific and highly publicized aspect of the child care crisis, rather than proactive, falls far short even of the minimum standards promulgated in 1980.

Since the Reagan administration left decisions about child care to the states and the Bush administration appears to be following suit, how well are the states protecting children? This issue is reviewed in detail by Young and Zigler (1986). These authors examined state licensing requirements for child care facilities and compared them with the 1980 federal standards. As might be expected, there is wide variability. Although all 50 states have some form of regulation and licensing requirement for day-care centers and 44 states also regulate family day-care homes, only 14 states regulate group day-care homes. Furthermore, not one state adheres to all the guidelines in the 1980 regulations! In particular, only three states meet the 1980 federal standards for infant:caregiver ratios and only one state meets these guidelines for both infants and toddlers. Fewer than one half of the states require the director of a day-care facility to have any training in child care or child development, and only eight states require that caregivers have any specialized training. Few states have program requirements that go beyond custodial care, and when they do, these requirements are vague and nonspecific. This suggests that federal standards will be necessary to establish uniformly adequate guidelines that are independent of cost constraints and type of setting. This raises problematic issues of funding and affordability that need to be addressed. However, the failure to make decisions about the minimum that constitutes adequate care for young children may well have serious economic and human consequences, both immediately and in the long-term, given the potential impact of inadequate facilities on the safety, health, and development of young children.

In view of the fact that women with children younger than 3 years are returning to work in increasing numbers, federal standards that mandate quality care, that is, care that facilitates children's emotional, social, and cognitive development, should be among our society's highest priorities. Although it is clear that there are some excellent facilities with caring staff, places in these facilities are hard to come by. It is not uncommon for working women to place their names on the waiting lists of high-quality child care centers as soon as they learn they are pregnant. Such centers are extremely expensive, and children living in less than comfortable circumstances rarely, if ever, have access to them. The increase in for-profit day-care facilities that are franchises, rather similar to a fast food chain, are also a cause for concern. Although these facilities are often glitzy and appealing in appearance, issues of ratios, staff training, and programming become particular concerns because it is unclear how the owners of such facilities balance children's and families' needs against their desire for profit. Finally, many family day-care settings are unlicensed and, therefore, may not even meet their state's minimum requirements for adequacy.

It seems obvious that professionals concerned with young children must join forces with parents to put pressure on politicians to establish and enforce adequate federal standards. Organizations such as the Children's Defense Fund and the National Association for the Education of Young Children have been vocal on this issue. Other educational, developmental, and mental health groups need to give this issue top priority. Furthermore, some form of subsidy to child care centers that serve middle and low income families and a more generous tax rebate for parents who must pay for child care seem to be important first steps in dealing with this crisis, which could have important long-term implications for the emotional health and well-being of a large segment of today's infants and preschoolers (see also Stipek & McCroskey, 1989).

Infant Care Leave and Flexible Work Schedules for Parents

The child care issue also interfaces with parental leave policies and flexible work schedules for parents with young children (Hopper &

Zigler, 1988; Stipek & McCroskey, 1989). There has been a renewed call for a national policy providing for paid parental leave for at least one parent at the time of the birth or adoption of an infant. For example, Zigler and his colleagues at the Bush Center for Social Policy at Yale have recommended that parents be granted 6 months of partially paid leave, continued benefits, and guaranteed job security. A less sweeping bill that would grant parents 18 weeks of unpaid leave and some degree of job security was considered by the 100th Congress and then tabled prior to the 1988 election. It will hopefully be revived in the next legislative session, although its fate (despite pre-election rhetoric) remains uncertain. As Hopper and Zigler (1988) note, this would be a step in the right direction, and it would deal effectively with some of the shortcomings of available and affordable infant care. Many parents who are forced to return to work would at least have the option of staying home with their newborn for the first few months, a time when early parent–infant relationships are being established. Certainly, it appears reasonable to grant paid or partially paid leave at least through the postpartum period (i.e., 3 months) so that women are not required to return to work when they are still exhausted from the physical and psychological demands of childbirth and newborn infants do not have to be placed in substitute care if their parents would prefer to remain at home. It is worth noting that most other Western democracies have some form of national policy on this issue that includes paid or partially paid leave and job security (Stipek & McCroskey, 1989).

Whereas the need for a parental leave policy is clear, there are also other changes in policy that seem important for families with young children. Because company-run, on-site day-care centers are rare, there is a need for more flexible work hours for families with young children. This issue is addressed in detail by Winett, Stefanek, and Riley (1983) who recommend part-time work arrangements that include flexible work hours and more opportunities to work at home. For example, these authors suggest that jobs that are 75% time would permit one parent to return home in the late afternoon to spend time with preschool-age or younger children, making it unnecessary for the young child to spend 40 or more hours a week in a day-care center. More flexible work hours would also permit parents to share child rearing, allowing one parent to be at home during part of the time the other worked, cutting down on the expenses of child care as well as the number of hours each week that children are in nonparental care. Although some parents have managed to work out such schedules, for example, if they do shift work or work in certain types of positions, flexible work hours are rarely considered as an option that may assist young families who are dealing with child care problems. However, there is some empirical evidence to suggest that flexible work hours ease the pressures on families with young children and increase the time parents spend with children, while not decreasing worker productivity (Winett et al., 1983). Certainly, more thought needs to be given to various flexible work schedules in both the public and private sectors.

Mental Health Programs for Preschoolers

As noted throughout this book, there is a serious lack of appropriate programs for preschoolers and their families. Although funds have been poured into various mental health screening programs for preschoolers, there are rarely adequate programs available to deal with problems once they are identified. This is particularly the case for preschool-age children with behavior and adjustment problems not accompanied by mental retardation, severe emotional withdrawal (e.g., autism), or marked poverty and psychosocial disadvantage. Thus, the working class or middle class family whose 3- or 4-year-old has a significant behavior problem really has few places to turn. Few workers in mental health centers are knowledgeable about the special issues that confront preschoolers and their parents. As already noted, parents are often told that the problems will be outgrown or they are coached in the use of behavior management procedures. Comprehensive treatment programs are almost nonexistent (see also Saxe, Cross, & Silverman, 1988, for a more general discussion of this issue and of the fact that most treatment programs are not based on our current knowledge of development or of what works). Thus, children who are too difficult to manage in a regular preschool program, who require more specialized programs, but who are not appropriate for programs for retarded or severely disturbed youngsters tend to fall between the cracks. There are few programs available for such children, and those that do exist often have long waiting lists. Children such as Jamie and Robbie require small classes with structured programs that help children develop prosocial behaviors, such as sharing, compromising, and playing cooperatively, and also help them to control their aggressive and angry impulses. Obviously, preschool programs that cater to such children must have a small teacher:child ratio; the staff must be knowledgeable about young children's development and trained to deal with impulsive and defiant behavior as well as social withdrawal. However, it is unknown whether aggressive and defiant preschoolers do better when mainstreamed into programs with children who are developing normally or whether they require a highly specialized program geared only to children with problems.

In addition, therapeutic preschool programs must meet the needs of the child's family as a whole to be effective as a mental health intervention. Thus, parent groups that provide both support and help with child rearing are a minimum requirement. As was made clear throughout this book, in most instances children's problems occur in the context of other family problems. Thus, a comprehensive program would need to provide individual or marital therapy when it appeared indicated, as well as referrals for help with other problems confronting the child or family. Although the literature reviewed in Chapter Seven suggested some of the ingredients that may go into a successful comprehensive program for preschoolers and their families, no treatment outcome studies have evaluated the effectiveness of a truly comprehensive therapeutic program for preschoolers with behavior problems. In general, programs dealt with one or two facets of a complex problem or were not sufficiently intense to determine whether the approach was viable or not. Because it is clear that relatively marked behavior problems in preschoolers have long-term developmental consequences for some proportion of children and their families, the need for early intervention programs seems obvious. Although comprehensive treatment programs for preschoolers may seem costly in the current economic climate, the successful amelioration of problems in young children should ultimately decrease the need for mental health and educational services later on.

Summary

Research and theory on young children's development and on early indicators of behavior problems were reviewed and integrated. The discussion in this chapter focused on several social policy implications of both the research and clinical findings. In particular, educational programs for parents and health care providers were discussed. Issues around child care and the need for uniform federal day-care standards were emphasized as major problems confronting families with young children. Parental leave and flexible work schedules were also mentioned as ways of helping parents with young children juggle the multiple demands of career and family while providing their children some needed time at home with at least one parent. Finally, the lack of comprehensive treatment programs for preschool children with significant behavior problems was noted.

Although there are a myriad of programs that serve infants and preschoolers (Garwood, Phillips, Hartman, & Zigler, 1989), and these run the gamut from nutritional supplements to educational screening and intervention, there has also been a notable lack of planning, direction, integration, or assessment of priorities and outcomes. One particular gap is in the availability of comprehensive treatment programs for behavior problem preschoolers. Because findings from several studies now converge to indicate that preschoolers with severe externalizing problems, especially those living in more dysfunctional or disrupted family environments, are at risk for persistent problems that may last into elementary school and beyond, the need for early intervention programs appears obvious. Programs that include educational and therapeutic work with the parents, as well as intensive, structured work with troubled children in a preschool setting, remain an ideal goal. Furthermore, a parental leave policy and the availability of adequate child care might help to alleviate the stresses on dysfunctional families or families with difficult children and make parents more available to meet their children's needs. In other instances, stable and nurturant caregivers might buffer some young children from the impact of parental unavailability, insensitivity, or rejection. It seems obvious that the ultimate cost to society that stems from not treating such problems early far outweighs the cost of instituting appropriately targeted intervention programs when children are young.

References

Abramovitch, R., Corter, C., & Pepler, D. (1980). Observations of mixed-sex sibling dyads. *Child Development, 51,* 1268–1271.

Achenbach, T. M., & Edelbrock, C. (1978). The classification of child psychopathology: A review and analysis of empirical efforts. *Psychological Bulletin, 85,* 1275–1301.

Achenbach, T. M., & Edelbrock, C. (1981). Behavioral problems and competencies reported by parents of normal and disturbed children aged four through sixteen. *Monographs of the Society for Research in Child Development, 46* (Serial No. 188).

Achenbach, T. M., & Edelbrock, C. (1983). *Manual for the Child Behavior Checklist and Revised Child Behavior Profile.* Burlington, VT: University Associates in Psychiatry.

Achenbach, T. M., McConaughy, S. H., & Howell, C. T. (1987). Child/adolescent behavioral and emotional problems: Implications of cross-informant correlations for situational specificity. *Psychological Bulletin, 101,* 213–232.

Ainsworth, M. D. S. (1969). Object relations, dependency, and attachment: A theoretical review of the infant–mother relationship. *Child Development, 40,* 969–1026.

Ainsworth, M. D. S., Blehar, M., Waters, E., & Wall, S. (1978). *Patterns of attachment.* Hillsdale, NJ: Erlbaum.

Aldenderfer, M., & Blashfield, R. (1984). *Cluster analysis.* Beverly Hills, CA: Sage.

Alexander, J. F., & Malouf, R. E. (1983). Intervention with children experiencing problems in personality and social development. In E. M. Hetherington (Ed.), P. Mussen (Series Ed.), *Handbook of child psychology: Vol. IV. Socialization, personality, and social development.* New York: Wiley.

American Psychiatric Association. (1980). *Diagnostic and statistical manual of mental disorders* (3rd ed.). Washington, DC: Author.

American Psychiatric Association. (1987). *Diagnostic and statistical manual of mental disorders* (3rd ed., rev.). Washington, DC: Author.

Anderson, D. R., Long, A., Leathers, E., Denny, B., & Hilliard, D. (1981). Documentation of change in problem behaviors among anxious and

243

hostile-aggressive children enrolled in a therapeutic preschool program. *Child Psychiatry and Human Development, 11,* 232–240.

Andrews, S. R., Blumenthal, J. B., Johnson, D. L., Kahn, A. J., Ferguson, C. J., Lasater, T. M., Malone, P. E., & Wallace, D. B. (1982). The skills of mothering: A study of parent child development centers. *Monographs of the Society for Research in Child Development, 47* (Serial No. 198).

Asher, S. (1983). Social competence and peer status: Recent advances and future directions. *Child Development, 54,* 1427–1434.

Axline, V. (1969). *Play therapy.* New York: Ballantine.

Barkley, R. A. (1981). *Hyperactive children: A handbook for diagnosis and treatment.* New York: Guilford.

Barkley, R. A. (1985). The social behavior of hyperactive children: Developmental changes, drug effects and situational variation. In R. McMahon & R. Peters (Eds.), *Childhood disorders.* New York: Brunner/Mazel.

Bates, J. E. (1980). The concept of difficult temperament. *Merrill-Palmer Quarterly, 26,* 299–319.

Bates, J. E. (1987). Temperament in infancy. In J. Osofsky (Ed.), *Handbook of infant development* (2nd ed.). New York: Wiley.

Bates, J. E., & Bayles, K. (1988). Attachment and the development of behavior problems. In J. Belsky & T. Nezworski (Eds.), *Clinical implications of attachment.* Hillsdale, NJ: Erlbaum.

Bates, J. E., Maslin, C., & Frankel, K. (1985). Attachment security, mother–child interaction, and temperament as predictors of behavior problem ratings at age three years. In I. Bretherton & E. Waters (Eds.), Growing points of attachment theory and research. *Monographs of the Society for Research in Child Development, 50,* 167–193.

Baumrind, D. (1967). Child care practices anteceding 3 patterns of preschool behavior. *Genetic Psychology Monographs, 75,* 43–88.

Bayley, N., & Schaefer, E. S. (1964). Correlations of maternal and child behaviors with the development of mental abilities: Data from the Berkeley Growth Study. *Monographs of the Society for Research in Child Development, 29* (Serial No. 97).

Beardslee, W. R., Bemporad, J., Keller, M. B., & Klerman, G. L. (1983). Children of parents with major affective disorder: A review. *American Journal of Psychiatry, 140,* 825–832.

Becker, W. C. (1971). *Parents are teachers.* Champaign, IL: Research Press.

Behar, L. B. (1977). The Preschool Behavior Questionnaire. *Journal of Abnormal Child Psychology, 5,* 265–276.

Bell, R. Q. (1968). A reinterpretation of the direction of effects in studies of socialization. *Psychological Review, 75,* 81–95.

Belsky, J. (1981). Early human experience: A family perspective. *Developmental Psychology, 17,* 13–23.

Belsky, J. (1984). The determinants of parenting: A process model. *Child Development, 55,* 83–96.

Belsky, J. (1988). The "effects" of infant day care reconsidered. *Early Childhood Research Quarterly, 3,* 235–272.

Belsky, J., & Rovine, M. (1988). Nonmaternal care in the first year of life and security of infant–parent attachment. *Child Development, 59,* 157–168.

Belsky, J., Rovine, M., & Taylor, D. G. (1984). The Pennsylvania Infant and Family Development Project, III: The origins of individual differences in infant–mother attachment: Maternal and infant contributions. *Child Development, 55,* 718–728.

Bennett, F. C., & Sherman, R. (1983). Management of childhood "hyper-activity" by primary care physicians. *Journal of Developmental and Behavioral Pediatrics, 4,* 88–93.

Block, J. H., & Block, J. (1980). The role of ego control and ego resiliency in the organization of behavior. In W. A. Collins (Ed.), *Minnesota symposium on child psychology: Vol. 13. Development of cognition, affect, and social relations.* Hillsdale, NJ: Erlbaum.

Block, J. H., Block, J., & Morrison, A. (1981). Parental agreement–disagreement on childrearing orientations and gender-related person-ality correlates in children. *Child Development, 52,* 965–974.

Bornstein, M. H., & Sigman, M. D. (1986). Continuity in mental development from infancy. *Child Development, 57,* 251–274.

Bowlby, J. (1969). *Attachment and loss: Vol. 1. Attachment.* New York: Basic Books.

Bowlby, J. (1973). *Attachment and loss: Vol. II. Separation.* New York: Basic Books.

Brazelton, T. B. (1974). *Toddlers and parents.* New York: Delta.

Bretherton, I. (1985). Attachment theory: Retrospect and prospect. In I. Bretherton & E. Waters (Eds.), Growing points in attachment theory and research. *Monographs of the Society for Research in Child Development, 50* (Serial No. 209).

Bretherton, I. (1987). New perspectives on attachment relations: Security, communication, and internal working models. In J. D. Osofsky (Ed.), *Handbook of infant development* (2nd ed.). New York: Wiley.

Brim, O., & Kagan, J. (1980). *Constancy and change in human development.* Cambridge, MA: Harvard University Press.

Brody, G. H., & Forehand, R. (1985). The efficacy of parent training with maritally distressed and nondistressed mothers: A multimethod assess-ment. *Behaviour Research and Therapy, 23,* 291–296.

Brody, G. H., Stoneman, Z., & Burke, M. (1987a). Child temperaments, maternal differential behavior, and sibling relationships. *Developmental Psychology, 23,* 354–362.

Brody, G. H., Stoneman, Z., & Burke, M. (1987b). Family system and individual child correlates of sibling behavior. *American Journal of Orthopsychiatry, 57,* 561–569.

Bronfenbrenner, U., & Crouter, A. C. (1983). The evolution of environmental models in developmental research. In W. Kessen (Ed.), P. H. Mussen (Series Ed.), *Handbook of child psychology: Vol. I. History, theory, and methods.* New York: Wiley.

Brown, A. L., Bransford, J. D., Ferrara, R. A., & Campione, J. C. (1983). Learning, remembering, and understanding. In J. H. Flavell & E. M. Markman (Eds.), P. Mussen (Series Ed.), *Handbook of child psychology: Vol. III. Cognitive development.* New York: Wiley.

Brown, G. W., & Harris, T. (1980). *Social origins of depression.* London: Tavistock.

Brownell, C. A. (1986). Convergent developments: Cognitive-developmental correlates of growth in infant–toddler peer skills. *Child Development, 57,* 275–286.

Brownell, C. A. (1988). Combinatorial skills: Converging developments over the second year. *Child Development, 59,* 675–685.

Buss, A., & Plomin, R. (1975). *A temperament theory of personality development.* New York: Wiley.

Buss, D. M. (1981). Predicting parent–child interactions from children's activity level. *Developmental Psychology, 17,* 59–65.

Buss, D. M., Block, J. H., & Block, J. (1980). Preschool activity level: Personality correlates and developmental implications. *Child Development, 51,* 401–408.

Campbell, S. B. (1976). Hyperactivity: Course and treatment. In A. Davids (Ed.), *Child personality and psychopathology* (Vol. 3). New York: Wiley.

Campbell, S. B. (1985). Hyperactivity in preschoolers: Correlates and prognostic implications. *Clinical Psychology Review, 5,* 502–524.

Campbell, S. B. (1987). Parent-referred problem three-year-olds: Developmental changes in symptoms. *Journal of Child Psychology and Psychiatry, 28,* 835–845.

Campbell, S. B. (1989). Developmental considerations in child psychopathology. In T. Ollendick & M. Hersen (Eds.), *Handbook of child psychopathology* (2nd ed.). New York: Plenum Press.

Campbell, S. B., & Breaux, A. M. (1983). Maternal ratings of activity level and symptomatic behavior in a non-clinical sample of young children. *Journal of Pediatric Psychology, 8,* 73–82.

Campbell, S. B., Breaux, A. M., Ewing, L. J., & Szumowski, E. K. (1984). A one-year follow-up of parent-identified "hyperactive" preschoolers. *Journal of the American Academy of Child Psychiatry, 23,* 243–249.

Campbell, S. B. Breaux, A. M., Ewing, L. J., & Szumowski, E. K. (1986). Correlates and predictors of hyperactivity and aggression: A longitudinal study of parent-referred problem preschoolers. *Journal of Abnormal Child Psychology, 14,* 217–234.

Campbell, S. B., Breaux, A. M., Ewing, L. J., Szumowski, E. K., & Pierce, E. W. (1986). Parent-referred problem preschoolers: Mother–child interaction during play at intake and one-year follow-up. *Journal of Abnormal Child Psychology, 14,* 425–440.

Campbell, S. B., & Cluss, P. (1982). Peer relations of young children with behavior problems. In K. H. Rubin & H. S. Ross (Eds.), *Peer relationships and social skills in childhood.* New York: Springer-Verlag.

Campbell, S. B., Endman, M., & Bernfeld, G. (1977). A three-year follow-up of hyperactive preschoolers into elementary school. *Journal of Child Psychology and Psychiatry, 18,* 239–250.

Campbell, S. B., Ewing, L. J., Breaux, A. M., & Szumowski, E. K. (1986). Parent-identified behavior problem toddlers: Follow-up at school entry. *Journal of Child Psychology and Psychiatry, 27,* 473–488.

Campbell, S. B., & Paulauskas, S. L. (1979). Peer relations in hyperactive children. *Journal of Child Psychology and Psychiatry, 20,* 233–246.

Campbell, S. B., Schleifer, M., Weiss, G., & Perlman, T. (1977). A two-year follow-up of hyperactive preschoolers. *American Journal of Orthopsychiatry, 47,* 149–162.

Campbell, S. B., Szumowski, E. K., Ewing, L. J., Gluck, D. S., & Breaux, A. M. (1982). A multidimensional assessment of parent-identified behavior problem toddlers. *Journal of Abnormal Child Psychology, 10,* 569–592.

Campos, J. J., Barrett, K. C., Lamb, M. E., Goldsmith, H. H., & Stenberg, C. (1983). Socioemotional development. In M. M. Haith & J. J. Campos (Eds.), P. H. Mussen (Series Ed.), *Handbook of child psychology: Vol. II. Infancy and developmental psychobiology.* New York: Wiley.

Cantwell, D., Baker, L., & Mattison, R. (1979). The prevalence of psychiatric disorder in children with speech and language disorders: An epidemiological study. *Journal of the American Academy of Child Psychiatry, 18,* 450–461.

Casey, R. J., & Berman, J. S. (1985). The outcome of psychotherapy with children. *Psychological Bulletin, 98,* 388–400.

Cassidy, J. (1986). The ability to negotiate the environment: An aspect of infant competence as related to quality of attachment. *Child Development, 57,* 331–337.

Chi, M. T., & Koeske, R. D. (1983). Network representation of a child's dinosaur knowledge. *Developmental Psychology, 19,* 29–36.

Clark, E. (1983). Meanings and concepts. In J. H. Flavell & E. M. Markman (Eds.), P. Mussen (Series Ed.), *Handbook of child psychology: Vol. III. Cognitive development.* New York: Wiley.

Clarke-Stewart, K. A. (1989). Infant day care: Maligned or malignant? *American Psychologist, 44,* 266–273.

Clarke-Stewart, K. A., & Fein, G. (1983). Early childhood programs. In M. M. Haith & J. J. Campos (Eds.), P. Mussen (Series Ed.), *Handbook of child psychology: Vol. II. Infancy and developmental psychobiology.* New York: Wiley.

Cochran, M., & Brassard, J. (1979). Child development and personal social networks. *Child Development, 50,* 601–616.

Cohen, N. J., Bradley, S., & Kolers, N. (1987). Outcome evaluation of a therapeutic day treatment program for delayed and disturbed preschoolers. *Journal of the American Academy of Child and Adolescent Psychiatry, 26,* 687–693.

Cohen, N. J., Davine, M. & Meloche-Kelly, M. (1989). The prevalence of unsuspected language disorders in a child psychiatric population. *Journal of the American Academy of Child and Adolescent Psychiatry, 28,* 107–111.

Cohen, N. J., Minde, K. (1983). The "hyperactive syndrome" in kindergarten children: Comparison of children with pervasive and situational symptoms. *Journal of Child Psychology and Psychiatry, 24,* 443–456.

Cohen, N. J., Sullivan, J., Minde, K., Novak, C., & Helwig, C. (1981). The relative effectiveness of methlyphenidate and cognitive behavior modification in the treatment of kindergarten-aged hyperactive children. *Journal of Abnormal Child Psychology, 9,* 43–54.

Coleman, J., Wolkind, S., & Ashley, L. (1977). Symptoms of behavior disturbance and adjustment to school. *Journal of Child Psychology and Psychiatry, 18*, 201–210.

Conners, C. K. (1980). *Food additives and hyperactive children*. New York: Plenum Press.

Conners, C. K. (1984, November). *Experimental studies of nutrient effects on brain, cognition, and behavior in children*. Paper presented at the American Medical Association Conference on Diet and Behavior, Arlington, VA.

Corsaro, W. A. (1981). Friendship in the nursery school: Social organization in a peer environment. In J. Gottman & S. Asher (Eds.), *The development of children's friendships*. New York: Cambridge University Press.

Corter, C., Abramovitch, R., & Pepler, D. (1983). The role of the mother in sibling interaction. *Child Development, 54*, 1599–1605.

Cowen, E. L., Pederson, A., Babigian, H., Izzo, L. E., & Trost, M. A. (1973). Long-term follow-up of early detected vulnerable children. *Journal of Consulting and Clinical Psychology, 41*, 438–416.

Cowen, E. L., Trost, M. A., Lorion, R. P., Dorr, D., Izzo, L. D., & Isaacson, R. V. (1975). New ways in school mental health: Early detection and prevention of school maladaptation. New York: Human Sciences Press.

Crnic, K. A., Greenberg, M. T., Ragozin, A. S., Robinson, N. M., & Basham, R. B. (1983). Effects of stress and social support on mothers and preterm and full-term infants. *Child Development, 54*, 209–217.

Crockenberg, S. B. (1981). Infant irritability, mother responsiveness, and social support influences on the security of infant–mother attachment. *Child Development, 52*, 857–865.

Crowther, J. K., Bond, L. A., & Rolf, J. E. (1981). The incidence, prevalence, and severity of behavior disorders among preschool-aged children in day care. *Journal of Abnormal Child Psychology, 9*, 23–42.

Cummings, E. M., Zahn-Waxler, C., & Radke-Yarrow M. (1981). Young children's responses to expressions of anger and affection by others in the family. *Child Development, 52*, 1274–1282.

Cummings, E. M., Zahn-Waxler, C., & Radke-Yarrow, M. (1984). Developmental changes in children's reactions to anger in the home. *Journal of Child Psychology and Psychiatry, 25*, 63–74.

Cutrona, C. E., & Troutman, B. R. (1986). Social support, infant temperament, and parenting self-efficacy: A mediational model of postpartum depression. *Child Development, 57*, 1507–1518.

Dadds, M. R., Schwartz, S., & Sanders, M. R. (1987). Marital discord and treatment outcome in behavioral treatment of child behavior problems. *Journal of Consulting and Clinical Psychology, 55*, 396–403.

Daehler, M. W., & Greco, C. (1985). Memory in very young children. In M. Pressley & C. J. Brainerd (Eds.), *Cognitive learning and memory in children*. New York: Springer-Verlag.

Damon, W. (1977). *The social world of the child*. San Francisco: Jossey-Bass.

Davenport, Y. B., Zahn-Waxler, C., Adland, M. L., & Mayfield, A. (1984). Early child-rearing practices in families with a manic-depressive parent. *American Journal of Psychiatry, 141*, 230–235.

DeLoache, J. S., Cassidy, D. J., & Brown, A. L. (1985). Precursors of mnemonic strategies in very young children. *Child Development, 56,* 125–137.

Devany, J., & Nelson, R. O. (1986). Behavioral approaches to treatment. In H. C. Quay & J. S. Werry (Eds.), *Psychopathological disorders of childhood* (3rd ed.). New York: Wiley.

DiPietro, J. A. (1981). Rough and tumble play: A function of gender. *Developmental Psychology, 17,* 50–58.

Dodge, K. A. (1983). Behavioral antecedents of peer social status. *Child Development, 54,* 1386–1399.

Douglas, V. I. (1983). Attentional and cognitive problems. In M. Rutter (Ed.), *Developmental neuropsychiatry.* New York: Guilford.

Doyle, A. B. (1982). Friends, acquaintances, and strangers: The influence of familiarity and ethnolinguistic background on social interaction. In K. H. Rubin & H. S. Ross (Eds.), *Peer relationships and social skills in childhood.* New York: Springer-Verlag.

Dumas, J., & Wahler, R. G. (1983). Predictors of treatment outcome in parent training: Mother insularity and socioeconomic disadvantage. *Behavioral Assessment, 5,* 301–313.

Dumas, J., & Wahler, R. G. (1985). Indiscriminate mothering as a contextual factor in aggressive-oppositional child behavior: "Damned if you do and damned if you don't." *Journal of Abnormal Child Psychology, 13,* 1–18.

Dunn, J. (1983). Sibling relationships in early childhood. *Child Development, 54,* 787–811.

Dunn, J. (1985). *Siblings.* Cambridge, MA: Harvard University Press.

Dunn, J., & Kendrick, C. (1981). Social behavior of young siblings in the family context: Differences between same-sex and different son dyads. *Child Development, 52,* 1265–1273.

Dunn, J., & Kendrick, C. (1982). *Siblings: Love, envy, and understanding.* Cambridge, MA: Harvard University Press.

Dunn, J., & Munn, P. (1985). Becoming a family member: Family conflict and the development of social understanding in the second year. *Child Development, 56,* 480–492.

Dunn, J., & Munn, P. (1986). Sibling quarrels and maternal intervention: Individual differences in understanding and aggression. *Journal of Child Psychology and Psychiatry, 27,* 583–595.

Dunn, J., Plomin, R., & Nettles, M. (1985). Consistency of mothers' behavior toward infant siblings. *Developmental Psychology, 21,* 1188–1195.

Earls, F. (1980). The prevalence of behavior problems in 3-year-old children. *Archives of General Psychiatry, 37,* 1153–1159.

Edelbrock, C., Costello, A. J., Dulcan, M. K., Kalas, R., & Conover, N. C. (1985). Age differences in the reliability of the diagnostic interview of the child. *Child Development, 56,* 265–275.

Egeland, B., & Farber, E. (1984). Infant–mother attachment: Factors related to its development and changes over time. *Child Development, 55,* 753–771.

Erikson, E. (1963). *Childhood and society.* New York: Norton.

Emery, R. E. (1982). Interparental conflict and the children of discord and divorce. *Psychological Bulletin, 92,* 310–330.

Emery, R. E., & O'Leary, K. D. (1982). Children's perceptions of marital discord and behavior problems of boys and girls. *Journal of Abnormal Child Psychology, 10,* 11–24.

Eyberg, S. M. (1987, August). *Assessing therapy outcomes with preschool children: Progress and problems.* Presidential Address to the Section on Clinical Child Psychology of the American Psychological Association, New York.

Eyberg, S. M., & Robinson, E. (1982). Parent–child interaction training: Effects on family functioning. *Journal of Clinical Child Psychology, 11,* 130–137.

Fagot, B. (1984). The consequences of problem behavior in toddler children. *Journal of Abnormal Child Psychology, 12,* 385–386.

Feingold, B. F. (1975). *Why your child is hyperactive.* New York: Random House.

Fergusson, D. M., Horwood, L. J., & Shannon, F. T. (1984). Relationship of family life events, maternal depression, and child-rearing problems. *Pediatrics, 73,* 773–776.

Field, T., & Reite, M. (1984). Children's responses to separation from mother during the birth of another child. *Child Development, 55,* 1308–1316.

Fischer, M., Rolf, J. E., Hasazi, J. E., & Cummings, L. (1984). Follow-up of a preschool epidemiological sample: Cross-age continuities and predictions of later adjustment with internalizing and externalizing dimensions of behavior. *Child Development, 55,* 137–150.

Flavell, J. (1963). *The developmental psychology of Jean Piaget.* Princeton, NJ: Van Nostrand.

Flavell, J. (1982). On cognitive development. *Child Development, 53,* 1–10.

Fraiberg, S. (1980). (Ed.). *Clinical studies in infant mental health.* New York: Basic Books.

Framo, J. (1975). Personal reflections of a therapist. *Journal of Marriage and Family Counseling, 1,* 15–28.

Frodi, A., Bridges, L., & Grolnick, W. (1985). Correlates of mastery related behavior: A short-term longitudinal study of infants in their second year. *Child Development, 56,* 1291–1298.

Gamble, T. J., & Zigler, E. (1986). Effects of infant day care: Another look at the evidence. *American Journal of Orthopsychiatry, 56,* 26–42.

Gamer, E., Grunebaum H., Cohler, B. J., & Gallant, D. (1977). Children at risk: Performance of three-year-olds and their mentally ill and well mothers on an interaction task. *Child Psychiatry and Human Development, 8,* 102–114.

Garmezy, N. (1987). Stress, competence, and development: Continuities in the study of schizophrenic adults, children vulnerable to psychopathology, and the search for stress resistant children. *American Journal of Orthopsychiatry, 57,* 159–174.

Garvey, C. (1977). *Play.* Cambridge, MA: Harvard University Press.

Garwood, S. G., Phillips, D., Hartman, A., & Zigler, E. F. (1989). As the pendulum swings: Federal agency programs for children. *American Psychologist, 44,* 434–440.

Gath, D. (1968). Child guidance and the general practitioner: A study of factors influencing referrals made by general practitioners to a child psychiatric department. *Journal of Child Psychology and Psychiatry, 9,* 213–227.

Gelman, R., & Baillargeon, R. (1983). A review of some Piagetian concepts. In J. H. Flavell & E. M. Markman (Eds.), P. Mussen (Series Ed.), *Handbook of child psychology: Vol. III. Cognitive development.* New York: Wiley.

George, C., & Main, M. (1979). Social interactions of young abused children: Approach, avoidance, and aggression. *Child Development, 50,* 306–318.

Gittelman, R., & Kanner, A. (1986). Psychopharmacotherapy. In H. C. Quay & J. S. Werry (Eds.), *Psychopathological disorders of childhood* (3rd ed.). New York: Wiley.

Gittelman, R., Mannuzza, S., Shenker, R., & Bonagura, N. (1985). Hyperactive boys almost grown up: Psychiatric status. *Archives of General Psychiatry, 42,* 937–947.

Goldsmith, H. H., & Alansky, J. A. (1987). Maternal and infant temperamental predictors of attachment: A meta-analytic review. *Journal of Consulting and Clinical Psychology, 55,* 805–816.

Goldsmith, H. H., & Campos, J. J. (1982). Toward a theory of infant temperament. In R. N. Emde & R. J. Harmon (Eds.), *The development of attachment and affiliative systems.* New York: Plenum Press.

Gopnik, A., & Meltzoff, A. (1988). The development of categorization in the second year and its relation to other cognitive and linguistic developments. *Child Development, 58,* 1523–1531.

Gottman, J. M., & Parkhurst, J. T. (1980). A developmental theory of friendship and acquaintanceship processes. In W. A. Collins (Ed.), *Minnesota symposium on child psychology: Vol. 13. Development of cognition, affect, and social relations.* Hillsdale, NJ: Erlbaum.

Greenberg, M. T., & Speltz, M. L. (1988). Attachment and the ontogeny of conduct problems. In J. Belsky & T. Nezworski (Eds.), *Clinical implications of attachment.* Hillsdale, NJ: Erlbaum.

Grest, D. L., & Wells, K. C. (1983). Behavioral family therapy with conduct disorders in children. *Behavior Therapy, 14,* 37–53.

Haith, M. M., & Campos, J. J. (Eds.). (1983). *Handbook of child psychology: Vol. II. Infancy and developmental psychobiology.* New York: Wiley.

Haley, J. (1976). *Problem-solving therapy.* San Francisco: Jossey-Bass.

Halverson, C. F., & Waldrop, M. F. (1976). Relations between preschool activity level and aspects of intellectual and social behavior at 7½. *Developmental Psychology, 12,* 107–112.

Harper, L. V., & Huie, K. S. (1985). The effects of prior group experience, age, and familiarity on the quality and organization of preschoolers' social relationships. *Child Development, 56,* 704–717.

Harter, S. (1983a). Developmental perspectives on the self system. In E. M. Hetherington (Ed.), P. Mussen (Series Ed.), *Handbook of child psychology: Vol. IV. Socialization, personality, and social development.* New York: Wiley.

Harter, S. (1983b). Cognitive-developmental considerations in the conduct of play therapy. In C. Schaefer & K. J. O'Connor (Eds.), *Handbook of play therapy.* New York: Wiley.

Hartmann, D., Roper, B. L., & Gelfand, D. M. (1977). An evaluation of alternative modes of child psychotherapy. In B. Lahey & A. E. Kazdin

(Eds.), *Advances in clinical child psychology* (Vol.I). New York: Plenum Press.

Hartup, W. W. (1974). Aggression in childhood: Developmental perspectives. *American Psychologist, 29*, 336–341.

Hartup, W. W. (1983). Peer relations. In E. M. Hetherington (Ed.), P. Mussen (Series Ed.), *Handbook of child psychology: Vol. IV. Socialization, personality, and social development*. New York: Wiley.

Hartup, W. W., Glazer, J. A., & Charlesworth, R. (1967). Peer reinforcement and sociometric status. *Child Development, 38*, 1017–1024.

Haskins, R. (1989). Beyond metaphor: The efficacy of early childhood education. *American Psychologist, 44*, 274–282.

Heinicke, C. M., & Strassmann, L. H. (1975). Toward more effective research on child psychotherapy. *Journal of the American Academy of Child Psychiatry, 14*, 561–588.

Hetherington, E. M. (1989). Coping with family transitions: Winners, losers, and survivors. *Child Development, 60*, 1–14.

Hetherington, E. M., Cox, M., & Cox, R. (1978). The aftermath of divorce. In J. H. Stevens & M. Matthews (Eds.), *Mother–child father–child relations*. Washington, DC: National Association for the Education of Young Children.

Hetherington, E. M., & Martin, B. (1986). Family factors and psychopathology in children. In H. C. Quay & J. S. Werry (Eds.), *Psychopathological disorders of childhood* (3rd ed.). New York: Wiley.

HEW federal interagency day care requirements. (1980). Washington, DC: U.S. Government Printing Office.

Hobbs, S. A., & Lahey, B. B. (1983). Behavioral treatment. In T. Ollendick & M. Hersen (Eds.), *Psychopathological disorders of childhood*. New York: Plenum Press.

Hopper, P., & Zigler, E. (1988). The medical and social science basis for a national infant care leave policy. *American Journal of Orthopsychiatry, 58*, 324–338.

Howes, C. (1981, April). *Patterns of friendship in young children*. Paper presented at the biennial meeting of the Society for Research in Child Development, Boston, MA.

Howes, C., & Olenick, M. (1986). Family and child care influences on toddler's compliance. *Child Development, 57*, 202–216.

Hubert, N. C., Wachs, T. D., Peters-Martin, P., & Gandour, M. J. (1982). The study of early temperament: Measurement and conceptual issues. *Child Development, 53*, 571–600.

Hughes, M., Pinkerton, G., & Plewis, I. (1979). Children's difficulties in starting infant school. *Journal of Child Psychology and Psychiatry, 20*, 187–196.

Hunt, J. McV. (1961). *Intelligence and experience*. New York: Ronald Press.

Jacobson, J. L., & Wille, D. E. (1986). The influence of attachment pattern on developmental changes in peer interaction from the toddler to the preschool period. *Child Development, 57*, 338–347.

Jenkins, S., Bax, M., & Hart, H. (1980). Behaviour problems in preschool children. *Journal of Child Psychology and Psychiatry, 21*, 5–18.

Jensen, A. (1969). How much can we boost IQ and scholastic achievement? *Harvard Educational Review, 29,* 1–23.

Kagan, J. (1971). *Change and continuity in infancy.* New York: Wiley.

Kagan, J. (1981). *The second year: The emergence of self-awareness.* Cambridge, MA: Harvard University Press.

Kagan, J. (1984). *The nature of the child.* New York: Basic Books.

Kagan, J., Kearsley, R. B., & Zelazo, P. R. (1978). *Infancy: Its place in human development.* Cambridge, MA: Harvard University Press.

Kagan, J., & Klein, R. E. (1973). Cross-cultural perspectives on early development. *American Psychologist, 28,* 947–961.

Kagan, J., & Moss, H. (1962). *Birth to maturity.* New York: Wiley.

Kavale, K. A., & Forness, S. R. (1983). Hyperactivity and diet treatment: A meta-analysis of the Feingold treatment. *Journal of Learning Disabilities, 16,* 324–330.

Kazdin, A. E. (1987). Treatment of antisocial behavior in children: Current status and future directions. *Psychological Bulletin, 102,* 187–203.

Klein, M. (1932). *The psycho-analysis of children.* New York: Norton.

Kohn, M. (1977). *Social competence, symptoms, and underachievement in childhood: A longitudinal perspective.* Washington, DC: V. H. Winston.

Kopp, C. B. (1982). Antecedents of self-regulation: A developmental perspective. *Developmental Psychology, 18,* 199–214.

Korner, A. F. (1971). Individual differences at birth: Implications for early experience and later development. *American Journal of Orthopsychiatry, 41,* 608–619.

Korner, A. F., Zeanah, C. H., Linden, J., Berkowitz, R. I., Kraemer, H. C., & Agras, W. S. (1985). The relation between neonatal and later activity and temperament. *Child Development, 56,* 38–42.

Kovacs, M., & Paulauskas, S. (1986). The traditional psychotherapies. In H. C. Quay & J. S. Werry (Eds.), *Psychopathological disorders of childhood* (3rd ed.). New York: Wiley.

Krasnor, L. R. (1982). An observational study of social problem solving in young children. In K. H. Rubin & H. S. Ross (Eds.), *Peer relationships and social skills in childhood.* New York: Springer-Verlag.

Ladd, G. W., & Price, J. M. (1987). Predicting children's social and school adjustment following the transition from preschool to kindergarten. *Child Development, 58,* 1168–1189.

Lamb, M. (1981). Fathers and child development: An integrative overview. In M. Lamb (Ed.), *The role of the father in child development* (2nd ed.). New York: Wiley.

Lamb, M. (1987). Predictive implications of individual differences in attachment. *Journal of Consulting and Clinical Psychology, 55,* 817–824.

Lazar, I., & Darlington, R. (1982). Lasting effects of early education: A report from the consortium for longitudinal studies. *Monographs of the Society for Research in Child Development, 47* (Serial No. 195).

Leach, G. M. (1972). A comparison of the social behaviour of some normal and problem children. In N. Blurton Jones (Ed.), *Ethological studies of child behaviour.* London: Cambridge University Press.

Lee, C. L., & Bates, J. E. (1985). Mother–child interaction at age two years and perceived difficult temperament. *Child Development*, *56*, 1314–1323.

Lee, V. E., Brooks-Gunn, J., & Schnur, E. (1988). Does Head Start work? A 1-year follow-up comparison of disadvantaged children attending Head Start, no preschool, and other preschool programs. *Developmental Psychology*, *24*, 210–222.

Lerner, J. A., Inui, T. S., Trupin, E. W., & Douglas, E. (1985). Preschool behavior can predict future psychiatric disorders. *Journal of the American Academy of Child Psychiatry*, *24*, 42–48.

Lerner, R. (1982). Children and adolescents as producers of their own development. *Developmental Review*, *2*, 342–370.

Lewis, M., & Brooks-Gunn, J. (1979). Toward a theory of social cognition: The development of the self. In I. Uzgiris (Ed.), *New directions in child development: Social interaction and communication during infancy*. San Francisco: Jossey-Bass.

Lewis, M., Feiring, C., McGuffog, C., & Jaskir, J. (1984). Predicting psychopathology in six-year-olds from early social relations. *Child Development*, *55*, 123–136.

Lewis M., & Starr, M. D. (1979). Developmental continuity. In J. Osofsky (Ed.), *Handbook of infant development*. New York: Wiley.

Lieberman, A. F. (1977). Preschoolers' competence with a peer: Relations with attachment and peer experience. *Child Development*, *48*, 1277–1287.

Lobitz, W. C., & Johnson, S. M. (1975). Parental manipulation of the behavior of normal and deviant children. *Child Development*, *46*, 719–726.

Loeber, R. (1982). The stability of antisocial and delinquent behavior. *Child Development*, *53*, 1431–1446.

Londerville, S., & Main, M. (1981). Security of attachment, compliance, and maternal training methods in the second year of life. *Developmental Psychology*, *17*, 289–299.

Loney, J., Kramer, J., & Milich, R. (1981). The hyperkinetic child grows up: Predictors of symptoms, delinquency, and achievement at follow-up. In K. Gadow & J. Loney (Eds.), *Psychosocial aspects of drug treatment for hyperactivity*. Boulder, CO: Westview Press.

Lytton, H. (1980). *Parent–child interaction: The socialization process observed in twin and singleton families*. New York: Plenum Press.

Maccoby, E. E., Kahn, A. J., & Everett, B. A. (1983). The role of psychological research in the formation of policies affecting children. *American Psychologist*, *38*, 80–84.

Maccoby, E. E., & Martin, J. A. (1983). Socialization in the context of the family: Parent–child interaction. In E. M. Hetherington (Ed.), P. Mussen (Series Ed.), *Handbook of child psychology: Vol. IV. Socialization, personality, and social development*. New York: Wiley.

Maccoby, E. E., Snow, M. E., & Jacklin, C. N. (1984). Children's dispositions and mother–child interaction at 12 and 18 months: A short-term longitudinal study. *Developmental Psychology*, *20*, 459–470.

MacDonald, K. (1987). Parent–child physical play with rejected, neglected, and popular boys. *Developmental Psychology*, *23*, 705–711.

MacFarlane, J. W., Allen, L., & Honzik, M. P. (1954). *A developmental study of the behavior problems of normal children between twenty-one months and fourteen years.* Berkeley: University of California Press.

Mahler, M. S. (1968). *On human symbiosis and the vicissitudes of individuation: Vol. 1. Infantile psychosis.* New York: International Universities Press.

Mash, E. J., & Johnston, C. (1982). Comparison of the mother–child interactions of younger and older hyperactive and normal children. *Child Development, 53,* 1371–1381.

Mash, E. J., & Johnston, C. (1983a). Parental perceptions of child behavior problems, parenting self-esteem, and mothers' reported stress in younger and older hyperactive and normal children. *Journal of Consulting and Clinical Psychology, 51,* 86–99.

Mash, E. J., & Johnston, C. (1983b). Sibling interactions of hyperactive and normal children and their relationship to reports of maternal stress and self-esteem. *Journal of Clinical Child Psychology, 12,* 91–99.

Masten, A. (1979). Family therapy as a treatment for children: A review of outcome research. *Family Process, 18,* 323–335.

Matas, L., Arend, R. A., & Sroufe, L. A. (1978). Continuity of adaptation in the second year: The relationship between quality of attachment and later competence. *Child Development, 49,* 547–556.

McCall, R. B. (1977). Challenges to a science of developmental psychology. *Child Development, 48,* 333–344.

McCall, R. B. (1979). *Infants: New knowledge about the years from birth to three.* Cambridge, MA: Harvard University Press.

McCall, R. B. (1981). Nature–nurture and the two realms of development: A proposed integration. *Child Development, 52,* 1–12.

McCartney, K., & Galanopoulus, A. (1988). Child care and attachment: A new frontier the second time around. *American Journal of Orthopsychiatry, 58,* 16–24.

McGee, R., & Silva, P. A. (1982). *A thousand New Zealand children: Their health and development from birth to seven.* Special Report, Series No. 8. Auckland, NZ: Medical Council of New Zealand.

McGee, R., Silva, P. A., & Williams, S. (1984). Perinatal, neurological, environmental, and developmental characteristics of seven-year-old children with stable behaviour problems. *Journal of Child Psychology and Psychiatry, 25,* 573–586.

McGee, R., Williams, S., & Silva, P. A. (1984). Background characteristics of aggressive, hyperactive, and aggressive-hyperactive boys. *Journal of the American Academy of Child Psychiatry, 23,* 280–284.

Milich, R., & Landau, S. (1982). Socialization and peer relations in hyperactive children. In K. D. Gadow & I. Bialer (Eds.), *Advances in learning and behavioral disabilities* (Vol. 1). Greenwich, CT: JAI Press.

Milich, R., Landau, S., Kilby, G., & Whitten, P. (1982). Preschool peer perceptions of the behavior of hyperactive and aggressive children. *Journal of Abnormal Child Psychology, 10,* 497–510.

Milich, R., & Loney, J. (1979). The role of hyperactive and aggressive symptomatology in predicting adolescent outcome in hyperactive children. *Journal of Pediatric Psychology, 4*, 93–112.

Milich, R., Wolraich, M., & Lindgren, S. (1986). Sugar and hyperactivity: A critical review of empirical findings. *Clinical Psychology Review, 6*, 493–514.

Miller, P. H. (1983). *Theories of developmental psychology.* New York: W. H. Freeman.

Minton, C., Kagan, J., & Levine, J. A. (1971). Maternal control and obedience in the two-year-old. *Child Development, 42*, 1873–1894.

Minuchin, S. (1974). *Families and family therapy.* Cambridge, MA: Harvard University Press.

Myers, N. A., & Perlmutter, M. (1978). Memory in the years from two to five. In P. A. Ornstein (Ed.), *Memory development in children.* Hillsdale, NJ: Erlbaum.

Olson, G., & Sherman, T. (1983). Attention, learning, and memory in infants. In M. M. Haith & J. J. Campos (Eds.), P. Mussen (Series Ed.), *Handbook of child psychology: Vol. II. Infancy and developmental psychobiology.* New York: Wiley.

Olweus, D. (1979). Stability of aggressive reaction patterns in males: A review. *Psychological Bulletin, 86*, 852–875

Ornstein, P. A. (1978). The study of children's memory. In P. A. Ornstein (Ed.), *Memory development in children.* Hillsdale, NJ: Erlbaum.

Osofsky, J. (1987). *Handbook of infant development* (2nd ed.). New York: Wiley.

Overton, W. F., & Reese, H. W. (1981). Conceptual prerequisites for an understanding of stability–change and continuity–discontinuity. *International Journal of Behavioral Development, 4*, 99–123.

Panaccione, V. F., & Wahler, R. G. (1986). Child behavior, maternal depression, and social coercion as factors in the quality of child care. *Journal of Abnormal Child Psychology, 14*, 263–278.

Parke, R., & Slaby, R. G. (1983). The development of aggression. In E. M. Hetherington (Ed.), P. Mussen (Series Ed.), *Handbook of child psychology: Vil. IV. Socialization, personality, and social development.* New York: Wiley.

Pastor, D. L. (1981). The quality of mother–infant attachment and its relation to toddlers' initial sociability with peers. *Developmental Psychology, 17*, 326–335.

Paternite, C. E., & Loney, J. (1980). Childhood hyperkinesis: Relationships between symptomatology and home environment. In C. K. Whalen & B. Henker (Eds.), *Hyperactive children: The social ecology of identification and treatment.* New York: Academic Press.

Patterson, G. R. (1980). Mothers: The unacknowledged victims. *Monographs of the Society for Research in Child Development, 45* (Serial No. 186).

Peery, J. C. (1979). Popular, amiable, isolated, rejected: A reconceptualization of sociometric status in preschool children. *Child Development, 50*, 1231–1234.

Pelham, W., & Bender, M. E. (1982). Peer relations in hyperactive children: Description and treatment. In K. Gadow & I. Bialer (Eds.), *Advances in learning and behavioral disabilities* (Vol. 1.). Greenwich, CT: JAI Press.

Pepler, D., Corter, C., & Abramovitch, R. (1982). Social relations among children: Comparison of sibling and peer interaction. In K. H. Rubin & H. S. Ross (Eds.), *Peer relationships and social skills in childhood*. New York: Springer Verlag.

Persson-Blennow, B., Naslund, B., McNeil, T. F., & Kaij, L. (1986). Offspring of women with nonorganic psychosis: Mother–infant interaction at one year of age. *Acta Psychiatrica Scandinavica, 73*, 207–213.

Peterson, L., & Roberts, M. C. (1986). Community intervention and prevention. In H. C. Quay & J. S. Werry (Eds.), *Psychopathological disorders of childhood* (3rd ed.). New York: Wiley.

Phillips, D. (1986). The Federal Model Child Care Standards of 1985: Step in the right direction or hollow gesture? *American Journal of Orthopsychiatry, 56*, 56–64.

Phillips, D. (1988). *Quality in child care: What does research tell us?* Washington, DC: National Association for the Education of Young Children.

Phillips, D., McCartney, K., Scarr, S., & Howes, C. (1987). Selective review of infant day care research: A cause for concern! *Zero to three: Bulletin of the National Center for Clinical Infant Programs*. Washington, DC: Superintendent of Documents.

Piaget, J. (1926). *The language and thought of the child*. London: Routledge & Kegan Paul.

Piaget, J. (1928). *Judgment and reasoning in the child*. London: Routledge & Kegan Paul.

Piaget, J. (1932). *The moral judgment of the child*. New York: Free Press.

Plomin, R. (1982). The difficult concept of temperament: A reply to Thomas, Chess, and Korn. *Merrill-Palmer Quarterly, 28*, 25–33.

Radke-Yarrow, M., Cummings, E. M., Kuczynski, L., & Chapman, M. (1985). Patterns of attachment in two- and three-year-olds in normal families and families with parental depression. *Child Development, 56*, 884–893.

Radke-Yarrow, M., Zahn-Waxler, C., & Chapman, M. (1983). Children's prosocial dispositions and behavior. In E. M. Hetherington (Ed.), P. Mussen (Series Ed.), *Handbook of child psychology: Vol. IV. Socialization, personality, and social development*. New York: Wiley.

Richman, N., Stevenson, J., & Graham, P. J. (1982). *Preschool to school: A behavioural study*. London: Academic Press.

Rickel, A. U., & Dyhdalo, L. (1981). A two-year follow-up study of a preventive mental health program for preschoolers. *Journal of Abnormal Child Psychology, 9*, 455–464.

Rickel, A. U., Smith, R. L., & Sharp, K. C. (1979). Description and evaluation of a preventive mental health program for preschoolers. *Journal of Abnormal Child Psychology, 7*, 101–112.

Ricks, M. H. (1985). The social transmission of parental behavior: Attachment across generations. In I. Bretherton & E. Waters (Eds.), Growing points of attachment theory and research. *Monographs of the Society for Research in Child Development, 50* (Serial No. 209).

Ross, D. M., & Ross, S. A. (1982). *Hyperactivity: Current issues, research and theory* (2nd ed.). New York: Wiley.

Routh, D., Schroeder, C. S., & Koocher, G. (1983). Psychology and primary health care for children. *American Psychologist, 38*, 95–98.

Rubin, K. H. (1982). Social and social-cognitive developmental characteristics of young isolate, normal, and sociable children. In K. H. Rubin & H. S. Ross (Eds.), *Peer relationships and social skills in childhood*. New York: Springer-Verlag.

Rubin, K. H., Fein, G. G., & Vandenberg, B. (1983). Play. In E. M. Hetherington (Ed.), P. Mussen (Series Ed.), *Handbook of child psychology: Vol. IV. Socialization, personality, and social development*. New York: Wiley.

Rutter, M. (1981). Stress, coping, and development: Some issues and some questions. *Journal of Child Psychiatry and Psychology, 22*, 323–356.

Rutter, M., & Garmezy, N. (1983). Developmental psychopathology. In E. M. Hetherington (Ed.), P. Mussen (Series Ed.), *Handbook of child psychology: Vol. IV. Socialization, personality, and social development*. New York: Wiley.

Rutter, M., & Shaffer, D. (1980). DSM-III: A step forward or back in terms of the classification of child psychiatric disorder? *Journal of the American Academy of Child Psychiatry, 19*, 371–394.

Sameroff, A. J. (1975). Early influences on development: Fact or fancy? *Merrill-Palmer Quarterly, 21*, 265–294.

Sameroff, A. J., & Chandler, M. (1975). Reproductive risk and the continuum of caretaking casualty. In F. D. Horowitz (Ed.), *Review of child development research* (Vol. 4). Chicago: University of Chicago Press.

Sameroff, A. J., Seifer, R., & Zax, M. (1982). Early development of children at risk for emotional disorder. *Monographs of the Society for Research in Child Development, 47* (Serial No. 199).

Sanders, M. R., & Christensen, A. P. (1985). A comparison of the effects of child management and planned activities training in five parenting environments. *Journal of Abnormal Child Psychology, 13*, 101–117.

Santrock, J. W., & Warshak, R. A. (1979). Father custody and social development in boys and girls. *Journal of Social Issues, 35*, 112–125.

Saxe, L., Cross, T., & Silverman, N. (1988). Children's mental health: The gap between what we know and what we do. *American Psychologist, 43*, 800–807.

Scarr, S., & McCartney, K. (1983). How people make their own environments: A theory of genotype–environment effects. *Child Development, 54*, 424–435.

Schaefer, C. E., & O'Connor, K. J. (1983). *Handbook of play therapy*. New York: Wiley.

Schleifer, M., Weiss, G., Cohen, N. J., Elman, M., Cvejic, H., & Kruger, E. (1975). Hyperactivity in preschoolers and the effect of methylphenidate. *American Journal of Orthopsychiatry, 45*, 38–50.

Schneider-Rosen, K., Braunwald, K. G., Carlson, V., & Cicchetti, D. (1985). Current perspectives in attachment theory: Illustrations from the study of maltreated infants. In I. Bretherton & E. Waters (Eds.), Growing points in attachment theory and research. *Monographs of the Society for Research in Child Development, 50* (Serial No. 209).

Selman, R. (1980). *The growth of interpersonal understanding*. New York: Academic Press.

Selman, R. (1981). The child as friendship philosopher. In J. Gottman & S. Asher (Eds.), *The development of children's friendships*. New York: Cambridge University Press.

Shantz, C. U. (1983). Social cognition. In J. H. Flavell & E. M. Markman (Eds.), P. Mussen (Series Ed.), *Handbook of child psychology: Vol. III. Cognitive development*. New York: Wiley.

Shantz, C. U. (1987). Conflicts between children. *Child Development, 58*, 282–305.

Shatz, M. (1983). Communication. In J. H. Flavell & E. M. Markman (Eds.), P. Mussen (Series Ed.), *Handbook of child psychology: Vol. III. Cognitive development*. New York: Wiley.

Shatz, M., & Gelman, R. (1973). The development of communication skills: Modifications in the speech of young children as a function of the listener. *Monographs of the Society for Research in Child Development, 38*(Serial No. 152).

Shepherd, M., Oppenheim, B., & Mitchell, S. (1971). *Childhood behavior and mental health*. New York: Grune & Stratton.

Shure, M. B., & Spivack, G. (1979). Interpersonal cognitive problem solving and primary prevention: Programming for preschool and kindergarten children. *Journal of Clinical Child Psychology, 8*, 89–94.

Slaughter, D. T. (1983). Early intervention and its effects on maternal behavior and child development. *Monographs of the Society for Research in Child Development, 48* (Serial No. 202).

Smith, P. K., & Green, M. (1975). Aggressive behavior in English nurseries and play groups: Sex differences and response of adults. *Child Development, 46*, 211–214.

Snow, C. E. (1972). Mothers' speech to children learning language. *Child Development, 43*, 549–565.

Sroufe, L. A. (1979). The coherence of individual development. *American Psychologist, 34*, 834–841.

Sroufe, L. A. (1983). Infant–caregiver attachment and patterns of adaptation in preschool: The roots of maladaptation and competence. In M. Perlmutter (Ed.), *Minnesota symposium on child psychology: Vol. 16. Development and policy concerning children with special needs*. Hillsdale, NJ: Erlbaum.

Sroufe, L. A. (1985). Attachment classification from the perspective of infant–caregiver relationships and infant temperament. *Child Development, 56*, 1–14.

Sroufe, L. A., & Fleeson, J. (1986). Attachment and the construction of relationships. In W. Hartup & Z. Rubin (Eds.), *The nature and development of relationships*. Hillsdale, NJ: Erlbaum.

Sroufe, L. A., & Rutter, M. (1984). The domain of developmental psychopathology. *Child Development, 55*, 17–24.

Stern, D. (1985). *The interpersonal world of the infant*. New York: Basic Books.

Stewart, R. B., & Marvin, R. S. (1984). Sibling relations: The role of conceptual perspective-taking in the ontogeny of sibling caregiving. *Child Development, 55*, 1322–1332.

Stewart, R. B., Mobley, L. A., Van Tuyl, S. S., & Salvador, M. A. (1987). The firstborn's adjustment to the birth of a sibling: A longitudinal assessment. *Child Development, 58,* 341–355.

Stipek, D., & McCroskey, J. (1989). Investing in children: Government and workplace policies for parents. *American Psychologist, 44,* 416–423.

Stone, L. J., & Church, J. (1984). *Childhood and adolescence* (5th ed.). New York: Random House.

Stoneman, Z., Brody, G. H., & MacKinnon, C. (1984). Naturalistic observations of children's activities and roles while playing with their siblings and friends. *Child Development, 55,* 617–627.

Sullivan, H. S. (1953). *The interpersonal theory of psychiatry.* New York: Norton.

Thomas, A., Chess, S., & Birch, H. (1968). *Temperament and behavior disorders in children.* New York: New York University Press.

Thomas, A., Chess, S., & Korn, S.J. (1982). The reality of difficult temperament. *Merrill-Palmer Quarterly, 28,* 1–20.

Tuma, J. M., & Sobotka, K. R. (1983). Traditional therapies with children. In T. Ollendick & M. Hersen (Eds.), *Handbook of child psychopathology.* New York: Plenum Press.

Turiel, E. (1978). Social regulations and domains of social concepts. In W. Damon (Ed.), *New directions for child development: Moral development.* San Francisco: Jossey-Bass.

Urbain, E. S., & Kendall, P. C. (1980). Review of social-cognitive problem-solving interventions with children. *Psychological Bulletin, 88,* 109–143.

Vandell, D. L., & Corasaniti, M. A. (1988). The relations between third graders' after-school care and social, academic, and emotional functioning. *Child Development, 59,* 868–875.

Vaughn, B. E., Egeland, B., Sroufe, L. A., & Waters, E. (1979). Individual differences in infant–mother attachment at 12 and 18 months: Stability and change in families under stress. *Child Development, 50,* 971–975.

Wahler, R. G. (1980). The insular mother: Her problems in parent–child treatment. *Journal of Applied Behavior Analysis, 13,* 207–219.

Wallander, J. (1988). The relationship between attention problems in childhood and antisocial behavior eight years later. *Journal of Child Psychology and Psychiatry, 29,* 53–62.

Wallerstein, J. S. (1983). Children of divorce: Stress and developmental tasks. In N. Garmezy & M. Rutter (Eds.), *Stress, coping, and development in children.* New York: McGraw-Hill.

Wallerstein, J. S., & Kelly, J. B. (1980). *Surviving the break-up: How children and parents cope with divorce.* New York: Basic Books.

Webster-Stratton, C. (1984). Randomized trial of two parent-training programs for families with conduct disordered children. *Journal of Consulting and Clinical Psychology, 52,* 666–678.

Webster-Stratton, C. (1985). The effects of father involvement in parent training for conduct problem children. *Journal of Child Psychology and Psychiatry, 26,* 801–810.

Weiss, G., & Hechtman, L. T. (1986). *Hyperactive children grown up.* New York: Guilford.

Weisz, J. R., Weiss, B., Alicke, M. D., & Klotz, M. L. (1987). Effectiveness of psychotherapy with children and adolescents: A meta-analysis for clinicians. *Journal of Consulting and Clinical Psychology, 55*, 542–549.

Wellman, H. M., Ritter, R., & Flavell, J. H. (1975). Deliberate memory behavior in the delayed reactions of very young children. *Developmental Psychology, 11*, 780–787.

Wellman, H. M., & Somerville, S. (1980). Quasi-naturalistic tasks in the study of congition: The memory-related skills of toddlers. In M. Perlmutter (Ed.), *New directions in child development: Memory development in young children.* San Francisco: Jossey-Bass.

Wenar, C. (1982). Developmental psychopathology: Its nature and models. *Journal of Clinical Child Psychology, 11*, 192–201.

Werner, E., Bierman, J. M. & French, F. E. (1971). *The children of Kauai.* Honolulu: University of Hawaii Press.

Werner, E., & Smith, S. (1977). *Kauai's children come of age.* Honolulu: University of Hawaii Press.

Werry, J. S., & Quay, H. C. (1971). The prevalence of behavior symptoms in younger elementary school children. *American Journal of Orthopsychiatry, 41*, 136–143.

Westman, J. C., Rice, D. L., & Bermann, E. (1967). Nursery school behavior and later school adjustment. *American Journal of Orthopsychiatry, 37*, 725–731.

White, B. L. (1985). *The first three years of life.* Englewood Cliffs, NJ: Prentice-Hall.

White, R. W. (1959). Motivation reconsidered: The concept of competence. *Psychological Review, 66*, 297–233.

Winett, R. A., Stefanek, M., & Riley, A. W. (1983). Preventive strategies with children and families. In T. Ollendick & M. Hersen (Eds.), *Handbook of child psychopathology.* New York: Plenum Press.

Wolkind, S. (1985). Mothers' depression and their children's attendance at medical facilities. *Journal of Psychosomatic Research, 29*, 579–582.

Woodhead, M. (1988). When psychology informs public policy: The case of early childhood intervention. *American Psychologist, 43*, 443–454.

Woollacott, S., Graham, P. J., & Stevenson, J. (1978). A controlled evaluation of the therapeutic effectiveness of a psychiatric day-centre for preschool children. *British Journal of Psychiatry, 132*, 349–355.

Yarrow, L. J., McQuiston, S., MacTurk, R. H., McCarthy, M. E., Klein, R. P., & Vietze, P. M. (1983). Assessment of mastery motivation during the first year of life: Contemporaneous and cross-age relationships. *Developmental Psychology, 19*, 159–171.

Young, K. T., & Zigler, E. (1986). Infant and toddler day care: Regulations and policy implications. *American Journal of Orthopsychiatry, 56*, 43–54.

Zahn-Waxler, C., Cummings, E. M., McKnew, D. H., & Radke-Yarrow, M. (1984). Altruism, aggression, and social interactions in young children with a manic-depressive parent. *Child Development, 55*, 112–122.

Zahn-Waxler, C., McKnew, D. H., Cummings, E. M., Davenport, Y. B., & Radke-Yarrow, M. (1984). Problem behaviors and peer interactions of young children with a manic-depressive parent. *American Journal of Psychiatry, 141*, 236–240.

Zahn-Waxler, C., Radke-Yarrow, M., & King, R. A. (1979). Childrearing and children's prosocial initiations toward victims of distress. *Child Development*, *50*, 319–330.

Zigler, E. (1987). Formal schooling for four-year-olds? No. *American Psychologist*, *42*, 254–260.

Zigler, E., & Valentine, J. (1979). *Project Head Start: A legacy of the War on Poverty*. New York: Free Press.

Zubin, J., & Spring, B. (1977). Vulnerability: A new view of schizophrenia. *Journal of Abnormal Psychology*, *86*, 103–126.

Index